The First-Time Mom's Guide to Managing Triggers

PRACTICAL STRATEGIES TO NAVIGATE DIFFICULT MOMENTS

Danielle Delorenzo, MSOT, OTR/L

ROCKRIDGE
PRESS

Interior and Cover Designer: Amanda Kirk
Art Producer: Meg Baggott
Editor: Samantha Holland
Production Manager: Holly Haydash
Production Editor: Melissa Edeburn

Illustration © Designdell/CreativeMarket
Author photo courtesy of Jenna Guzman Lowery @belchingbabe
Paperback ISBN: 978-1-64876-475-2 | eBook ISBN: 978-1-64876-476-9
R0

Luke, you made me a mom.
Seeing the world through your eyes
is a new adventure every day.
Being your mama is my
favorite occupation. I love you.

Contents

Introduction

As a first-time mom, I am no stranger to triggering experiences.

My son, Luke, was three days old when I awoke to the sound of him choking. (Even as I write, I can still feel the emotions of that experience as if it happened yesterday.) I screamed and picked him up, and immediately he cleared his throat and fell back asleep. He was fine, but I refused to put him down for hours—I was an anxious mess. Even though this was one of many triggers I experienced as a first-time mom, I knew I had to add some strategies to my tool kit to help support my overall emotional well-being.

Motherhood changes you. It's not good or bad; you just evolve. You are now completely in charge of taking care of someone else, which comes with many "triggers" that can sway your emotions at any time. What is considered triggering is unique to each individual and experience, but essentially, it can be anything—an event, situation, feeling, or person—that activates an intense emotional reaction. Being triggered might look like yelling, sudden anger, unrelenting anxious thoughts, tension in your body, uncontrollable crying, or any strong emotional response due to a stressful situation.

Motherhood is such a transitional adjustment. Things you never thought would be a "trigger" are now exactly that—the dishes piling up in the sink, the never-ending to-do list, parenting conversations with friends, etc. While motherhood is filled with its fair share of overwhelming emotions, it also brings some of the most loving, intense, and beautiful feelings.

I have been a pediatric occupational therapist for 11 years, and I am currently pursuing a post-professional doctorate degree (which I will be finishing up when this book is published!). I am the co-founder of mindfulness in mOTion, Inc., which focuses on integrating movement, gratitude, and mindfulness into your daily life. My professional and personal lives collided when my son sustained trauma at birth and was later diagnosed with autism at two and a half years old. Due to his traumatic birth, I was diagnosed with postpartum anxiety and PTSD. I have been where you are—alone, sad, anxious, triggered by almost anything at any moment. If my story resonates with you, you have come to the right place. This is just one season of your life. Give yourself grace along this journey of raising a tiny human.

Even though the strategies in this book are geared toward first-time mothers with younger children, they can be used by anyone looking to respond rather than react during triggering situations. The strategies build on one another, but it's not necessary to read in the order they are presented. Feel free to skip around to whatever feels most relevant to you at the time. This book is not meant to give you all the answers; rather, it is meant to guide you, pose real-life situations, and offer a variety of supportive tools to help you identify what you need to respond rather than react during stressful or triggering interactions during motherhood. The most important part is that you are here with an open mind, ready to learn how to support your emotional well-being along your journey of motherhood.

Note: *This book is not a replacement for therapy or other forms of clinical treatment. If you are experiencing any feelings of anxiety, depression, sadness, or anger that are impacting your engagement in your daily occupations (what occupational therapists call "meaningful and instrumental daily activities"), please consider contacting your doctor to explore your treatment options.*

TRIGGERS 101

Let's dive into a deeper understanding of triggers and how they relate to the stressors you may experience as a first-time mom, as well as some basic techniques with which to handle them. This section serves as foundational knowledge that will support your understanding of the strategies in later chapters.

CHAPTER 1

Understanding Your Triggers

The moment a trigger occurs—that feeling in your gut we all know well—it is driving your emotional response, not logic. When you learn to increase your awareness as to which "triggers" impact your ability to stay calm during interactions with your child, responding instead of reacting will begin to feel like second nature.

What Are Triggers?

Everyone has their own unique set of "triggers" that cause quick shifts in their internal emotional state—one minute you're feeling happy, and then something happens that makes you feel stressed, upset, angry, or frustrated. It's like when you drop a bunch of things on the ground; you go to pick them all up, but they keep falling out of your hands. It feels like you can't catch a break! You will experience many triggers throughout your life, but by becoming aware of what they are, you will learn how to respond in more mindful ways. Let's explore the various categories of triggers and how they relate to motherhood.

DIRECT AND INDIRECT

During any interaction, we receive feedback from ourselves (physically and emotionally) as to how that interaction made us feel. Direct triggers have an instant response—no time to think, just react. For example, you are walking with your child, but they lose their balance and trip, so you swoop in to prevent the fall. This is an instantaneous response to your child tripping. Indirect triggers take more time to register an emotional response, like when you hear a child crying in the store and begin to feel anxious or upset.

There will be many triggers, direct and indirect, along your journey of motherhood, your child's responses being one of them. Remember, their behavior is independent from you, and they will trigger you sometimes. Identifying your triggers, whether direct or indirect, and being more mindful in your reactions will help you respond to the situation more calmly.

EXTERNAL AND INTERNAL

External triggers consist of anything within your environment (outside your body) that impacts your overall well-being. This could be your child crying, the TV being too loud, dropping your baby's bottle on the floor, piles of laundry . . . pretty much anything that disrupts your current mental state. Internal triggers are brought on by your thoughts and feelings. These negative thoughts can trigger the central nervous system when stressors occur, making you more likely to react rather than respond during heated interactions with your child.

Identifying both external and internal stressors will increase your awareness of triggering situations. The strategies you'll learn in this book will help you maintain a state of calm in those overwhelming moments.

CONSCIOUS AND UNCONSCIOUS

Conscious stressors are the things you already know can trigger you, especially if you're experiencing a stressful day, like when your baby screams in the car every time you go for a drive but you still must complete your errands. You already know when these situations occur; they can trigger feelings of anxiety, frustration, anger, and sadness. Unconscious reactions occur from past feelings and experiences, ingrained habits, or unpleasant memories, all triggered by a random event or momentary interaction. For example, your past traumas can negatively impact your relationship with your child, triggering experiences that bring emotions to the surface.

Knowing what your conscious and unconscious triggers are will help you understand where your reactions are coming from. This will help you shift your emotions back to the current interaction rather than reacting with misplaced emotion.

REAL AND IMAGINED

Real triggers occur in the moment—the stress of your day, the mental load of motherhood, bumps in your healing process after giving birth, etc. Imagined triggers are stressors you think about that are not actually happening to you. Thoughts about all the worst-case scenarios, all imagined in your head, can be just as stressful as real triggers.

Many first-time moms live in constant protection mode, always trying to ensure the safety of their child. Try to stop thinking about projected outcomes or negative experiences that may never occur. Instead, stay focused on what is happening in the present moment.

The more you tune in to your child and tune out the imagined scenarios, you will begin to understand your child's responses when they are having difficulty expressing their wants, needs, and emotions—but most important, how to not let those responses trigger you.

IN THE MOMENT AND FROM THE PAST

Trauma, memory, and childhood wounds can be triggering, especially in the context of motherhood. A trauma might be any event that occurred during your childhood or anytime in your life when you felt danger or experienced pain. This could be an unexpected accident or an experience with death, abuse, or loss. Additionally, many first-time mothers also experience inequities and social, racial, economic, and structural disparities. These can greatly impact their overall health, well-being, and the parent-child relationship.

There is a connection to unresolved trauma and insecure attachments within the parent-child relationship that can result in recurring triggering situations. But even when unresolved trauma is present, mothers who actively work toward securing a more positive attachment and building a stronger relationship with their child, in fact, do so.

My traumatic birth experience ignited an anxiety that was not familiar, and it greatly interfered with my mental health and parenting experiences. I was anxious during every parenting decision, often hesitating to leave (or never leaving) the house for fear something would happen to me or my baby. Trauma is unique to each person; your own traumatic experiences impact your mental health and overall well-being.

If you are feeling signs of anxiety and depression during pregnancy and postpartum, express these concerns to your doctor. Society often overlooks mothers experiencing post-partum depression and anxiety. You are your best advocate! You're an amazing mother, and your mental health matters.

The Unique Stresses of Being a First-Time Mom

My environment is set up in a way that aligns with my daily routine and flow, and it greatly impacts my overall well-being. If my environment is out of order, so is my mind. At this point in your life, you have lived *without* a child far longer than with one. There were so many more things within your control pre-baby than there are postpartum. The more out of control you feel, the more intense triggering situations will be.

When you become a first-time mother, your mental status and your physical environment change significantly. Baby cribs, changing tables, toys, diapers, wipes—the list truly does feel endless. You notice this shift from supporting yourself to supporting someone else both in your environment and in your mind. What was once *your* space and thoughts now needs to accommodate another human. All this is happening while you're going through the hormonal and emotional changes of transitioning to motherhood, which make the presence of triggers even more prevalent.

Let's dive a little deeper into some of the more common stressors many first-time mamas face.

NO MORE "YOU" TIME

When you become a mother, there isn't enough time in the day to get everything done, let alone take some "you" time. As a new mom, I remember a conversation with a friend about how I had no time for myself anymore. It was a rare occurrence when I could take a five-minute shower. My friend responded, "Taking a shower is not 'you' time. That is your daily self-care routine." When mothers neglect their self-care routines and the activities they love, they can feel depleted, which leaves them more vulnerable and overwhelmed during stressful interactions with their children.

When you become a mother, you naturally gravitate toward giving up what you once loved to transition into this new role. Taking "you" time is not showering or eating or washing your hair—these are your basic self-care needs. It is important to clarify the distinction between the two. This will help you begin carving out time in your schedule not only for your basic self-care needs but also for your meaningful occupations (the life activities you engage in daily), which will continue to support your optimal well-being. Shift your mindset toward making "you" time a daily priority, even if it is just for a few minutes.

AN EVOLVING RELATIONSHIP WITH YOUR PARTNER

For parents with partners, a new baby presents a big change in your relationship. Figuring out how to manage household and parenting responsibilities, navigating sexual experiences during this time of transition and healing, adding new daily tasks to a to-do list, etc.—the list of changes within your relationship can feel never ending.

Your relationship will be tested in ways it never has before. Evolve together and figure out your groove as new parents.

Your partner is not a mind reader, so communication is key. It is important to feel comfortable and confident in expressing your feelings, especially when frustrated. If you are having difficulty figuring out how to express your feelings, write them down or send an email. Don't stop trying to communicate in ways you know your partner will understand. You are both in this together.

AN UNCEASING PROTECTIVE INSTINCT

Protective-mom mode begins the moment you find out you are going to be a mother. I wish I could say my protective instinct is calm now that my son is a little older, but it has decreased significantly. When Luke was a baby, I felt this constant need to protect him. It created such anxiety in my body when he would cry or appear stressed.

There will be times when these protective instincts will come in handy, but when we are in protection mode all the time, our bodies can experience negative, stressful responses. I would stare at Luke for hours to ensure that he was still breathing. I convinced myself that if I looked away for more than a few seconds, I would miss something. These moments of focused anxiety can greatly impact your mental health. When difficult situations arise, you will already be in a heightened state, making you more susceptible to reacting in a way you never intended with your child.

Throughout the book, we'll go over some practices, like journaling, mindfulness, and guided imagery, that can help you channel your constant need to protect your child into productive energy. This will ultimately help build a stronger relationship with your child.

IT'S HARDER THAN YOU THOUGHT

As a career-driven woman, I used to tell my coworkers that nothing would change once I became a mother. I imagined myself as a mom with a permanent glow, efficiently balancing work and my new motherhood duties gracefully. We hear stories from family and friends, and on social media and parenting blogs, all hailing the glories of motherhood, and we may think this will be the norm. I wish I could go back to my pregnant self, sit her down, and tell her that her life was going to get much harder. That was true! But the experience of being a mother has also brought me so much joy.

It can be challenging to think about all the amazing things that come with being a mother when life gets difficult. Your priorities will change. Your mindset will begin to shift toward your child's needs, putting them at the forefront. Previous routines and everyday activities will be interrupted. Remember: This is just one season of your life—a transitional moment. There are going to be times when you feel overwhelmed and triggered by how hard motherhood can be. Take it a moment at a time and breathe.

THE TIRED THAT NEVER ENDS

I used to laugh when my sister-in-law told me that I would never not be tired again. She was so right. Motherhood brought a new level of sleep deprivation I had never felt before. Every minute was filled with something to do rather than time to rest, recover, and sleep.

In the very beginning, pregnancy prepares our bodies to grow a human. During this time, many women experience difficulty sleeping. This is your body's way of preparing you for the long, sleepless nights ahead. From the moment your baby is born, there is a new list of "things" you're responsible for. Your day is filled with feeding the baby, changing the baby, rocking the baby, carrying the baby, preparing meals, creating a safe environment, changing and washing the baby's clothes, and so on. Then you experience the mental fatigue from the constant stream of thoughts in your head, like, "Did I remember to do (blank)?" And then combine that with everything else going on in your life. But don't worry—this book will help you declutter your mind, recharge your batteries, and find moments to relax.

THE COMPARISON CONUNDRUM

As soon as you become a mom, it feels like you have more questions than answers. Everyone in your life will have a different opinion when it comes to your child, and how these opinions are presented can be triggering in itself. For instance, let's say you're having difficulty breastfeeding and you reach out to one of your friends for support. They tell you how easy it was for them to breastfeed and not to stress about it, it will come naturally. In reality, 92 percent of mothers struggle with breastfeeding, according to the Centers for Disease Control and Prevention (CDC). But in that moment, all you think is, "What is wrong with me? Why isn't this easy for me? Am I doing something wrong?"

Try not to compare yourself or your baby to anyone else. Remember, you know yourself and your baby best. Write your own rulebook for parenting and do what works for you, regardless of what anyone else thinks. This is your life, your experiences, and your triggers. What matters is that you are able to identify what challenges you're experiencing and apply strategies when needed to support a healthy relationship between you and your child.

POSITIVITY CULTURE

Your new baby is something people will want to celebrate and dote over; babies are little miracles. Meanwhile, as the mother, you are going through extreme internal and external changes. For every tired, frustrated, anxious, scared thought expressed, a "you can do it" type of response is returned. People mean well, but this can make you feel like you aren't being heard.

I am all for positivity, but it's also important to understand that focusing on only the positive and ignoring your complex emotions will fill your fourth trimester (the first three months of your baby's life after birth) with unnecessary stress.

Mothers often hear common phrases that depict a limitless "positive only" vibe. This can be overwhelming for new moms, increasing their anxiety and making them feel overwhelmed and guilty for having negative thoughts. Negative thoughts do happen, and no amount of positive bumper stickers will make them go away. In fact, it is within these negative experiences and stressors that true, positive change can be made. These experiences allow for a period of healing, growth, and honoring the good, the bad, and the ugly. Be mindful when you're feeling overwhelmed from all the positivity. Take a step back and redirect the conversation.

THE "MENTAL LOAD" OF MOTHERHOOD

The "mental load" of motherhood is like an invisible running list of never-ending tasks and thoughts—the things you need to anticipate with your child, the tasks and responsibilities that need to be done to keep your household in order, keeping up with your work, etc.

Society has unrealistic expectations and understandings of motherhood. The fourth trimester is a time of true transition where you're healing from the birth experience—physically, mentally, and emotionally—while also learning how to care for your baby. It is something most people don't realize should be embedded in our health care, educational, and organizational systems' policies and procedures.

As reported in *The Guardian*, a 2019 UNICEF report labeled maternity leave policies in the United States as the worst among the world's richest countries. Compared to 41 other wealthy countries, the United States is the only one that does not have some type of national paid maternity policy. Other countries offered an extensive amount of time off, such as Austria with 49 weeks, Japan 36 weeks, Sweden 35 weeks, and Chile 30 weeks. Estonia was ranked number one with 84 weeks of leave.

Certain states have paid maternity plans in place, but it is not enough. Many mothers are faced with the burden of figuring out how to have a child and ensure financial stability at the same time. Mothers need to bond with their children and navigate this new path in life. But instead, many must return to work before they are ready, filled with anxiety and sadness that impact all areas of their life.

Societal norms, expectations, and institutions fail mothers after their baby is born with lack of maternity leave and beyond. The mental load increases so much once you have a baby. Work environments remain inflexible, leaving mothers exhausted, overwhelmed, and at higher risk for mental health problems.

Give yourself the space and time to process your emotions. Remember, you are forging your own path and beginning to manage the mental load of your life as a new mom. Being more mindful is the first step in navigating a system that is set up against you. Be kind to yourself.

The Way You're Feeling? It's Valid.

The mental, emotional, and physical experience of being a first-time mom is something you're navigating with no other real-life context to provide perspective. Everything you are going through is a first, and these "first" moments are filled with intense emotions. You may often feel overwhelmed, anxious, and stressed out. But don't worry, these feelings are completely valid!

I know that I'm a great mom to my son, but the new emotions I felt at the beginning made me doubt myself at every turn. I still have those moments, but with what I have discovered along my motherhood journey, I have learned to shift my mindset, and so can you! Despite the unprecedented joy and excitement of your new baby, being a mom is still incredibly stressful. Right now, we'll discuss some of the negative feelings that are commonly associated with being a first-time mom. Remember, your feelings are valid. It's okay to feel big emotions. Take a deep breath—you are a great mom, and you are doing your best.

FEAR

I am no stranger to fear. I would say out of all the feelings experienced by first-time mothers, fear is the emotion I have felt the most: *Are they breathing? Is that normal?* My husband would try to help me calm or redirect my thoughts, but there was no stopping them. Suddenly, I felt like I could never look away. There is this sense of urgency that occurs the second you meet your baby. From that moment, your thoughts are filled with rational and irrational fears that can impact your life.

When you become a mom, you might be more irritable, upset, and on edge. Fear impacts your ability to take care of your physical, mental, and emotional needs. You want to do everything right because a little life literally depends on you to take care of them. As a first-time mom, I know how fiercely you are trying to ensure a safe environment for your child, but this can negatively impact your emotional state.

ANXIETY

I've always struggled with anxiety, but when I became a mom, I felt anxiety on an entirely different level. When you become a mother, your anxiety level intensifies, as if your fight-or-flight response is activated at all times. Engaging in daily tasks, going to the grocery store, not feeling comfortable in your body or clothes, feeling like you are being judged, even doing the things you love—all of these may now be anxiety-filled thoughts and experiences. These experiences can transition into triggers during any social interaction, not just with your child. It may feel like you cannot break the anxious cycle in your head, but you absolutely can.

I knew I had to find a way to better manage my anxiety, not just to support more positive interactions with my son, but for my own mental health. Through ongoing therapy and implementing the strategies mentioned in this book, I was able to truly get a handle on the coping techniques that worked and supported me during intense interactions with my child and everywhere else in my life. My hope is that by reading this book, you will, too.

ANGER

New mothers often have preconceived notions about what our kids should already be able to do on a developmental and emotional level. In the moment, we can easily forget they are still learning and growing, right alongside us. Together, we are trying to figure out our new roles as mothers, and our children are learning how to navigate their environment, test limits, and understand how the world works.

Anger can also stem from and/or lead to other emotions such as shame, guilt, and self-doubt. It is important to manage your anger so that it doesn't transition into rage. Anger is a warning sign to your brain indicating something needs to change, and it builds with each triggering event. Your kids are going to do many things that can elicit an angry response from you. Be mindful to focus on where the anger is coming from: Did you sleep well the night before? Have you eaten anything? Are you behind with work or other responsibilities? Is something else bothering you? Once you can identify the source of your anger, you will begin to process it and channel those emotions in a more positive and productive way.

SELF-DOUBT

If I had a quarter for every time I asked my husband if I was a good mom, I would be rich. Many first-time mothers feel self-doubt and are constantly wondering if they are doing enough. Whether it's working late and not being able to see your kid at the end of the day, being distracted when you are with your child, or yelling during a stressful situation, all of these feelings lead to self-doubt.

The societal projections of motherhood constantly make us question whether we are making the right choices. New mothers find themselves questioning every decision they make and wondering, *Is this right? Will this be enough?* For me, it felt like those questions never went away. Anytime I learned something new or discovered I'd been doing something the "wrong" way, I began to doubt myself.

Every day your thoughts will be filled with doubt, especially when receiving unsolicited opinions from others, but trust your gut even when it feels like your brain is telling you otherwise. Self-doubt may never completely go away, but with the right support, you will feel more confident in your parenting choices.

HOPELESSNESS

Earlier on, I was concerned about my son's development and felt like I was not able to give him the support he needed at the time. I felt stuck. When you are constantly engaging in triggering situations that leave you with little resolve, you can feel hopeless—as would anyone.

There will be days when you're at a loss for what to do. In those moments, give yourself a hug. Be kind to yourself and allow your overwhelming feelings to come to the surface. As terrible as hopelessness is, it can also be scary to live *with* hope, afraid that no matter how much you hope for something, it may never happen. But I can say from experience that living a life without hope is much scarier.

When I look back on those moments, I am thankful I had the right support in place. I had an amazing group of friends, the support of other like-minded parents raising autistic children, and strategies to help me shift my mindset away from hopelessness and toward hopefulness. This allowed me to put more focus on my relationship with my child. This can happen for you, too!

GUILT

"Mom guilt" can stem from our preconceived notions and the expectations we put on ourselves, but that doesn't make it any less real. Whether you're feeling guilty for wanting a break after being with your child all day, leaving to go to work, neglecting your job or other responsibilities, or snapping at others and beating yourself up for it, guilt will happen. Guilt impacts your ability to respond positively in the moment and can intensify any emotions you're feeling.

First-time mothers often feel guilty about asking for help, taking time for their basic needs, and engaging in their meaningful occupations. Have you ever stayed in the bathroom a few minutes longer just to get some peace and quiet? We have all been there. All you want is to do what's best by your child, but acting out of guilt can also lead to feelings of anxiety, stress, and sadness. The guilt will subside as you learn how to manage your everyday stressors and practice self-compassion.

SHAME

Guilt and shame are often felt together, but they are not interchangeable. Guilt occurs when you feel you have done something wrong, whereas shame is the feeling that your whole self, everything you are doing or are, is wrong. I felt a lot of shame surrounding the birth of my son. It didn't go exactly how I planned, and I wasn't able to deliver him vaginally, as I wanted.

First-time mothers can be so hard on themselves. The amount of information coming at you can feel like a freight train. Vaccinate your kids, don't vaccinate your kids; co-sleep, don't co-sleep; stay at home, go back to work. No matter what choice you make, someone will have an opinion about it. And don't get me started on "mom shaming." As first-time mothers, we are already feeling our share of shame. This is the time when we need support the most, not to be shamed by other mothers.

Surround yourself with people who will empower, uplift, and support one another rather than perpetuate a guilty mindset. Find other moms who listen to your fears and let you process your emotions free of judgment.

What Happens When We're Triggered?

Picture this: It was a typical Sunday morning. I was exhausted from staying up late working on a grad school assignment the night before and wished I had more time to sleep, but I wanted to wake up early and start the day off right. I set my son's breakfast on his table and left a puzzle out for him to play with. He came running out of his room, knocked over the table, and spilled his food on the floor. The dog ran over and ate the food off the floor, and then Luke dumped his entire cup of water on the dog's head. I could feel myself starting to get upset. I was so tired and felt defeated. It seemed like nothing I did could get Luke calm and settled. I tried music, hugs, his favorite toys, even his favorite TV show—but he was not amused by any of it. It had been a day of three-year-old shenanigans that would make any parent want to run and hide in the bathroom.

After triggering or stressful situations, your heart may be racing, your breath may be short and labored, and you might be feeling a sense of overall sadness, anger, or irritability. Full of regret and shame, you may feel as if you failed in that moment because you never wanted to act that way in the first place (and the fact that you did is an emotion to process in itself). Every mom will react to a trigger differently. Some may shut down, some may yell, some may cry. First-time mothers may find it difficult to express their true emotions to their family and friends, for fear of being judged or dismissed. There are already so many societal pressures, as discussed earlier (page 12), and these negative interactions can make a new mother feel isolated, trying to process all these difficult emotions alone.

The body can experience stress responses in a physical way. This greatly impacts mental, physical, and emotional health. Untreated stress in the body can lead to anxiety, depression, cardiovascular issues, and other health conditions. That's why it is so important to honor all your emotions and embrace all your feelings, even the negative ones. Remember, stressful moments with your child can be difficult to manage. It is okay to feel sad. It is okay to be mad. It is also okay to take a minute and process your emotions. In part 3, you will learn strategies and techniques that can support you in the moment to respond positively, rather than reactionarily, during triggering situations.

The First-Time Mom's Triggers Tool Kit

In this chapter, we'll go over some general tools and techniques you can add to your kit to help you better manage your response to triggers. Then, in parts 2 through 4, we'll dive deeper into more detailed strategies and ways to support yourself.

No Two Moms Handle Triggers the Same

There are several healthy ways to manage triggers as a first-time mom. Since we all experience stress differently, our responses to stressors are unique as well. Assuming that there is a single correct way to do something is not realistic, as motherhood is not a one-size-fits-all approach. Too often, we mothers get caught up with figuring out the "right" way to do anything and everything. In our tech-focused and social-media-based world, it's hard not to compare yourself and try to adopt other methods of parenting and managing stress. But there is no one right way to manage our own stress and raise our children.

I am grateful to be surrounded by so many amazing mothers in my life, each on their own journey of motherhood. We love to share motherhood's amazing moments with one another, but being able to talk freely about our individual triggers is what keeps us sane. We are each triggered by different experiences, emotions, and actions that make us react in the moment with our kids, and we each need our own strategies that work best for us.

There is no right way to manage your triggers, as you will respond differently than someone else in a similar situation. But you can discover the strategies that will work best for you. The following are basic, preventive tools that will help decrease intense emotional responses in the moment. When you begin to develop an awareness and an understanding of your triggers, you will be able to identify the most helpful ways to respond.

MINDFULNESS

Scientist, writer, and meditation teacher Jon Kabat-Zinn defines mindfulness as "paying attention on purpose, in the present moment, non-judgmentally." Being present in the moment and honoring where your body is in relation to other areas of your life can help increase awareness during conflicts or unpleasant emotions. Becoming more aware of the present helps our bodies and minds develop healthy techniques that promote emotional regularity when stress decides to creep in.

Mindfulness also keeps your mind from wandering toward the future or the past, focusing instead on the present. Allow yourself to feel whatever emotions come your way, experiencing each one as it happens. Life is a wave of emotions; the tricky part is finding the balance between high and low tides. The more we practice mindfulness, the more the emotional rift between our highs and lows decreases. Our brains and bodies begin to adjust to a more mindful way of viewing life.

As a parent, mindfulness will help support your optimal wellness. Modeling and implementing mindfulness techniques when interacting with your child will allow you to stay in the present moment without missing anything.

BREATH WORK

Your breath is your superpower. Sometimes we just need to take a minute to reground ourselves. Being aware of our breath is the quickest and most effective way to reach a state of calm. You have the ability to decrease your heart rate and restore normal breathing patterns, all by focusing on your breath. It is imperative to find breath work that works with your body and helps you calm down during stressful situations.

There are many different breathing exercises, but ocean breathing is one of my favorites. It works like this: Close your eyes and imagine you are on a beach, gazing out at the ocean. You watch the waves ebb and flow, as they move to the shore and then back out to sea. As you imagine the waves crashing on the shore, take a deep breath in. Then breathe out through your mouth slowly as you picture the waves returning to the sea.

The more often you practice breath work, the more your body will be ready to keep calm, rather than reacting during a stressful interaction with your child. You can practice breathing exercises as soon as you wake up, at the end of your day to recenter your emotions, or whenever you need it.

MINDFUL MOMENTS

One thing I find helpful during stressful situations with my son is pausing and thinking about a happy memory. Some of my go-tos are the first day I got to hold him, his excitement about his first trip to the beach, and the first time he called me "Mom." These memories help bring me back to a state of happiness and peace so I can calmly respond to what is triggering me in that moment.

When triggered, our bodies are physically reacting to a stressful situation, which can impact our voice volume, movements, and word choice. Take a moment to think about happy memories and you will notice those physical responses begin to subside. Thinking about what brings you peace will help you focus on a more appropriate response.

Once we understand the patterns of our responses to triggers, we can use these happy thoughts to detach us from those moments, to see our responses as gut reactions based on our current mood. When you separate yourself from the triggering moment, you will be able to react more appropriately to what's triggering you.

GUIDED IMAGERY

This strategy uses all of our senses: visual, auditory, olfactory (smell), gustatory (taste), tactile, vestibular (where your head is in relation to your body), proprioceptive (how the joints and muscles perceive where your body is in space to properly navigate the environment), and interoception (our feelings of thirst, hunger, and fullness). For more information on understanding your senses, check out the Resources section on page 148.

With guided imagery, you want to reach a state of harmony through a mind-body connection using some or all of your eight senses, whether in your mind or out in nature. Within your mind, imagine a place that fills you with calmness and peace. You might imagine a beach, the mountains, anywhere that makes you feel grounded. You can also refer back to the mindfulness tools on page 22.

Guided imagery brings your body back to a state of stillness, transitioning from a triggering moment to baseline—an emotional state where you feel calm and organized; a reset. More important, it can help you become acutely aware of your environment and how it supports your ability to self-regulate. This can bring awareness to your triggers and set the foundation for more successful implementation of your strategies.

JOURNALING

Journaling is a great way to release the mental load of emotions you're carrying, as it clears your brain from stressful and negative thoughts and allows space to process your emotions. I have dabbled in journaling since I was a young child. My journal was always there for me when the thoughts in my head were too overwhelming to sort through. Getting your thoughts down on paper helps to reduce anxiety and create clarity, which can be very beneficial after experiencing triggering interactions with your child.

If you have never journaled before, try a guided journal. Guided journaling can help when you do not know exactly where to start. The guided prompts initiate the journaling process and help you sort through your feelings and emotions. There are so many different journal options. Depending on your preference, you might choose an empty notebook and write freely, or write short phrases on sticky notes. The goal is to find a journal that fits *your* needs, one that supports your ability to write down and work through triggering situations so you can respond differently next time.

POSITIVE SELF-TALK

Our bodies can experience negative physical and physiological symptoms based on the narratives we create in our minds. When we are being our worst critic and engaging in negative self-talk, it can impact our immune system and overall well-being. But when your inner voice is more positive, acting as your advocate, it can support self-regulation and optimal emotional wellness. Shift a negative narrative to one that is filled with grace, love, and self-acceptance to increase your overall mental well-being.

Try not to think about your days, situations, or experiences as good or bad. Instead, remind yourself that you will show up, do your best, and give yourself grace every day for whatever life throws at you. Some days will be more difficult than others, but keep practicing positive self-talk and it will start to become a habit. Try coming up with an affirmation that is short and simple, and encompasses what you're trying to manifest. I have a sticky note on my computer that says, "I am worthy. My body is capable. My experiences do not define me." What would yours say?

BASIC NEEDS CHECKLIST

Motherhood is filled with days that feel effortless at times—when everything seems to be going right. Then there are days that are filled with tears and frustration no matter what you do. We have all been there. Sometimes it's because we're playing a guessing game: *What does my child want? Why are they crying? Why isn't anything I do helping?* This can trigger a great deal of frustration for parents.

Take a deep breath and pause. Now write down a checklist of your child's basic needs for when you're too exhausted or triggered to think. Is your child thirsty, hungry, tired, over-stimulated, or do they need a diaper change? Or all of the above? When we ensure our baby's basic needs are being met, we can then focus on our own needs and check in with ourselves: Can you eat while your child is eating or incorporate daily tasks in multiple steps throughout the day? Sometimes this may be just enough to bring a better flow to your day.

SELF-CARE

Self-care is the act of taking care of one's own overall health (both preventive and ongoing) by supporting individual emotional and physical needs. Taking care of your emotional needs can look like learning to say no more, scheduling time for yourself, or allowing your feelings to be present without judgment. Physical self-care refers to your bathing, grooming, and the overall health and wellness tasks you engage in daily. Many first-time mothers put physical self-care on the back burner once baby arrives.

There will be days when you feel like you don't have time to take care of yourself, but as moms, we must prioritize our health and well-being by keeping these needs at the forefront of our minds. It's important to engage in self-care activities that support your overall mental and physical health to help you be the best version of yourself for your children—and for you.

Write down a realistic self-care routine on a sticky note: "Take a shower, wash my hair, eat a healthy meal, take a walk," whatever you need to do to take care of yourself. Post it somewhere you'll see it every day. This visual reminder will help you find time throughout the day to prioritize yourself.

BUILD A SUPPORT NETWORK

Surround yourself with people who accept your true, authentic self without judgment. Sounds so simple, right? Unfortunately, it is not as easy as you might think. Before becoming a mother, you had a life filled with family, friends, and experiences. Once your baby is born, your relationships and activities evolve through a variety of factors.

It is important to identify when these relationships are shifting in a direction that impacts your mental well-being. It is also imperative to use tools to support your ability to distance yourself from stressful or toxic relationships, like judgmental friends or family (more on this later). Finally, surround yourself with individuals that fill your cup with light and love. This may look like joining nonjudgmental mom groups, attending local events for kids and their families, and following positive social media accounts. See chapter 19 for more detail on ways to cultivate a strong support network.

TAKING A MINUTE

It is okay to take space from your child. I repeat: It is okay to walk away and take a minute away from your child. As long as your child is safe, secure, and in line of sight, you can pause and embrace a moment of stillness. I have my go-to techniques I access during triggering moments, but depending on how overloaded and overwhelmed I am, they might not always work as effectively and efficiently. There are days you won't be able to tap out, days where it feels like your cup is overflowing like a waterfall. These are the times when you should take a minute and channel your breath.

When I need to take a minute, the easiest thing I can do is focus on my breath. Be kind to yourself. Parenting is hard! Discover ways to help regulate your reactions, even if it's just to survive the day. Have techniques available as needed. Take a minute to breathe, walk outside, close your eyes, read a page of a book or magazine, or scroll through social media. Just do something to step away mentally and physically for a moment. Your brain will thank you.

USING THESE TOOLS GOING FORWARD

We just processed a lot of information about what triggers are and how they impact motherhood, as well as some strategies to help you begin to shift your mindset when trying to identify your own triggers. You will learn more strategies and techniques—tools to fill your tool bag in the moment and beyond—to help you identify, shift, and manage your triggers along your motherhood journey.

Next, we'll jump into what you can do in the moment to help you understand and defuse your triggers.

IN-THE-MOMENT STRATEGIES FOR DISARMING TRIGGERS

M otherhood is filled with so many emotions that can lead to intense reactions during triggering situations. But remember, there are tools and strategies that can help. You'll get this! In this section, you will learn techniques to quickly and positively disarm triggers rather than react to them during stressful situations.

Raising Self-Awareness

Leslie's husband was recently transferred to a new job in a new city, far away from family and friends, leaving Leslie alone with her two-year-old son, Harper, all day. Leslie was feeling increasingly stressed out during her interactions with her son. She often found herself wondering why she got mad at every little thing he did. He was waking up earlier from his naps or not napping at all, leaving his toys all over the house, and protesting every request. He was also waking up in the middle of the night several times and going into Leslie's room. Her days were filled with exhaustion and her nights were interrupted. She never had any time to recoup.

One day, Harper wanted to paint his friend a picture. Leslie told him to be very careful so as to not spill any paint. Harper agreed, went to get the paint out of the closet, and dropped it. The paint went everywhere— the carpet, the cabinet, and the wall. Leslie yelled at Harper, stressed about the mess on the carpet and how long it would take to clean. Harper began to cry and express how sorry he was.

Leslie's eyes welled up with tears, and she felt sick to her stomach. She knew it was an accident, and her response was completely invalidating to Harper's feelings. She was aware how irritable she felt during the day, along with not sleeping at night. She realized she was taking out all her feelings on Harper. He made an honest mistake and she yelled at him for it. This was a turning point for Leslie.

She apologized to Harper, explaining that even mommies make not-so-great choices. She reassured him that it was an accident and she never meant to hurt his feelings, and she loved him. Harper then hugged Leslie as she sat with Harper to help him paint a picture for his friend.

It is during these moments of self-awareness that true change is happening. Leslie was aware she was becoming increasingly stressed and knew it was making her act in a way she didn't like with Harper. She chose to increase her self-awareness, pause in the moment, shift her anger to sadness and acceptance, and transition to a place of peace and happiness with her son. Sometimes it may be easy to move through a triggering situation, and oftentimes, when there are compounding stressors, it can be hard to come to this level of awareness in the moment.

STRATEGY SESSION

In this section, you will discover techniques to help increase your self-awareness, identify how to be more aware of what triggers you, and understand what you need to support yourself in that moment.

Get out of your head. It's so easy to get lost in the moment, especially after a tense situation. You may find yourself stuck, replaying the stressful situation in your head. Negative or stressful thoughts can cause a physical and emotional response in the body, even when you're engaging in a happy task (page 19). Take note of the stressors that hang around long after the triggering event occurred. Try a mindful breathing exercise when your stress takes over.

Take stock of your needs. As you become more aware of your triggers, it is also imperative to understand how to nourish your sensory system, that is, use your senses to help you reach a grounded, calm, "just right" emotional state. You could make a list of how you respond to sensory information, delegate responsibilities to others to lessen your mental and daily load, or engage in self-care tasks. Here are some tips to get started:

→ When you start to feel dysregulated—when you're having trouble managing your emotional responses— have three go-to strategies to lessen the intensity and duration of your dysregulation. Mine are deep breathing, standing outside in the sun, and taking a bath with essential oils.

→ Tell those around you what you need in moments of overstimulation to help you get calm and organized. You can communicate to others what your triggering signs are and ways they can help you. Even toddlers can understand "Mommy needs a minute" or "Mommy needs a hug." This is a great time to use a "mindful moment" (page 23) to help detach yourself from the trigger.

→ What's on your to-do list? Write down what's overwhelming you or stressing you out. Is there anything you can delegate? Do your priorities need refocusing?

→ When you advocate for your own sensory needs, you will start to see a shift in your overall regulation.

Own your triggers. Healing starts with self-awareness. Once you become aware of what your triggers are, you can use what supports will help you. Don't get caught up in what you think should or should not be a trigger; rather, just acknowledge what stresses you out and write it down. Review this list weekly and see if the same things are still bothering you or if you have found tools to support you in those specific moments.

Be intentional. Try to be intentional rather than reactive with your actions. During triggering situations, it is so easy to fall back on ingrained behaviors and react. In these moments, instead of thinking in terms of good or bad, switch the narrative to intentional or reactive.

When you act with intention instead of reacting to triggers, you are mindful of your emotions in the moment and more aware of what a responsive approach would be. For example, think about how Leslie yelled at Harper. A responsive approach would have been to pause (even though she may have been yelling in her head) and then calmly reassure Harper that accidents happen.

Mothers put so much pressure on themselves that it can leave us feeling exhausted and unable to process our true overwhelming emotions. Motherhood brings both good and bad days, so instead of labeling each day or experience as good or bad, label it for what it is—a temporary moment in time.

Trigger Technique

So often when we engage in stressful situations or interactions, we recognize that we should pause and take a break, yet, we choose to keep pushing through (which is rarely a good idea). Take that break! Doing something as simple as standing outside and letting the sun hit your face for a minute, going for a brisk walk, or mindfully drinking a warm cup of tea can greatly shift your mood in a positive direction.

KEEP IN MIND

- Be proud of yourself! You are actively searching for the meaning of your triggers. The more awareness you have about your own triggers, the better equipped you will be at selecting and implementing strategies to stay calm in the moment.

- If you're having trouble being self-aware, keep notes on triggering instances. This will help you practice self-awareness and be more in tune with what you need to work through that emotion.

- Imagine watching one of these instances as though it is occuring in a movie. Now step into the scene and hit pause. Explain to your past self that this is just a moment in time, and everything will be okay. This is a great technique to work on forgiving yourself and letting go of your patterns.

- When working on identifying your triggers, lean into every point of discomfort and embrace the intensity of all your emotions. Meet that intensity and honor it as part of your transition. Remember, you can't own your triggers until you know what they are. You are on your way!

CHAPTER 4

Naming Your Triggers

Camila was a 31-year-old single mom eagerly awaiting the birth of her child. A few weeks before Camila was due to give birth to Sofia, her mother suddenly passed away. Her mother was a huge part of her life and had played an active role in influencing Camila as a mother. The loss added a huge amount of stress and overwhelming emotions during an already emotional time. Camila found herself feeling increasingly anxious as the birth of her daughter approached.

It seemed like it was constant chaos from the moment Sofia arrived. Camila tried so many things to balance all her new roles, but she just could not get into a good rhythm with Sofia.

On one particular day, Camila woke up to the sound of her baby crying, a very familiar trigger. She knew it was going to be another long day. She stared at the blank ceiling, wishing for a few minutes of extra sleep. She turned over to her crying baby, fed her, and held her for a while, then transitioned to her daily routine.

Camila cooked breakfast, making her favorite meal, which had been her mother's favorite as well. Afterward, feelings of grief crept up on her spontaneously throughout the day. These unconscious triggers greatly impacted her mood and ability to regulate her emotions.

Camila couldn't stop thinking about her mother and wanting her to be present, to experience all Sofia's "firsts," be a listening ear, offer motherly advice, and provide a shoulder to cry on. Most important, her new baby was a constant reminder of her mother's absence. Camila wanted a way to work through these intense feelings of grief and anger and not let them impact her emotionally. Camila identified the loss of her mother as a trigger that was impacting her relationship with her baby. She was able to identify the foundation of what triggered her and actively worked on managing her grief, for example, by pausing and taking a mindful breath.

Triggers come in all shapes and sizes. Some may feel small and insignificant. Others will feel heavy, as Camila's were. When trauma is present, it can exacerbate those triggers.

Naming your triggers is a foundation for a healthy and constructive mindset, which can help enable you to maintain optimal regulation in stressful situations.

STRATEGY SESSION

There are many reasons triggers occur. You have already learned to increase your self-awareness; now let's learn how to name your triggers.

Step 1: Clear Your Head

Mindset is key during the process of identifying your triggers. This is a time when your brain can feel like a tornado of intense emotions spiraling out of control. Tune in to your body and see where you're holding tension. Start at your head, face, and shoulders, moving through each part of your body, and focus on letting go of each area where you're holding tension. Even though your body and brain may want to react to the trigger, try not to let it, or lessen its emotional intensity. You know this will happen, so now you can anticipate it in the moment.

Step 2: Identify Your Triggers

We talked about ways to keep track of your triggers in chapter 3 by writing them down or typing them using a notes app on your phone (page 35). Refer back to that list, or write down your techniques on a piece of paper. Then arrange them in order from least to most intense. This will help you identify which triggers to focus on first.

Step 3: Time to Debrief

When changing your emotional responses in the moment, it is imperative to reflect on why the "trigger" is a trigger in the first place. In Camila's case, she experienced direct and indirect triggers separate from her child, but her emotions still impacted their relationship. Follow these steps to analyze your triggers and the feelings associated with them.

1. Take out a blank piece of paper. In the middle of the page, draw a circle and write out one trigger from your

list within the circle. For example, let's say you have identified "working late" as a trigger. That would go in the center of the circle.

2. Draw lines out from the circle and label each with a feeling that goes along with that trigger, such as, "Not enough 'me' time," "Zoned out during family time," or, "Difficulty being present in the moment after work ends."

3. Pick a few things you can do to start managing these feelings when you must work late. For example, after writing down your feelings associated with the trigger, write down a couple of ideas to begin to manage these feelings when this stressful situation occurs, like meditating for 15 minutes or taking a short break to grab coffee before transitioning into "mom mode."

Step 4: Visualize Your Triggers

Clear your mind and think about triggering experiences as if you were there repeating the moment. You can also write them down. The idea is to visualize these situations so you can begin to understand what exactly the trigger was. Make sure to take time to pause if you are feeling overwhelmed. When you have the triggering situation in mind, ask yourself the following questions:

→ Was it something someone said? Or the way they said it?

→ What were the feelings behind the anger (e.g., sadness, worthlessness, defensiveness, frustration, etc.)?

→ What is the source of the trigger? Trace it back until you find its origin.

→ What could be done differently?
This is the first step toward diffusing your sympathetic nervous system and allowing your parasympathetic nervous

system (which is responsible for decreasing stress, returning breathing to a normal rate, and supporting a relaxed state) to calm and organize you. Triggering situations activate your fight-or-flight response. When you relive these experiences, you can begin to identify whether they were actually dangerous situations or if they just triggered that type of response.

Trigger Technique

Now that we have named our triggers, let's pick one and begin to dissect its components. Think of a situation or trigger you would like to break down. For example: *You haven't had "you" time since the baby was born.* Now list the following conditions as they relate to the trigger:

Thoughts: *Will this ever get easier? I had no idea having a kid would be like this. Am I a horrible mother because I think this way?*

Emotions: *Exhaustion, pain, emptiness, anxiety, fear*

Bodily sensations: *Rapid heartbeat, shortness of breath, fatigue*

Behavior: *Zoning out, emotionless, tearful*

Choose your own trigger and break down where these feelings are coming from. Start to identify ways you could support the underlying need, such as a breathing activity, meditation, a mindful pause, or any strategy you feel will pair best with each trigger.

KEEP IN MIND

- Many feelings will arise when you are identifying your triggers. But it's necessary to shift your internal narrative toward healing, self-compassion, and a mindset ready to use tools to help you manage your triggers in the moment and ongoing.

- These triggering moments won't last forever. Repeat this gentle reminder to yourself as you feel your emotions intensify.

- Remember to break down the anatomy of your trigger and determine the root of the problem (page 40). This way, you can begin to know which triggers are true to the situation or occurring because of other reasons, like past trauma. This will help you reshape your anger in a more positive and healthier way.

- Remember to give yourself grace; this is a marathon, not a sprint. There will be setbacks, but that is normal! You are making a lifestyle change, and it is not as glamorous as social media makes it out to be. If you get discouraged, channel your strategies to bring your emotions back to baseline.

CHAPTER 5

Keeping Calm

Amy wished she had a moment of peace, but three-year-old River was constantly on the go and wanted Amy to play with her 24/7. Anytime Amy tried to get her to play independently, she would cry, and Amy would feel guilty.

After a day of distractions, Amy finally had a few minutes to sit down and write. She thought River was bouncing on the trampoline, but once Amy stopped paying attention, it felt too quiet. Amy turned around to see that River had pulled out her toy box and begun to climb the shelves in the living room.

Instead of reacting, Amy redirected River multiple times. She checked for tension in her own body and released it using breathing techniques (see the STAR strategy on page 47) to help reground herself. It did not completely regulate her, but it kept her emotions from overwhelming her and allowed her to be "mom" until River went to sleep.

Stressful situations can sometimes have an ingrained cycle of stressors, emotions, and responses. If these situations repeat often, you may have developed certain habitual responses. These responses may take more time and intention to shift. We can feel them coming, and even though we do not want to lose control of our actions, it happens anyway. It's as if we are watching outside our body, saying, "No, I don't want to do this."

These situations can be turning points. Self-awareness during these moments help increase your ability to do something different next time you're heated. You become aware of something, you want to change it—and the next time, you can use tools to help you achieve that change.

Think of your tool kit of strategies surrounding yourself like a protective bubble with many layers: Each strategy is a specific tool you have learned along the way to help you channel your inner calm during triggering interactions with your child. Once you are more in tune with your self-awareness, you can begin to learn your calm down cycles. How do they start? How do you feel during the cycle? How do you return to a state of stillness? When we are still, we are truly present in the moment and able to have the most control over our overwhelming emotions.

STRATEGY SESSION

This strategy is all about techniques to help you calm down without using the words "calm down." This phrase can be triggering because your emotions and their intensity are expressions of your feelings. The goal shouldn't be to not feel your emotions, just to be able to feel and process them in a more regulatory way. The more you can use your tools and strategies in the moment, the more you will feel your inner mindset shifting. Keep up the awesome work!

What Does Calm Mean to You?

We often forget that the inside of our body controls our emotional responses. When you're stressed, you activate your body's survival responses, shifting into fight-or-fight mode. Hormones called "catecholamines" jump into action, speeding up your heart and preparing you to better respond to dangerous situations. A hormone called "acetylcholine" will then respond, slowing your heart rate and bringing you to a state of calm.

Visualize the inside of your body, all its synapses, muscles, veins, and nerves. Picture it alive and working, filled with chemical reactions. This will help you remember that you have the control to relax when trying to manage your emotions. We want the body to relax and know that it is okay to pause.

Honor Your Emotions

You are going to experience frustration, sadness, and anger as a mother, as well as happiness and joy. It is okay for you to feel sad or mad. It is also okay to take a minute and process your emotions.

You are experiencing a fight-or-flight reaction right along with your child. Many times, you and your child will demonstrate uncontrollable emotions simultaneously. In those moments, maintain this inner dialogue: "I am doing my best. My emotions are valid. My child's emotions are valid. My child needs me right now to be their anchor. I can do this. I am a good mother who cares about her child's well-being."

Don't Tell Yourself to "Calm Down"

When has anyone ever really calmed down after being told to do so? This has been one of the hardest things for me when interacting with my son. All day long I am his anchor to support his emotional regularity, and if I am feeling irritated or emotional, it makes it much more difficult to help him. When I reflect on the times someone told me to calm down or I told myself to "calm down," it's clear it did not make me feel great. In fact, it invalidated my feelings. There is something triggering about the words "calm down." Begin to shift your mindset to erase these words from your vocabulary and replace them with a different word, such as "pause."

Channel Your Inner STAR

When you feel the urge to tell yourself to calm down, instead pause and then practice STAR.

Scan: Scan your body for tense spots.

Target: Find your tense spots. Breathe into them as if you were filling up a balloon with air in the exact spot of the tightness/tension.

Anchor: Release your breath, pushing your feet into the floor. Reground yourself.

Respond: Take a mindful breath and respond to the situation without your emotions taking the reins.

Trigger Technique

The more you are aware of your emotional state, the more you can self-regulate during heated situations. When you are feeling exhausted, overwhelmed, and ready to react in an interaction with your child, pause and try this 4-7-8 breathing exercise.

1. Breathe in through your nose for a count of four.

2. Hold your breath for seven seconds.

3. Breathe out through your mouth for eight seconds.

4. Repeat two more times, or as needed.

5. Say the following: "I am calm. I am Mom. I can do this," or replace this phrase with a positive affirmation of your choosing.

KEEP IN MIND

- Don't feel guilty if you need to spend a few minutes away from your child. In these moments of intense emotion, the goal is to calm down in order to move forward through the situation as gracefully as you can. Take a few seconds and visualize what your intentions are for the next five minutes. Try not to think past a few minutes into the future. What needs to be accomplished or prioritized? Most often, things can wait, which allows you time to process your emotions and tackle the duties of the day when you are in a more stable emotional state.

- Triggers will happen, impacting your ability to stay calm during stressful situations. Practice does not equate to perfect, but it does give you opportunities to implement the strategies you have learned so far that are supportive to you.

- It might be helpful to write a mantra on a sticky note affixed to your computer. It could be something like "Breathe" or "Take a mindful minute." Write something meaningful to you and post it somewhere visible to you each day. Read it first thing in the morning and whenever you are having triggering thoughts. Keep reminding yourself that you can do this!

Reframing Your Anger

R ick and Dominique had been fighting for days. They were stressed and overworked, and the recent birth of their daughter had strained their relationship. This was the first time that Rick and Dominique were not on the same page. Every conversation made them feel like they were stuck in a perpetual state of frustration, anger, and sadness. They had no family close by, and they were managing their careers and their household and transitioning to life with an infant.

Every little thing triggered an argument. One night after they got into a huge fight over something that had gotten blown out of proportion, Rick and Dominique began to realize their fights were stemming from something deeper: They were truly and utterly exhausted from their new roles as parents, along with having two full-time careers.

Even though they were tired, they chose to stay up late one night and talk things out after a fight. They got out a piece of paper and organized how they were feeling. They were both able to express themselves calmly and safely, communicating their frustrations in a way that was understood by both parties. Together, they identified steps they could each take to work on what was bothering them in their own lives. Rick was going to try to not shut down and be a more active listener. Dominique was going to give Rick more time to process what she had to say, and if she was feeling heated, she would take a minute to pause before continuing. They discussed ways they could support each other and manage their work schedules, new responsibilities, and parental roles while still leaving time for themselves.

Whether it's a conflict with a friend, family member, partner, or coworker, negative interactions can affect our anger in stressful situations with our children. Many of us were stressed enough before motherhood, with work, school, friendships, social calendars, health concerns, and everyday roles and responsibilities. When you become a mom, your anger may reach a level you never thought it could.

As you learn about yourself as a mother, possible unresolved anger issues from your past may start to impact your present and future. This is why reframing your anger is so important. It is necessary to be able to move forward in your role as a mother and manage how you previously processed anger. When you identify where your anger is coming from, you will notice that the things making you angry may not actually be what's occurring in the moment.

STRATEGY SESSION

The following strategies will help you reshape your anger in a way that reflects the true meaning behind these triggers and why they make you angry.

Get Grounded

Anger has a way of creeping in and making you feel unsettled, like when an earthquake hits. This is a simple exercise you can do in the moment to help stay grounded when you're angry.

1. Pause once you experience that first sense of anger or triggering experience.

2. Look around the room and name three objects you see.

3. Listen to what's around you and name two sounds you hear.

4. Take a deep breath in and name what you smell.

During stressful or triggering situations, the brain can sometimes get stuck in fight-or-flight mode, unable to move forward. This exercise stops this negative feedback loop in your brain and grounds you, so you can process your emotions and move through the rest of your day with emotional stability.

Know Your Baseline

The body begins to experience physical and emotional symptoms of anger immediately. When anger is not dealt with in the moment, or is ongoing, it can turn into rage. Be mindful of where your anger baseline level is. Check in with yourself several times a day, especially if you are already feeling heightened. On a scale of one (less intense) to five (most intense), rate how angry you are. Notice the triggers you rate as fours or fives. This will help you determine which strategies will be most beneficial for those instances.

Identify Your Anger Symptoms

Everyone expresses and feels anger differently. Be mindful of the specific physical and emotional symptoms you feel when angry. Do you feel differently during certain triggering situations? In a notebook or a journal, write down all the symptoms you feel. Some common symptoms are:

→ Heavy breathing

→ Sweating

→ Tense body language

→ Quick speech

→ Shift in mood

→ Changes in facial expression (tension in jaw, furrowed brow)

It is also important to be mindful of the physical and emotional symptoms of your child's or partner's anger. Family members can help regulate each other when there is a mutual understanding of everyone's unique triggers and what each person needs to fill their cup.

Write It Out

Take out a piece of paper, just like Rick and Dominique did. Make two columns:

→ In the first column, write about how you see yourself. Think about when you get angry. Imagine you are looking at yourself in a moment of anger. As you watch yourself, describe what you feel and where you feel it. You can also write down your triggers and identify the emotions behind each.

→ In the second column, write about what you had rather done. For example, "Instead of storming away and slamming the door, I wish I had paused and taken a deep breath." Knowing where you are and where you want to go is the foundation for choosing which strategies will help you get there.

It will take time to reframe your anger. Writing down your ongoing triggers will help you see which strategies work to diffuse triggering situations.

Trigger Technique

The goal of any stressful interaction is to move through it as best as you can and return to baseline with your emotions. A body scan is an amazing tool to help you reset, identify specific areas in the body that are holding tension, and ground yourself.

Start by sitting in a chair or lying down. Close your eyes and feel your feet or body on the floor. Take three mindful, slow breaths, in through your nose and out through your mouth. Begin softening every part of your body, starting with the top of your head and moving down to your toes. Take note of where the tension is. Breathe into the tension until you feel it begin to lessen. If you still feel restless, you can move into a progressive body scan (see **STAR**, page 47).

KEEP IN MIND

- When you reframe how anger impacts your emotions, your body and brain will fight you. When this happens, remind yourself that you are prepared. You are rewiring neuronal connections and forming new habits. You are equipped to win the fight against your old habits as you take small steps toward shifting your mindset.

- Anger can be all-consuming. It can shift your inner monologue toward reacting emotionally rather than responding calmly. In the brief moment before you act on it, shift your mindset and respond in a different way. Take a few breaths and ask yourself, *What is the result I desire, and what action can I take to get there in a positive way?*

- You have every right to feel anger. These are your feelings, and no one can tell you otherwise. What matters is the intensity of your anger, how your anger impacts your responses, and how it affects your daily interactions and relationship with your child. The goal is to help you handle your anger more effectively, so it doesn't turn into rage and affect your mental health and relationships.

CHAPTER 7

Finding Humor in the Situation

Edna was CEO of a company in the city. A career-driven woman, she never wanted kids, but life had other plans for her. She became pregnant with her son, Julian, and transitioned into the role of motherhood. Luckily, she worked at a company that was very flexible and allowed her to bring Julian to work.

One day, Julian was crying frantically whenever he was away from his mother. This also happened to be the day Edna had a major deadline, and she was scheduled to present important material to the board. Edna wanted to leave Julian home that day with the nanny, but Julian was not having it. She felt scattered trying to get all Julian's things arranged to bring him into work, barely being able to get herself together. Soon she showed up at work, with baby in tow, and began to prepare for the meeting.

On top of everything else, Julian was in the cluster feeding stage. Edna found herself stopping several times throughout the workday to feed her son. When it was time for the meeting, she could have tried to pass off Julian to her secretary to hold during the presentation, but Julian only would have screamed the entire time. Out of options, Edna walked into the meeting breastfeeding her baby and said, "Well, nothing like a working mom in action." Everyone laughed. Edna was able to be a mom and rock her meeting at the same time. She could have broken down, given in to the unconventional stares of some board members, left Julian crying at home, or passed him off to her secretary, but she didn't do any of those things. She got herself together and used laughter to diffuse the situation and give her child what he needed, all at the same time.

Laughter has so many benefits for our health. In the short term, it decreases your stress response and can ease tension. In the long run, it can lead to an overall increase in mood, help alleviate pain, and support better immune health. Motherhood can pull you in multiple directions at any time. Laughter can be a way to quickly lighten the mood and switch gears from stress to smiles. Sometimes it might be hard to find the laughter during these situations, but it just might be the emotion you need in that moment.

Here are a few ways to use laughter to diffuse intense situations.

Smile

When you smile, you set off a series of chemical reactions that release dopamine and serotonin. Dopamine elevates happy feelings as serotonin helps reduce stress. So often when we are upset, our facial expressions are held tight and reflect anger, sadness, and frustration. Our kiddos see these expressions on our faces, and they begin to model our emotional responses, which is exactly how kids learn—by imitating us. In these moments, when you feel your anger rising and your facial expressions tensing, just smile. A smile often leads to laughter and can quickly lighten any mood. It halts the emotionally charged situation and provides an immediate redirection toward positive feelings.

Create Humor in the Situation

Oftentimes, it's difficult to find the humor in stressful situations. Try to think about something that just occurred that would be funny if you were not so mad. The most important thing is to ensure you are honoring everyone's emotions while trying to lighten the mood with respect and dignity. When we model to our children that it is okay to have big and frustrating emotions and still be able to transition into a state of laughter and peace, it helps them understand that their emotions are fluid, not permanent, and they are in control of shifting their emotions from one feeling to the next.

Play a Funny Scene in Your Head

My go-to is a scene from the show *Parks and Recreation*. Leslie Knope, the main character—a hardworking, kindhearted, overachiever—is stranded with her team at a bed and breakfast, and one of her friends locks her in a room filled with 50 cats so she can relax and get some sleep after frantically trying to solve a problem all day. The scene cuts to her peeking out through one of the windows in distress, and the next time you see her, she has a burst of energy and hundreds of ideas for solving the problem. When I think of this episode during intense situations, I'm able to laugh to myself and I see a shift in my mood.

What is a favorite scene or line of dialogue from a show or movie you like? Find your funny scene and add it to your tool bag for the next time you need a good laugh during a stressful situation. You can even write on a sticky note a line or phrase that reminds you of the scene and keep it handy for triggering moments.

Laugh

Did you know that one minute of anger weakens your immune system for up to four to five hours, while one minute of laughter boosts your immune system for over 24 hours? Laughter can support your overall mental health and well-being. Remember that phrase and keep it somewhere prominent—like your phone background or your fridge—as a reminder to laugh more. Try to include things in your day that will make you smile or have a good laugh, like watching baby animal videos.

Trigger Technique

Sometimes, a good laugh can lighten tense situations. During a triggering interaction with your child, place a random object on your head and pretend to sneeze, so the object falls off. I have used this trick so often with my three-year-old, and it works almost every time. You can also make silly faces and talk about how silly your faces look when mad, adding humor to the situation for both of you.

KEEP IN MIND

- Laughter is a natural cure everyone has access to, just like our breath. Analyze the situation and determine if using one of these strategies can turn that frown upside down.

- There are times when using laughter as a strategy may not diffuse a situation. It is important to be mindful of your child's or partner's emotional reaction to laughter and whether it will escalate or calm the situation. Pause, and honor their emotions so they understand you aren't dismissing them. To ease tension, acknowledge their feelings by saying something like, "I see you are getting more upset. I wasn't trying to laugh at you, I was only trying to cheer us up."

- Be an observer in your own environment. Be mindful of the things your child and partner find funny. Be aware of their emotional responses in situations. This will show you how best to lighten the mood when anger arises.

- Remember, if all else fails, smile to yourself. Let out a forced laugh and hold your face in a smiling position for a few seconds. If you can reset yourself, you have a better chance of being an anchor for your child or partner during stressful situations.

CHAPTER 8

Learning to Respond, Not React

L una became a first-time mom at 35. She had always heard of the terrible twos, but it was not until she experienced it firsthand with her two-year-old son, Jack, that she truly grasped the inherent truth in that saying. Every mom has been there—the never-ending "no no nos," toys everywhere, tantrums and meltdowns (we get to this more in chapter 18), etc.

Luna's job as a special education teacher was very demanding and left her feeling burned out most of the time. One day, when she was arriving home from work, Luna could hear Jack screaming from outside the door. This seemed to be a recurring theme in her house lately. She was already dreading going inside. Upon entering the house, she tripped over a toy Jack had left in front of the door. She yelled at Jack to clean up his toys right away, as she threw her arms up in distress.

Instead of cleaning up his toys, Jack became even more upset and began to throw his toys while screaming even more loudly.

While Luna yelled at him to calm down, Jack screamed in protest, refusing to pick up his toys. This exchange ended with both of them in tears and overwhelmed. Of course, Jack's toys were still all over the floor. Luna shut down. Filled with anger and sadness, she picked up Jack's toys. She felt that, despite her intention of staying calm and getting Jack to clean up, she had achieved the opposite. She never wanted to yell at Jack, but she had reacted rather than responded. Luna paused and made a choice to change the rest of this interaction with Jack. She did a quick breathing exercise to reset and then walked over to him, got down on his level, and said she was sorry.

Luna's intentions were always positive. Her main goal was to be the best mother she possibly could be, every single day. Isn't that the intention of every mother, to be able to support their child as best as they can? It can be challenging to respond rather than react in heated moments. The most important thing to remember is that once you begin to bring awareness to your triggers, in the moment you will be armed with the tools to help you respond rather than react. Even if you may have started an interaction with your child in a frustrating or negative way, the tools you will learn to implement will help you pause and support shifting your mindset to better respond.

STRATEGY SESSION

You are your child's anchor in their sea of strong emotions. These techniques will help you stay calmer during heated interactions, which will help your child be calm in those moments as well. Now, let's learn how to respond, not react, during triggering interactions with your child.

The powerful pause. When you feel the emotional pressure rising, pause and take a mental step out of the situation. Pausing is so powerful that it can be the key to changing the direction of an interaction. By pausing, you stop yourself from reacting immediately, and you give yourself the room to make a choice. You can then choose how to use other techniques to respond rather than react.

Body language matters. Young children can read your emotions through your body language. When they see their mom with hands clenched or a rigid posture, it can heighten their fight-or-flight reactions. Think about bringing all your movements inward, closer to the body. To help you reorganize in that moment, try giving yourself a tight hug while squeezing your arms, starting closer to your shoulders, and moving toward your hands. You can teach this strategy to your child when they are calm. Then in a heated moment, model it, and encourage your child to imitate you. This will help them regulate their emotions, too.

Monitor your voice volume. When your child is yelling, crying, or expressing big emotions, it can trigger you to raise your voice. Instead, do the opposite and bring your volume way down, almost to a whisper. This will show your child you are present in the moment, calm, and accepting of all their emotions. This, in turn, will help them calm, organize, and regulate their emotions. This powerful technique is called "coregulation." It is the ability to use yourself as a therapeutic agent, the anchor for your child, by providing a warm and positive response when your child is experiencing frustrating emotions.

Validate what your child is trying to communicate. When a child is experiencing big emotions, it has nothing to do with you even though it can often feel like a personal attack. Most often, there is a breakdown in communication between you and your child. Nonetheless, the situation can still be triggering. Pause. Honor your child's emotions. Give your child the words when they are unable to express their emotions. Tell your child, "I see that you are mad. I see that you are sad. It is okay to be upset." It is important to validate their feelings so they can begin to express their feelings more calmly in the future.

Trigger Technique

Throughout the day, find your anchor—your way of returning to a state of stillness and feeling grounded. Meditation is a grounding practice that can support you in doing just that. The Resources section includes a mediation that I find helpful to anchor myself called "Finding Your Anchor" by Michelle Amussen (page 148). The practice will explore your connection to your breath and the sensations felt throughout your body to help you be mindful in the moment and get grounded. You can use the meditation anytime during the day, and it only takes 10 minutes. Remember, you are taking 10 minutes toward better self-care to support optimal well-being and self-regulation.

KEEP IN MIND

- A regulator, like one on a scuba tank, controls the release of the pressure inside. When we are regulated, we can experience intense emotions without having intense reactions, because we can control how quickly we let the pressure out.

- Your goal is not to eliminate your emotions, but to regulate the release of emotional pressure. Your emotions are valid, and they inform you that your child is likely having similar emotions.

- Think about situations that are likely to cause triggering interactions. Remind yourself of your power to choose your response before the triggering interaction starts.

- Children do not calm down simply because they are told to. The mind does not work this way. You also cannot expect to calm yourself simply by remembering to calm down. The techniques you've learned will remind your body how it feels to be calm, and your brain will follow suit. Likewise, show your child how to calm their body, and their brain will follow.

- Pausing is a necessary step, and it must be intentional. It gives you power to choose a response instead of reacting. If you remember one thing when you feel the emotional pressure rising, remember to pause.

- Practice does not make perfect, but it will make you more aware. No one can respond rather than react 100 percent of the time, so be kind to yourself. You are raising a tiny human with big emotions. The goal is to be consistent, act with intent, and be mindful with your responses as best you can.

3

ONGOING STRATEGIES FOR MANAGING TRIGGERS

So far, you have learned about the different types of triggers and some strategies that can help you respond rather than react during stressful situations. Even though these strategies are presented in the context of motherhood, they can also be helpful in your everyday life. We all encounter stressful situations; the goal is to have a variety of tools in your tool kit that are easily accessible during any interaction. In this section, you will continue to discover ongoing strategies that will help you manage your triggers more mindfully. Let's get started!

Managing Expectations

E velyn and their partner, Sara, couldn't wait to have kids of their own someday. They had been trying to get pregnant for a few years, so when they found out Evelyn was pregnant, they were beyond excited.

Evelyn and Sara had always been in harmony when managing the day-to-day responsibilities of their life and home together, but when Evelyn gave birth to their daughter, Amaya, their lives turned to chaos.

Evelyn and Sara owned a local business downtown. When Evelyn was pregnant, they had created a plan based on what they expected to experience when their baby arrived. Evelyn would stay home with the baby and take care of the day-to-day responsibilities. They enlisted Evelyn's niece to help out after school during the week, both with the baby and at the store. Sara would manage the store and come home on breaks to spend time with the family. It all looked perfect on paper.

Oftentimes, we create certain expectations of parenthood in our mind. We even may think back to our own childhood—what we loved about it, what we'd like to share with our kids, what we plan to do differently, and how we'll manage our time. Sometimes, though, when you actually transition to that life, it isn't anything like you envisioned. Those blissful days spent dreaming of family outings, bonding through "mommy and me" time, or catching up on housework while the baby sleeps can become a blur of tantrums or meltdowns in the grocery store.

That is exactly what happened to Evelyn and Sara: Evelyn's niece joined a sports team and couldn't help out, Evelyn was overwhelmed by being at home with the baby, and Sara was struggling to manage everything at work.

The transition to motherhood is filled with many challenges and can have you questioning your abilities as a mother and in other roles of your life. You may feel like you're not a good mom or that you don't know what you're doing. The truth is that you are and you do; you are just adjusting to the new realities of motherhood and reconciling them with your earlier expectations.

Being a mom is not easy! Be mindful of what you need each day and what you want to do. Determine which expectations are realistically attainable and necessary and which ones are more like good intentions. The following strategies can help you manage the ongoing expectations of motherhood and help support a better balance in your life.

Daily to-do lists and the mental load of all your roles can be overwhelming, even before motherhood. Add in the responsibilities of being a new mom, and even the most motivated individual can feel defeated.

Instead of labeling your expectations as a "to-do" list, reframe them as "intentions" and take it one day at a time. Living with intention means actively being present in the moment, taking time to respond, and responding in a way you truly feel is right in that moment. Looking at a to-do list can be a trigger in itself—the actual words "to-do," to be specific. But when we shift our mindset to the word "intention," it changes our internal narrative to be more mindful of what needs to be done each day and what a realistic expectation would be.

1. **Write down your intentions.** Begin by writing down all the intentions you want to accomplish. These can be daily tasks or weekly tasks—any intention (expectation) you want to assess to see what would be realistic. Once you have that list, label each item as a want or a need—what needs to occur on a daily basis, and what can be done weekly? The goal is to determine what you truly "need" to do in your life (and when) and what you "want" to do.

2. **Fill your cup.** In the morning, ask yourself, *What do I need to fill my cup today?* Refer back to the techniques that help you stay calm during stressful situations. Adjust your needs based on the day, and be mindful of how you're feeling. Do you feel a rapid pulse, labored breathing, tension in your body, low energy, foggy brain, extreme tiredness, or other symptoms of stress? Employ a strategy, such as a breathing exercise, to support your ability to stay calm in that overwhelming moment.

3. **Engage in mindfulness.** Engage in a five-minute mindfulness activity to set your intention. It can be as simple

as taking a few mindful breaths or naming something you are grateful for. Do an internal scan. Pay attention to your breath—is it fast-paced or even? Are you feeling any discomfort or pain? Be mindful about the food you eat, too, and listen to what your body is telling you.

4. **Prioritize.** As you are navigating your day, if you feel like it is getting harder to manage, ask yourself in that moment, *Can this wait until tomorrow?* This can be a powerful way to give yourself the grace you deserve when the day is not going as planned. Ask yourself if the task can be done tomorrow, and set a realistic time frame for completion the next day. This will also help you assess your ongoing daily intentions and adjust your expectations as necessary.

5. **Be kind to yourself.** Honor every single thing you accomplished during the day, no matter how small. We often think we need to be supermoms, but the truth is we just need to figure out how to manage the expectations of life, while also meeting our child's needs. The positive emotional attachment you form with your child will be an emotional anchor when life gets chaotic.

These steps can also be a great starting point when you are navigating the strategy in chapter 11 on page 82.

Trigger Technique

Managing expectations can be very overwhelming. Insight Timer is a free app that provides thousands of meditations to explore when searching for ways to be more mindful in the moment. Though any guided meditation that focuses on breathwork can help, I recommend "Meditation for Managing Expectations" by Jessy Coleman, a link to which can be found in the Resources section on page 148. The seven minutes it takes to practice this 4-2-4-2 breathing exercise and meditation can help you reground, refocus, and better manage the expectations in your life. Try it today!

KEEP IN MIND

- If you're finding it difficult to be present in the moment, pause. Take a minute to breathe, and, if you are able to, step away. Even if the baby is crying, the phone is ringing, or notifications are going off, pause. Be present and take it one intention at a time.

- Remember, many of the strategies in this book can be used in a variety of situations to support you. You get to determine which supports work best in each situation. The more tools in your tool kit, the better equipped you will be to handle different stressors.

- It's okay if your expectations differ from how things actually turn out. That's just part of life. It's okay to feel sad and frustrated, and to mourn the reality you thought you'd have. Remember: You *are* doing a good job, and you *will* adjust to your new role.

- Just because you may be feeling sad or frustrated with yourself for not meeting your own expectations, does not mean you are a terrible parent. Think about this next time you are overwhelmed. It can help to lighten the mood instantly, steer you away from any thoughts of failure, and bring some humor to the situation.

Unpacking Emotional Baggage

Padma had struggled with anxiety since she was a child. Her parents never understood why she was always anxious, and they also had no idea how to support her, which just made Padma feel even more isolated and alone.

As she grew older, she tried to explore strategies and supports to help her manage her anxiety, but it was an ongoing challenge. When Padma met her husband, Bill, in her late 30s, she was still struggling with intermittent anxiety. Even so, their relationship progressed quite quickly. Padma finally found someone who tried to support her anxiety rather than judge her for it— something she's never experienced before. Within a year they had moved in together, gotten married, and were expecting their first child.

Padma's anxiety increased during pregnancy. Bill was patient with her, trying to provide support in any way he could. But he could not help Padma manage her anxiety, which was starting to strain their relationship.

A few months after the birth of their daughter, Padma found that her anxiety was also affecting her ability to manage her expectations as a mother. She would often have flashbacks to the anxiety she felt throughout her life. She couldn't change how the flashbacks made her feel; she could only work toward the things within her control.

One day in particular, her anxiety was so high she could not even leave her house. As she sat there, holding her crying baby, she realized her anxiety was interfering with her ability to regulate her emotions during triggering interactions. She began using the 4-7-8 breathing activity (see page 48) and discovered it was helpful in the moment.

Later that night, she opened up to Bill and apologized. She acknowledged that it was not his responsibility to fix her anxiety; his support and understanding was all she needed. With that insight, she could explore other options to honor, understand, and work through her anxiety.

It is imperative to identify, recognize, and work toward unpacking your emotional baggage when entering relationships, especially when transitioning to motherhood.

When you understand where your emotions are coming from, you can stay grounded when more intense emotional interactions arise between you, your partner, and your child—or in any relationship. It can be emotionally draining to relive traumatic experiences from your past.

Remember, you do not have to do it all at once. Reflect and process as much or as little emotion at any one time and circle back when you feel ready. The goal is to make sure you are striving to be the best version of yourself, focusing on what you can control, and working toward optimal emotional wellness.

STRATEGY SESSION

Dialectical behavior therapy (DBT) is a form of cognitive therapy that supports your ability to manage your emotions and lessen triggering reactions when interacting with others, especially your child. Even though DBT was originally used to treat personality disorders, the tools that DBT encompasses are very useful in supporting anxiety and behavior in anyone looking to take a more mindful approach to managing their emotions.

DBT helps you become more present in the moment, honor your negative emotions rather than pretending they do not exist, determine strategies and supports that can help you during intense emotional responses, and find ways to connect with others through effective and respectful conversations. When working through the trauma and emotions from experiences, focus on the following concepts:

Mindfulness. To stay present in the moment, figure out which of three mindsets you are in. In the "reason" mindset, facts and logic prevail. In the "emotion" mindset, feelings prevail. In a "wise" mindset, both reason and emotion are present. Try to adopt a wise mindset.

Interpersonal effectiveness. This examines your relationships with others and how you manage conflict within each one (partner, child, friends, etc.). Determining what is impacting or getting in the way of your interpersonal effectiveness skills will help you see what areas you should focus on.

When we examine how we interact with others and the emotions that arise, we can begin to notice our reactions, identify the roots of our emotions, and work toward not letting those emotions interfere during frustrating or stressful situations.

Distress tolerance. This refers to how you manage your distress. When trauma or negative emotional experiences occur throughout your life, it can be difficult to accept the feelings that were consequential to your specific traumas.

Accepting and honoring your pain and discomfort as a part of life is the foundation for learning to regulate your emotions. As you navigate these feelings when they arise, you will increase your emotional tolerance during stressful moments. This is also an important part of the healing process.

Emotional regulation. Maintaining complete control of your emotions all the time is an unrealistic expectation, but you can figure out what strategies will support you when navigating stressful situations. The goal is not to be rid of your emotions but to be in control as much as you can when they vary during stressful situations. You can also refer to the breathing exercises, journaling, and mindfulness exercises found throughout this book for help with emotional regulation.

As always, before beginning any techniques or strategies, breathwork is a great place to begin. It only takes a few minutes but can set the foundation for your practice.

Trigger Technique

Diaphragmatic breathing is the foundational breathing practice used in most meditation and mindfulness techniques. It may also be referred to as "deep breathing" or "deep belly breaths." Not only does this type of breathing strengthen the diaphragm, but it can also be a way to reduce stress and support emotional regulation.

Find a comfy and relaxing spot. You can either sit or lie down during this exercise. Check in with your body and release all tension. Place one hand on your chest and the other on your belly. Take a deep, steady breath in through your nose. Be mindful to keep your chest still as your stomach moves outward. Slowly exhale for two seconds. Repeat as needed. Keep your chest still as you feel your breath move outward and inward in your belly region.

KEEP IN MIND

- Be mindful when navigating past traumas, emotional experiences, or any other emotion that has become a trigger for you. It will push you to reflect and gain more insight into your actions, responses, and feelings. It can be tempting to close your eyes and turn away—but don't. This means you are on the brink of change.

- Sometimes writing down your emotions is easier than talking about them. It may be helpful to write down your thoughts in a journal or a notebook when you begin to unpack your emotions. You can always keep these pages in a safe space. Let your writing be a reminder of your emotional journey and why you are trying to better yourself, for you, and your family.

- Show yourself endless compassion when revisiting past trauma and any triggering situations you are presently working through. It is much easier for us to continue responding reactively in stressful situations, but you are trying to change that. This work takes strength, determination, and motivation—you are amazing!

Calming and Redirecting Your Inner Critic

Geraldine was very hard on herself, always striving for perfection. She would analyze every aspect of her life and try to do everything right. Her friends often told her she was her own worst critic and she needed to be less hard on herself. Anytime she made a mistake, her inner narrative was filled with negative comments.

When Geraldine was pregnant with her first child, Jesse, she would constantly judge herself for every little thing she did that was not in line with the latest and greatest trends for a healthy pregnancy. Before she became a mother, she had high expectations of what the experience would be like; but after Jesse was born, she felt unable to fulfill the expectations that came with motherhood.

Geraldine found herself criticizing every parenting decision she made. She loved being a mother, but her daughter was an extremely fussy baby and always seemed upset. She would cry well into the night and early into the morning—sometimes it felt like Jesse would just cry all day long. Geraldine tried to think of ways to calm her, but nothing seemed to work. She blamed herself for her daughter's outbursts and thought she was a bad mom because she couldn't soothe her daughter. She felt emotionally drained. Geraldine believed she would be able to handle being a mom, but her inner critic was sabotaging her instead of supporting her.

Geraldine expressed her concerns during a conversation with one of her friends, who was also a first-time mom. To Geraldine's surprise, her friend said she felt the same way and offered her advice on not being so hard on herself. In that moment, Geraldine realized she was sabotaging herself and wanted to figure out how to shift away from that mindset. She also began to realize that the way she managed her time wasn't intentional, or allowing her to spend meaningful, quality time with her family. She began to think about and implement strategies to help her readjust her day-to-day activities and allow for more quality time, while still maintaining her daily responsibilities.

Motherhood will be filled with various moments that won't go right or as planned, but that is in no way a reflection of your parenting skills. There will be times that, no matter what you do, there is not a solution to the problem. Talking down to yourself will only perpetuate the cycle of negative thoughts and emotions. If you can learn to let go of the concept of fixing, forgive yourself with kindness, and work to support and honor all the messy moments, it will help shift your internal narrative into something more positive. It will also strengthen your emotional connection with your child, especially during triggering situations.

STRATEGY SESSION

Have you ever calculated the time you spend talking negatively to yourself on any given day? If not, take a moment to ask yourself about your inner monologue. Do you criticize everything you are doing? What specific things are you negative about?

Looking deeper into your inner critic can help guide you toward solutions that will halt that negative feedback loop in your head during stressful interactions with your child. Your inner monologue can either support you or sabotage you, if you let it. Make a habit out of redirecting your inner critic.

It takes 21 days to form a habit, so over the next 21 days, analyze which strategies you've implemented the most, which ones made you feel like your best self, and what things you were doing that might not have had such a positive impact. Challenge yourself to embed supports and strategies into your daily and life routines. This will help you turn your internal critic into your biggest support system.

Figure out which habit you'd like to start with. You can work on any habit or routine, but for the purposes of this chapter, let's focus on positive self-talk. Create a positive affirmation or simply practice gratitude all day—whatever strategy you choose, whether it's for one day or all 21 days, take it one day at a time and see what actually helps you transform your inner critic into your inner advocate. Here are a few tips:

Shift the internal script. Pick a short phrase you can say in your head to intercept, acknowledge, and shift a negative thought process when you feel your internal monologue becoming critical. It can be something as simple as, *Hello. I see you. I hear you. And I allow myself to let go of this thought.* Sometimes, giving yourself permission to not speak negatively to yourself can help transition your mindset to a more supportive one.

Remember that change takes time. Be mindful that your internal narrative has been present for quite some time. There will be moments where it feels like the strategies in this book may not be working or you find yourself slipping back into a negative feedback loop in your head. This is completely normal. In those moments, remind yourself that you knew this could happen. Try to shift your internal script and tell yourself, *I was prepared for this*.

This 21-day period is all about learning how to shift your mental mindset from one drowning in negative self-talk to one that focuses on the positive. Enrich your internal monologue with meaningful conversations and positive self-talk, such as funny catchphrases, supportive, affirming thoughts—or even a simple *I got this!*—to shift that negative feedback loop in your head.

Trigger Technique

Maintaining a visual of which strategies and supportive techniques you have been using over the 21-day period can greatly help you. You can use a habit tracker (see page 148) to help you track your habits over time, determining which habits are supporting or hindering your emotional state and which strategies you are using the most or least often. This will further support the habits you want to focus on and be mindful of so you can calm your inner critic.

KEEP IN MIND

- Remember, a negative narrative within your head can negatively impact the body, both emotionally and physically. On the other hand, when your internal monologue is positive, it can have an amazing impact on your overall emotional well-being.

- The goal is to shift your internal narrative so it supports your overall well-being. Otherwise, it will further perpetuate reactive responses during triggering interactions in all relationships in life, not just those with your kids.

- Think of one moment with your child that brings you happiness. Reflect on how it represents all the ways you support your child. Be proud of your intentional choices to create a positive relationship with your child. The next time a negative narrative tries to creep into your head, think of that moment.

- Take the pressure off yourself as you start the change process. Go into it with an open mind, ready to use your chosen strategies to make small daily shifts that create a positive state of mind.

CHAPTER 12

Encouraging Your Inner Advocate

Yuki found herself criticizing everything she did once she became a mother. Whether her daughter, Lulu, was content, happy, sleeping, frustrated, or crying, Yuki was always putting herself down. In fact, Lulu had begun to pick up on some of Yuki's emotions and would become increasingly fussy when Yuki was irritable, feeling down, or anxious.

One night, Yuki was trying to finish up the loads of laundry that had been piling up since the previous week. She found herself yelling out loud, unable to manage her emotions, with her fight-or-flight responses in full effect. Lulu overheard her mom yelling and began to cry. But this time, Yuki felt a shift in her mindset. As Lulu cried, it became clear the way Yuki spoke to and treated herself was greatly impacting her mental health, as well as her interactions with her daughter, preventing her from sustaining coregulation (staying calm to help calm her daughter) when Lulu was frustrated and expressing her wants, needs, and emotions.

Yuki was ready to shift the narrative inside her head to one that was supportive and loving for both herself and her daughter. So Yuki paused and took a few deep, mindful breaths. She calmly walked over to her daughter, picked her up, and held her. She felt grounded, and Lulu calmed down, too. Yuki was provided with the best reinforcement—seeing the positive effects of being able to coregulate with her daughter. It was a step toward encouraging her inner dialogue, which made her feel like a good mom.

Even when you are in a state of calm and ready to shift that narrative in your head, you may not receive a reinforcing response, such as when Yuki was able to calm Lulu. When this happens, find one thing that does work (for example, Lulu may not have stopped crying, but she did cry less), write it down, and remind yourself that you are an amazing mother.

Now that you have learned how to calm your inner critic and encourage your inner advocate, let's turn that knowledge into positive life habits that will support not only your well-being, but also the relationship you have with your child during stressful situations.

STRATEGY SESSION

If you're trying to change your habits in 21 days (page 82), you're already beginning to identify some ways to shift your internal critic to one that is more supportive, that advocates and cheers you on, especially during stressful times. Now let's focus on when and where to embed these strategies throughout your day to support your inner advocate.

Start with a simple dialogue. Each time your internal narrative wants to slide down the negativity slope, say a simple three-to-four-word sentence such as, "I am kind," or, "I am capable." You can say these words either out loud to yourself or in your head, depending on what you are comfortable with.

Do one nice thing for yourself every day. Even if it's something as simple as setting out your clothes the night before for a smooth morning or taking a few extra minutes to sit in the car before coming into the house, do something that makes you happy. One of my favorite things to do is buy myself sunflowers so I have something beautiful to look at when taking a minute to pause during stressful situations.

Set boundaries. We will talk more about this in part 4, but it's important to notice when your inner voice tells you to set boundaries and why. When you're feeling overwhelmed, it can be challenging to be a support to others or be around people that may actually heighten your anxiety. Be mindful of what you need on any given day and make sure to communicate your wants and needs to others clearly and respectfully. Boundaries are a great way to follow through and establish your wants and needs (see page 144).

Believe in yourself. I am sure you have heard some version of this concept: Before you can take care of someone else, you must take care of yourself. One way to practice self-nourishment is to actually believe what you are telling yourself. It may be hard to do this at first, so practice focusing on all the things you are doing right, even if you are still battling negative self-talk. Make a list of encouraging messages to yourself, such as, "I am a good mom because I want the best for my child," or, "I am learning to meet my child's needs." No one else gets to tell you how to use that voice in your head, so make sure you are actively choosing to use it to advocate for your wants and needs and to express your feelings in a more mindful way.

Trigger Technique

Take out a piece of paper. Every time a negative thought creeps into your head, write it down. Then, next to it, write three positive things about yourself. They do not have to be anything major; something short, simple, and to the point will suffice. Once you have your positive things, cross out the negative thought—there is no longer any room in your mind for it. The goal is always to remind yourself that one negative thought or emotion does not define who you are and should not be given the power to influence your emotional regulation on a day-to-day basis.

KEEP IN MIND

- Imagine you are speaking to yourself with pure kindness, grace, understanding, compassion, and love. What would that do for your self-esteem, for your faith in yourself, and for your ability to use these strategies in the moment? Think of it as nourishment for your emotional soul.

- Your inner voice can be your advocate. Use it to encourage yourself.

- During stressful situations, the body goes into overdrive. It is imperative to take a moment to rest. Go outside, complete a breathing activity, listen to your favorite song, take a nap, etc. Our bodies want to keep going, but try not to give in. Resting and using the strategies you've learned so far will help you reach your goal of cultivating your inner support system.

CHAPTER 13

Accepting Responsibility for Your Actions

K ayla was juggling a lot with her son, work, and grad school. Most recently, her job had transitioned to remote work, and she had lost day care for her 28-month-old son, Jeremiah. Her husband, Mark, worked a full-time job that required overtime, so she was alone most of the time with Jeremiah.

Unfortunately, Mark and Kayla were not the best communicators. Kayla often got mad at Mark for not empathizing with her situation or for not trying to help more. She would often yell at Mark and was irritable and anxious whenever they talked. He typically avoided conflict, and lately, he was annoyed anytime Kayla vented her frustrations to him. This further fueled Kayla's already intense negative emotions.

Kayla's stress was at an all-time high. It was difficult for her to attend virtual meetings and get her work done each day, all the while attending to her son's needs. During a meeting, Jeremiah was in her office. He poured a cup of water on top of her work documents. Kayla gasped, turned the camera and mic off in her meeting, and yelled at Jeremiah. Jeremiah began to cry. Kayla turned on the video but kept the sound muted, and returned to her meeting. She fought back tears of frustration, sadness, shame, guilt, you name it—everything started to build up.

When Mark got home, Kayla told him what happened and how she felt compelled to yell at Jeremiah. Mark stayed quiet, and his responses were short. She expected Mark to say the right thing or do something to support her, but that didn't happen. This triggered her to put herself in Mark's shoes. She realized all her venting and yelling, even though she felt justified in the moment, was not the appropriate response and was causing Mark to burn out and shut down. Kayla excused herself and took a minute to breathe. Once calm, she apologized. It was the first time in a long time that Mark was receptive to Kayla's feelings.

Unfortunately, life is full of stressful situations, but you cannot keep responding in the same, unpleasant way when stressors arise. Why? Because motherhood will stress you out! If you don't take steps to break that cycle, it will only make you feel worse.

Triggering situations are out of your control, but your actions *are* within your control. Justifying negative behavior will only continue to lead you toward the same mistakes and behaviors you are trying to change. There will be many times during your motherhood journey when you act in ways you are not proud of, ways that really make your heart feel heavy. That is okay; we've all been there. The goal is to shift out of the shame and guilt mindset and into a place where you can accept responsibility for your actions, give yourself grace, and be more mindful going forward.

STRATEGY SESSION

Spend time reflecting on the changes you want to make in your life and why. The first step is accepting ownership of your words and actions, especially if they are hurtful toward others. In the moment, it might be challenging to accept responsibility for your actions; however, if you are able to reflect on why what you did or said was harmful, then you can actively change how you handle situations going forward.

The following exercise can help you separate yourself from your behavior. We can get caught up in intense emotions when we make a mistake, which can then cause negative thoughts to ruminate in our minds. Separating yourself from the behavior will help stop these all-consuming feelings of guilt, shame, anger, and frustration.

1. On a piece of paper or in a notebook, draw a table with four columns (see the example table on page 93).

2. In the first two columns at the top, write out "What happened?" and "Why did it happen?" In the third and fourth columns, write "What do you think of yourself?" and "What do you think about your behavior?"

3. Then reflect on a situation, either recently or in the past, when you acted in a way you now regret, or anything that you feel shame or guilt for. Write about them in the "What happened?" column.

4. Next, ask yourself why you acted that way, and put your answers in the second column ("Why did it happen?"). Is there an underlying reason you are upset? Were you tired and stressed that day? Did you feel like you deserve better, or did your reaction feel valid? Take yourself out of the equation and think about the action itself. What personality characteristics does it reflect?

5. Now think about what caused the behavior. In the third column, write about how your actions made you feel. How did you think of the way you reacted in that moment?

6. In the last column, write about what you think of your behavior, now that you've taken some time to reflect. Was it helpful or unhelpful?

WHAT HAPPENED?	WHY DID IT HAPPEN?	WHAT DO YOU THINK OF YOURSELF?	WHAT DO YOU THINK ABOUT YOUR BEHAVIOR?
Ex. *I snapped at Mark.*	*I was anxious and expected Mark to resolve the situation.*	*I wasn't being a thoughtful partner.*	*Snapping at Mark was not helpful and caused him to shut down.*

What can you conclude from this activity? Reflect on what resonates with you the most.

One more thing to keep in mind: When learning how to navigate taking responsibility for your actions, it's important to practice self-compassion, especially when revisiting memories from the past and reflecting on how you have handled accepting responsibility throughout your life.

Trigger Technique

The previous exercise can be emotionally triggering in itself.
If you begin to feel overwhelmed, pause, breathe deeply,
and take a movement break. Go for a walk, or rearrange your
furniture. Sometimes just shifting positions or moving to
a different area of your environment can help you refocus
your attention on the exercise rather than the intense
emotions behind it.

KEEP IN MIND

- There will be many times you wish your partner, your friend, or a family member would say the right thing or do something in the moment so you feel understood and heard. But ultimately, the responsibility falls on you to truly make that change, regardless of what's going on in your surroundings or how other people respond.

- When support is not available, look to your child. When they smile at you or engage with you, that should be all the reassurance you need—your child is over the moon in love with you and can feel your love.

- You are strong. You are capable. You can make these changes. By acknowledging that your actions are reflections of unresolved triggers in your own life and you take responsibility for changing them, you can begin to choose and implement strategies in future triggering situations.

- Focus less on your expectations of others and more on attaining your own goals. That is, focus on the things you can control.

Coming to Terms with Mom Guilt

It had been five months since Judy returned to work. Her son, Greg, was attending day care for extended hours to accommodate Judy's busy work schedule. It felt like she barely had any time with Greg. She also began to witness Greg developing more of an attachment with his day care providers than he had with her, which made Judy feel even more guilty about working so much.

Often, Judy was playing catch-up with what Greg preferred at this stage. His day care providers tended to know more about what he was eating, what he liked to play, or whether he was having a bad day than she did.

The days felt like they were running into one another, and she was stuck in a cycle of dropping off Greg, going to work, being away from him for 12 or more hours a day, picking him up, struggling through their night-time routine, and then crashing into bed and doing it all over again. She would think, *I should be home more. I should have pushed through the excessive tiredness and been calmer for Greg when he was upset.* She placed blame on herself for not being able to connect more with her son.

On top of all of that, Judy had not been out with her friends since before she was pregnant. She had almost no energy or time to even think about meeting for a cup of coffee. Judy was feeling overwhelming "mom guilt" for "failing" at so many things. She even felt guilty for doing her job, which was starting to make her feel depressed. It was time to make some changes and restructure the guilt she had been feeling. She decided to reach out to a babysitter for a few hours a week so she could take a yoga class or go to the occasional happy hour with her friends.

Mom guilt is something mothers inflict upon themselves when they feel they are not meeting the standards of someone else's (or society's) expectations or that they are a failure within their own motherhood experience. This could not be further from the truth.

Mom guilt can be attributed to the many stressors and triggers that are found along the journey of motherhood, especially for first-time moms. There are times you will fall into the mom guilt trap and experience the various emotions that go along with it—sadness, a sense of failure, frustration, and anger. We'll examine the source of your guilt with techniques to reshape your internal narrative, making those moments of mom guilt few and far between.

STRATEGY SESSION

Notice when mom guilt shows up and when you feel your mindset shifting in a negative way. This will help you begin to analyze why and when the guilt is occurring. The following strategy will help you reframe guilt.

1. **Channel it.** Focus on your feelings of guilt. Where are you feeling guilt in your body? Perhaps you can try a quick body scan to discover areas where you're holding tension.

2. **Embrace it.** Instead of letting the guilt suck you down like quicksand, embrace it. Get to the root of the guilty emotion. You'll find this guilt often stems from wanting to be the best mom possible for your kid, along with having to manage all the other expectations and responsibilities that come with life.

3. **Ask yourself why this is happening.** Talk to your guilt. Ask it why it is here and what its purpose is. Get to the root of why you are feeling guilty in this moment. Now that you have embraced your guilt and honored your emotions, complete the following journaling exercise to help continue with the reframing of your guilt.

4. **Write it down.** In a notebook or journal, write down the answers to the following questions:

   → **Where are you feeling the guilt?**

   → **Why are you feeling guilty right now?**

   → **What is your guilt's purpose?**

5. **Every time the word "should" appears, cross it out.** There is no time machine to take you back to change the past, so don't waste time in the future feeling guilty about what you "should" have done. The goal is to learn from your past experiences, not to erase them.

Instead, cultivate thoughts like, *I was so sad about _____ that it caused me to act this way. Next time, I will_____*. Find ways to manage your guilt when it creeps in by starting your day with positive self-talk, especially if you feel guilty when you wake up. Being able to shift your mindset first thing in the morning can help you set the foundation for your day to be filled with more emotional stability.

Trigger Technique

When you turn in for the evening, reflect on the guilty feelings you had during the day. Now imagine a scenario that would make that guilt ultimately disappear. Is it realistic to attain? Are there tiny changes you can make to begin to shift your day toward a more positive mindset? Think of it like this: *Rather than feeling guilty, here's what I can do, which is all I can give today.* Start there.

Sometimes when we imagine everything we're feeling guilty about, we think, *If only I had XYZ, things would be better.* It's often the case that XYZ isn't as attainable as we think it should be. Instead of focusing on what you wish were different, stay mindful in the moment and control what you can. When guilt arises, analyze whether it is truly necessary to be experiencing these feelings.

KEEP IN MIND

- As mothers, we put extra stress on ourselves because of societal expectations about how we should be and other outside factors. And then when life happens and things take a negative turn toward frustration and anger, we are left feeling guilty about not upholding these standards. But *we* set the standards for ourselves. All we can ever do is appreciate the person we are today and strive to be better tomorrow.

- If you are always coming from a place of love, understanding, empathy, and conscious parenting, you will never ever have anything to feel guilty about, no matter what mistakes you might make.

- When "mom guilt" creeps up, embrace it with a big hug. Dive into the guilt and try to identify the source. Review the strategies on page 98 that can help shift your mindset on how you embrace guilt, to learn from it, understand it, and give yourself grace.

CHAPTER 15

Dealing with Shame

Teresa had been struggling to breastfeed her daughter Ophelia for weeks. For every good latch, there were several painful, emotionally charged ones. Teresa was part of a mom support group that provided tips and tricks to support the breastfeeding journey, but week after week she watched all the other moms learning to breastfeed their children while she struggled to figure it out.

Teresa became extremely frustrated. She felt ashamed and guilty about not being able to feed her child. Though she never meant any ill will toward them, she started to get upset whenever she would see other mothers breastfeeding their children. She decided to transition Ophelia to formula. Regardless of how badly she wanted to breastfeed her daughter, she needed to keep her baby fed. Still, she could not help but feel broken, like she had failed as a mother. She couldn't stop comparing herself to her friends and what she felt society considered "normal." She spiraled, feeling shame, guilt, and overwhelming anxiety.

Even when her friends tried to comfort her, Teresa's feelings of shame continued to grow. She would lash out at her friends whenever they tried to help her. Not only was she feeling guilty for not being able to feed her child the "right" way, but she was hurting her friendships now, too. One day, Teresa was scrolling through social media and mom blogs, and to her surprise, she realized that many mothers have similar emotions and reactive responses. She needed to figure out a way to work through her shame.

Shame can greatly impact your motherhood journey. It perpetuates an internal narrative that you are unworthy and flawed in some way, which can lead you to feel even more intense negative emotions such as anger and rage. As discussed in chapter 1, shame is typically felt after you recognize guilt and feel embarrassed for something you did or how you acted based on how you see yourself and how you think others will see you. Teresa was so caught up with not being able to breast-feed her child that she let her feelings of guilt transition to shame, which impacted her relationships with her friends and her daughter.

STRATEGY SESSION

Guilt materializes when we feel we're deserving of blame about something we've done; we feel bad about the action or situation. Shame goes deeper into our core; we're so embarrassed and humiliated, we almost feel as if *we* are bad.

Remember, shame is a byproduct of guilt. To decide which stress-relieving techniques will be helpful to you, you first have to determine if your guilt has transitioned to shame.

1. Take out a piece of paper and divide it into four columns. Label the columns "Situation," "Guilt," "Shame," and "What Comes to Mind." (See table below.)

2. In the "Situation" column, list some of your triggering situations.

3. Then put an "X" in either the "Guilt" or "Shame" column, depending on what you're feeling about the situation.

4. In the last column, reflect on what comes to mind when you think about your triggering situations and feelings.

SITUATION	GUILT	SHAME	WHAT COMES TO MIND
Ex. *I am never home*	X		*Failure as a mom and as a partner; no time to relax; limited fun time*
Ex. *When I was stressed out, I yelled at my son.*		X	*Overworked; exhausted; anxiety; sadness; want to be different*

Separating your emotions into guilt and shame can help you further identify triggers responsible for these feelings. This will help you find strategies with which to pair them. For example, if you feel like you don't have time to relax, take a day off or carve out five minutes each day just for you.

When you're stuck in a shame spiral, you may not even feel like change is possible, but it is! After getting to the root of your shame, use the techniques that helped you channel your inner advocate (page 85) to remind yourself that you are worthy of being a mother and you are able to take care of your kid.

Trigger Technique

To help further shift your mindset from shame, write down some of the things you like about yourself and the ways you are a good mom. You might write something like, "I am a good listener to my child," or, "My kid loves my silly songs." And if that doesn't work, try incorporating a self-care activity you love that put you in a better state of mind. An example might be taking a spa day for yourself, whether that's DIY at home or going to a spa for a massage or sound bath. Take some time for you, because you deserve it. Remember, you are a great mom!

KEEP IN MIND

- Whether you are a victim of "mom shaming" or are feeling shameful during triggering interactions within any relationship, try not to stay in that shame for long. That sinking feeling in the pit of your stomach is not a reflection of who you are as a mother. Even if you are feeling trapped or like there is no way out of your emotions, there is.

- Be mindful of the guilt you carry and whether it's fueling any shame you're experiencing. Being able to address your underlying guilt can help you peel back the layers to identify the triggers behind it before it evolves.

- Don't let yourself continue to feel shame for something you are actively trying to change. When discovering the foundation of your shame, ask yourself, *Can I let this go?* More often than not, the answer will be yes.

- Stop causing yourself unnecessary trauma over the things you have done and focus on what you can control in the present. Be kind to yourself and give yourself grace.

CHAPTER 16

Practicing Self-Compassion

Wanda was so excited when she found out she was pregnant. She felt overjoyed going to her first ob-gyn appointment and seeing the ultrasound for the first time. To her surprise, she was carrying not one but two babies! Wanda immediately felt a sense of urgency, anxiety, and a flood of other emotions all at once.

Wanda was a lawyer. Her husband traveled often for his job, leaving Wanda alone on weeknights. Most of her day-to-day activity involved providing intense therapeutic interventions to other families and supporting parent-child relationships. Wanda had only been planning to have one child. Now, with the unexpected baby number two, she was unsure of how she was going to manage all the expectations at home and at work.

Wanda's twins were born prematurely, and she had some complications with the birth, which caused her to be out of work longer than she anticipated. She had sustained some injuries during her delivery, and her babies had a long neonatal intensive care unit (NICU) stay, about three months. Each day, Wanda was trying to heal, be strong for her babies, and be supportive of the person who was covering her job while she was on leave. She had only planned on being out for six weeks, and her treatment plans were only covered until then. With her husband gone most weeks, she found herself alone and experiencing postpartum depression.

Wanda started to feel defeated and found it very difficult to give herself any kind of grace. One day she was sitting in the NICU with her babies, and a nurse came in and said to her, "You're doing a great job. Try not to be so hard on yourself. This is such a stressful time." In that moment, Wanda realized those words of compassion were words she should be saying to herself. She began to think about all the things she was doing for herself, her family, and her clients. And even though it wasn't at the level she wanted it to be, she began to give herself grace and compassion for her situation. This allowed her to process all the emotions of what she had been going through and use her internal narrative to be supportive and compassionate toward her situation.

To navigate all the demands of parenting, we must practice self-compassion. We can all be our own worst critics. That voice inside your head no one else hears can wreck your emotions in a flash. Cultivating a healthy inner narrative is key to creating a foundation for self-compassion. The following activity will help you practice more self-compassion throughout your day.

STRATEGY SESSION

To begin practicing self-compassion, try this self-love activity. I suggest practicing this activity when alone, or somewhere that you feel comfortable, so you can let go of all your inhibitions and focus on your self-compassion journey.

1. Stand in front of a mirror, or take a self-recording video.

2. Look at yourself and smile. Watch yourself take a deep breath in and a deep breath out. Be intentional with your breath.

3. As you take a few minutes to be still with your breath, begin to tell yourself about the amazing things you did throughout the day–anything positive that happened or something you'd like to remember.

4. If you find yourself thinking about things that were challeng-ing during the day, remind yourself that this is just another part of life to navigate. It is also important during these moments to tell yourself that everything will be okay. There will always be moments in motherhood you may regret, but you're taking amazing steps in the right direction.

5. Later in the day, make a video on your phone reminding yourself to be kind to *you*. Sometimes we can be our own worst critics. But, as discussed in chapter 12, we want our inner voice to become our advocate. We can do this by talking kindly to ourselves and being the voice we need to hear during stressful situations. Refer back to this video during stressful times to support your cultivation of self-compassion.

Video modeling is a great technique that helps you learn a new skill. If practicing self-compassion is something that you are newly embarking on, this can be a great visual reminder to support embedding this practice into your everyday life.

Trigger Technique

Create a vision board by finding a corkboard or posterboard and filling it with images, photos, affirmations, and quotes that inspire you. Use any materials you like and make this a creative, fluid process rather than one filled with structure and direction. The goal is to create something that is a reflection of what is meaningful to you. It should help you channel your inner compassion for your meaningful occupations (activities) and practice compassion toward yourself and what's important to you. This will help you become less self-critical in stressful interactions.

After you have completed your vision board, keep it in a place that will catch your eye and serve as a daily reminder.

KEEP IN MIND

- Showing compassion toward others is always easier than being compassionate to ourselves. Think about times that you showed compassion to others. Why would you not want to take your own advice and be more compassionate to yourself? Especially during frustrating situations, when you need your inner advocate the most!

- Be kind to yourself; you are your biggest cheerleader. Believe me, I have used all the strategies in this book and continue to use many of them on a daily basis. The days can still be filled with stressors, but having shaped my habitual responses to be more responsive rather than reactive has truly set me on a path of love, light, gratitude, acceptance, and stillness. You got this, Mom!

- Being a mother is an ongoing transformation process full of various phases. No matter what phase of motherhood you are in, you will be able to take away at least one strategy, if not several, that you can begin using now. Thank you for being here. You are doing an amazing job.

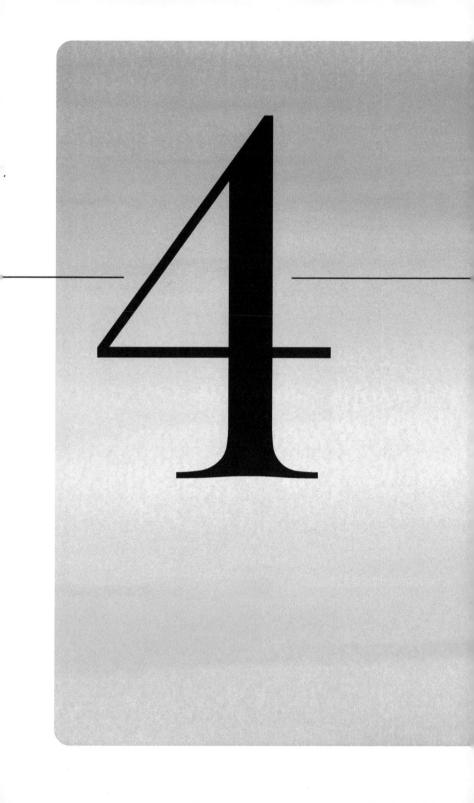

PART 4

SPECIFIC STRATEGIES FOR COMMON MOM-RELATED TRIGGERS

E ven though each parenting journey is different, there are some parent-related triggers everyone will experience at some point. In this section, you will discover techniques and strategies for dealing with situations that can commonly trigger emotional reactions in first-time moms—or parents in general.

CHAPTER 17

Challenging Behavior

Gwen screamed at her son Joseph to stop squeezing the cat's tail as she cleaned up the cereal he dumped on the floor. Joseph was a very energetic one year old. He ran through the house swiping things with his hands, threw objects too hard, and used excessive force when manipulating toys and other household items, which usually resulted in him breaking something. This led to Gwen and Joseph getting into back-and-forth struggles several times during the day when Gwen wanted Joseph to listen to her.

"No" was Joseph's favorite new word. It was no, no, no—to everything. When Gwen would ask him to clean up or try to transition away from his favorite activities, it was highly likely that a toy would be thrown, he would try to hit Gwen, and/or he would fall to the ground and scream.

This made it very difficult for Gwen to channel her inner calm on a daily basis. In fact, Joseph's behavior was so triggering, she felt a shift in her overall mental state and mood. She was becoming increasingly more anxious and easily irritable, including with others in her life.

Later that night, Gwen was taking a few minutes for herself while Joseph played independently in the next room. She wanted to end the day on a positive note, so at bedtime, Gwen talked about everything they did that day: They played with cars, baked banana muffins, and swam in the pool. She expressed to Joseph that it's okay to be mad or sad during the day and reminded him of what he could do when he gets upset, such as taking a deep breath, giving himself a hug, or stomping his feet. Gwen started to use bedtime to review coping strategies with Joseph so he could learn how to process his emotions and go to bed in a much calmer state.

Challenging behaviors will continually arise with young children, which can lead to you feeling frustrated, sad, guilty, and even ashamed. But you've learned how to counteract those feelings in the previous chapters. Now try shifting your mindset to think of these challenging behaviors as communicative responses instead. Ask yourself: What is your child trying to tell you? Do they need or want something? What happened just before the triggering interaction?

So often these types of behaviors are considered problems, when they really are just complex interactions because young children are still trying to figure out how to express their wants, needs, and emotions. Moreover, it is important to determine if the child is experiencing a tantrum or a meltdown (more on this in chapter 18).

Redefine your internal monologue regarding "challenging behaviors" and interpret these interactions as your little one reaching out to you for support. I know you are tired. I know it can feel all-consuming at times. As best as you can, try to transform your mindset so it supports connection, acceptance, understanding, and calm during these stressful situations.

STRATEGY SESSION

Young kids are learning how to express themselves, and, as moms, it is our job to help them learn how to regulate their emotions. The following strategies will help you channel that inner calm during these stressful moments so you can coregulate with your child.

Take a Water Break

My go-to strategy in triggering situations is to pause and grab a glass of water. Water makes everything better. Whether it's drinking a glass of water, using a guided imagery exercise, looking at the ocean, or engaging in water play activities with your child (like jumping in puddles), water can help bring both you and your child back to a state of calmness and clarity. And if your child doesn't like water, try something else they enjoy that will help them channel their inner calm.

Say Yes Instead of No

Deviating from the schedule and following your child's lead can drastically shift the tension in any room. For example, let's say you wanted to go grocery shopping, but your kiddo refused to get into the car. Instead of engaging in a 15-minute power struggle, ask yourself, *Do I really need to do this now?* or, *Is a no absolutely necessary?* Then ask your child what they'd like to do.

Incorporate what they'd like to do into what you need to do during the day, including chores and household tasks. Obviously, some things need to get done at certain times, but the more you allow yourself to go with the flow of the day, the more you'll be able to be present in the moment and help diffuse the frustrations your young child is facing.

Use the times your kiddo is engaging in their most preferred activities as opportunities to introduce coping strategies and talk about their big feelings through role-playing and calm discussion. To help you and your child identify feelings and find support to reach a calm state, check out the Zones of Regulation strategies (see the Resources section on page 148 for more information).

Reset Together

Set aside time each day to talk about all the good things that happened with your child. Then transition into what occurred during any stressful interactions. Kids need to be able to practice coping strategies when they are calm just like adults do. Bedtime is also a great opportunity to practice, as Gwen does with Joseph earlier in the chapter (page 115).

Practice Mindfulness

When your little ones see and hear you living in the moment, they, too, will begin learning and implementing mindfulness throughout their day. I see Luke watch me when I pause and do a yoga pose. Likewise, I see him pausing and being mindful of the world around him. Embracing mindfulness practices at a young age can support positive social-emotional development skills. When children learn to be present in the moment, especially in an upsetting situation, they learn to accept that moment for what it is and better control their own emotional responses, with you as their role model.

Start with this simple mindfulness exercise with your child: Ask them to tell you one thing they hear, smell, see, and feel, and talk about how it feels. Continue encouraging your child to express what they notice in the moment and how it makes them feel. This helps them become more aware of how they process information from the world around them.

Trigger Technique

Try to avoid the words "no," "stop," and "don't." These words can be triggering for some kids and can escalate their behavior. Take a moment and reflect on why you are about to say "no," "don't," or "stop," and choose to tell your child what they should be doing instead.

Also avoid saying "be careful," which can lead to anxiety in your child.

KEEP IN MIND

- Remember: Behavior is neither bad nor good—it is simply communication. Once we stop labeling our child's responses as "bad," we can begin to see this as their way of communicating. This will help us stay calmer in stressful moments and focus on what our child is trying to express.

- Stay mindful during the various shifts in your daily routine, especially on days when emotions are high. The more mindful you are of these moments, the better you can identify strategies to help you coregulate with your child and help them communicate their wants, needs, and frustrations with love.

- There will be moments when nothing works, no matter what strategy or technique you use. That's okay. Keep looking for opportunities to validate feelings and reset. The more your child sees you as someone who tries to act with intention in times of stress, the more they'll learn to do the same. Remember, the goal is not perfection but intention.

CHAPTER 18

Redefining Tantrums

L izette had not slept well the night before. She was up early editing an article for the magazine she worked for, and was watching her 27-month-old son, Nick, while her partner was at work. Nick woke up crying because he wanted pancakes and became increasingly upset and impatient, as it was taking Lizette longer to make the pancakes than he wanted.

While she was in the kitchen gathering ingredients, Nick screamed at her, swinging his arms as he ran in her direction. She was already irritated and told him repeatedly to wait. Nick continued to yell and tried to hit her while she was cooking. Once she was done and Nick had his pancakes, he immediately stopped yelling, was calm, and sat at the table to eat his food.

Every interaction that day felt triggering. In the evening, Nick wanted more pancakes. Lizette told him to get ready for bed and that he could have some tomorrow. Nick threw himself to the ground and screamed, while rolling on the floor in distress. Lizette was so tired.

She relented and gave Nick a pancake, but it did not help; he would not calm down. Lizette sat on the floor with him and let him process his emotions. After about 30 minutes, he climbed into his mother's lap, and they just sat still, both in tears while they embraced each other. They took a few deep breaths, then transitioned to bedtime.

Crying, screaming, yelling, pinching, hitting—these are just a few communicative expressions children sometimes demonstrate when they are upset. These behaviors can be very triggering for parents. I know; I have experienced them in my house, too. What has helped is gaining a better understanding of how my child communicates so I can help him express his wants, needs, frustrations, and emotions in a more positive way. You can do this with your child, too.

Each child is unique and has their own preferences as to what helps them calm, organize their emotions, and get back to a regulated emotional state. As parents, we can help our kids explore their sensory preferences by giving them a quiet area to rest, providing noise-canceling headphones or a weighted blanket, giving them a hug, playing some calm music, or introducing a movement break or breathing activity. These supports can increase their ability to self-regulate as they grow and maintain an optimal level of arousal (a "just right" state of mind) to support positive emotional expression and decision-making.

Your child has strong feelings, and so do you. Be mindful of how you feel when you are being triggered, you aren't feeling heard, you're stressed out, or you're having any number of negative feelings. Remember, your kiddo is learning how to navigate those feelings, too. Tantrums and meltdowns can be overwhelming to experience, but this strategy can help.

STRATEGY SESSION

Not all tantrums are actually tantrums; some may be meltdowns. Tantrums occur when a child gets frustrated and angry, and might kick, hit, yell, or cry. With a meltdown, the same behaviors may occur, but they are in response to being overloaded with sensory information from the child's daily demands, interactions, and environmental experiences. They may also include other emotions like extreme frustration. A tantrum will typically end once the child has been given what they want, whereas during a meltdown, the child will still have trouble regulating their emotions. During a meltdown, the goal is to support the child as they are getting back to a grounded state, which will happen gradually, not instantly.

Whether your child is having a tantrum or a meltdown, this strategy will help support them during stressful interactions. If your child is experiencing a meltdown, provide a safe space for them to process their feelings, honor where they are, and don't try to stop the meltdown.

1. **First, pause with your child.** Get down on your child's level and just be present. Sometimes words aren't necessary. Refer back to the coregulation strategy from chapter 8. Even if everything feels like it's going wrong, pause, assess the situation, and transition to something that can help everyone get back on track.

2. **Go outside.** A change of scenery is always good for the soul. Whether it's a walk around the block or exploring a new park, getting outside can be an instant mood shift for everyone and will help support a state of calm after an

intense situation. The connection between movement and being outside facilitates a child's ability to process and regulate their emotions more effectively. In our backyard, we have a variety of preferred sensory activities for our son to access, such as a sand table, swing, climber, bike, scooter, and chalk. Playing with all his favorite things helps him calm, organize, and regulate his emotions.

3. **Less is more.** When talking to your child during their tantrum or meltdown, use minimal language, lower the volume of your voice, and use your body language to express that you are in a state of calm, which will help you coregulate emotions with your child. Your child may even need complete silence, especially if they are having a meltdown.

4. **Keep it positive.** Tell your child what they *should* be doing rather than telling them what they *should not* be doing. Shift your language in a more positive direction to help set the stage for coregulation and to support your child's ability to stay calm and organize themselves. For example, if your child is trying to sit on the table, you can simply say, "Chairs are for sitting. We sit on chairs."

Trigger Technique

When your child is experiencing a tantrum or a meltdown, remember to pause and breathe. There are going to be times when you will need to recover from the emotions experienced in the triggering situation and bring yourself back to a state of regulation. Check out the "What Do You See" chart (page 148) to assess what happened before the frustrating moment and how you were able to support your child. You can use this chart to see if any of your strategies were helping or hindering you and make adjustments as needed.

KEEP IN MIND

- It can feel overwhelming when you are trying every-thing to help your child and nothing seems to work. Understanding the "why" behind your child's tantrum or meltdown will help you better respond to them. Break down why the tantrum or meltdown is happening by using the chart on page 148. You'll be able to track what happened just before, what the behavior looked like, and what did or did not work to support your child.

- Tantrums are not bad; they are your child's way of communicating with you. Through conscious parenting, we can help our children express their big emotions in a calm, positive way. Once you think of tantrums as a way to express emotions, you will notice a shift in how you respond during challenging situations. Remember, your child is trying to communicate with you in any way they can.

- By shifting your mindset toward understanding what your child needs to find calm, you will begin to feel compassion needed to support a more coregulated parent-child relationship.

Handling a Lack of Parental Support

G loria was excited to become a mother. She had just given birth to her daughter, Ana, and had everything she needed for the baby; she was embracing her journey of being a first-time mom. Gloria was obsessed—sharing photos of Ana with friends and family, talking about her milestones. And then, at 16 months, Ana stopped meeting those milestones.

Gloria became concerned. Her daughter was increasingly withdrawn, was avoiding interactions with others, and was more easily frustrated. Ana had spoken a few words already, but Gloria had not heard her say them in a while. Gloria used to be able to take Ana anywhere, but recently, Ana seemed to get overwhelmed when going out in the community. She would cover her ears and freeze in place when things were too loud, would drop to the ground screaming when Gloria tried to leave before Ana was ready, and was hyper focused on certain items when navigating any environment.

Whenever Gloria tried to talk about her concerns for Ana, she was met with comments that she was overreacting or that nothing was wrong with her daughter, and she'd grow out of it. It felt like no matter who she talked to—her family, friends, partner—she was faced with redirection rather than compassion, understanding, or support.

Gloria didn't feel like she was overreacting. She was reaching out for help with her daughter, and no one was listening to her. Gloria discussed her concerns with Ana's pediatrician, and even they expressed that everything sounded fine. But Gloria still knew that Ana needed additional support. She began to research professionals with a neurodiversity framework and found positive supportive social media accounts to follow, which helped her feel validated. She also began to advocate for Ana's needs whenever someone tried to downplay or redirect Gloria's words.

Some people have a difficult time sitting with others' emotions. Gloria's family and friends meant to be helpful, but to her, their words and actions felt dismissive. It can be very isolating when all your friends are raising children who do not have a disability and you're not feeling supported. No one mother has the same story, regardless of common experiences, but many first-time moms do share feelings of shame, guilt, sadness, and loneliness when they experience a lack of support.

No matter what your situation is, there are strategies to support you along your journey.

STRATEGY SESSION

Whether or not your child has a disability, when you feel unsupported as a parent, it can feel very frustrating and overwhelming. It may also be challenging for you to detach from the negative experience you are having and be able to increase your self-awareness in the moment. Preparing yourself for these difficult conversations with family and others in your life, as well as keeping in mind these strategies to use when support is absent, can help you navigate those interactions. Here are some tips:

Stay true to yourself. If you feel guilty or ashamed or your need for support is dismissed, you do not have to accept those emotions as your truth. Sometimes it can be hard for others to be active listeners and provide the support you need in the moment. These are your emotions and your feelings; no one else can tell you what or how you should be feeling.

Be confident in your parenting decisions. Honor the way you are choosing to parent your child and feel confident in your parenting decisions, even when it seems like no one agrees with you. You are Mom. You know what is best for your child. There is no one right way to parent. Stay true to your values, especially during these interactions.

Protect your energy and emotions. Reaching out for help can be a very vulnerable moment. It might be time to reevaluate relationships with people who respond negatively.

Be mindful of the company you keep. Try surrounding yourself with people who love and support you. Be wary of the ones who hinder your goals.

Get informed. There are many ways parents can seek out and cultivate an awesome support network. Facebook, Instagram, and local community support groups are good places to start.

Keep in mind that the internet is full of overwhelming and inaccurate information that may perpetuate more isolating emotions. See page 149 for a list of online supports that are beneficial in adopting a positive mindset when raising a disabled child.

Beware of who you follow on social media. As mentioned, the internet is an amazing way to connect with people; however, sometimes our social media feeds can be flooded with unhelpful information that fuels anxiety and can greatly impact your interactions with your child. Here are some dos and don'ts to consider:

→ Do follow people who bring a smile to your face. Look to connect with people who help you feel validated, provide you with new information to learn/unlearn, and support your overall mental, physical, and emotional health in a positive way.

→ Don't follow people who make you feel like a "bad" mom. No one has time for that, and all it does is keep you in a negative mindset.

→ Do unfollow people when they no longer serve a purpose for your overall optimal well-being.

→ Don't feel bad or guilty for choosing to follow or unfollow, connect or not connect.

→ Do block people who continue to enter your space in a negative way, especially if you have already asked them to stop.

→ Don't engage in unproductive or toxic debates online. You cannot control how other people respond, but you can control the level of involvement that you have in the conversation. Ask yourself, *What do I hope to gain from this?*

Trigger Technique

Now, let's practice a social media detox. Scroll through your social media accounts and assess the accounts, people, and organizations you follow. Who provides soul-enriching content, and who facilitates negative thoughts? Sometimes we feel guilty for unfollowing people or not wanting to sustain an ongoing relationship (whatever that relationship may be). However, that can cause more harm than good. The point is to be mindful about the time you spend on social media, and how the people you follow encourage either your inner advocate or your inner critic. Choose to fill your time with things that continue to support and nurture your soul in a positive way.

KEEP IN MIND

- Try not to let the opinions and actions of others take up emotional space and time within your thoughts. The more you trust yourself and your decisions, the less others will be able to negatively sway your emotions.

- If you are a parent raising a neurodivergent or a disabled child, remember that this initial diagnosis period is just a season of your life, and with the right support, you can learn to navigate and knock down barriers. Please know that your child is amazing, and you can help them be the best version of themselves, even when it feels like the world is against you.

- You may feel bombarded with information as a first-time mom, especially if your child is neurodivergent. Navigate your search for information toward autistic individuals, disabled individuals, and neurodiversity. This will help you begin to live in the moment and fill your life with authenticity, compassion, understanding, and empathy. For more resources on neurodiversity, see page 148.

- There may be moments when no one understands what you are going through or is able to support you in a way that you need. These situations are temporary. You are navigating these feelings and experiences as you go. You are allowed to change your mind in parenting, choose the less popular path, and be the mother that you want to be. Trust your ability to be a parent and continue to seek out opportunities to connect with others who will respect and support you along the way.

Balancing Work and Motherhood

Madison knew the struggle of balancing motherhood and her job all too well. She was a career-driven woman and got pregnant with her first child at age 38. Madison had always been the last person at the office, working well into the night and going above and beyond at her job—this was just her nature. When she was pregnant, one of her friends said everything would change once she had a child, that her priorities would shift dramatically. Madison was skeptical; she felt she could totally balance motherhood. But she had no idea what it was actually going to be like.

After the birth of her child, Madison was overwhelmed with feelings of anger and frustration. She wasn't feeling well-adjusted during this transition to motherhood. The responsibilities of caring for a newborn while still healing from her labor and delivery brought constant instability with big emotions every day.

Madison was only able to spend six weeks at home with her daughter, Addie, before returning to work. She wasn't ready. When she was at work, all she wanted to do was be at home, and when she was home, she felt guilty for not being present with her daughter. The sleepless nights, waking up early, and working all day left her feeling drained and depressed, like she was failing in both her personal and professional life.

Madison wished she could go back to the late-night work sessions that had been so productive for her, but that time was now devoted to caring for Addie. Madison knew she had to do something to balance the responsibilities in her life. After completing a time survey of how she spent her day (see "Strategy Session," below), she was able to carve out moments for her self-care and meaningful activities, set aside time to catch up on work, and set boundaries for herself to maximize the time she did have. This allowed her to make her time intentional, whether at home or at work.

When you become a mom, it may seem like you cannot handle everything on your plate *and* figure out how to balance motherhood with your other priorities and responsibilities. Instead of trying to find the perfect balance, think of it more like finding grace within the balance you can achieve each day. In overwhelming moments, all you may want is balance, but true balance does not exist. Reframe your narrative toward setting attainable, realistic expectations every day and living with intention.

STRATEGY SESSION

This strategy will help you manage your time better—which will support your ability to respond and be more present during stressful parenting situations. Don't get lost in the illusion that everything will be perfect if you can just figure out how to find balance in your life. Instead, start by analyzing the things you are trying to balance and determine their level of importance.

Remember, time is everything. A professor in graduate school once made me complete a time survey, and it was life-changing. For two days, I tracked everything I did minute to minute. We then analyzed it together to see how I was spending my time. It was revelational! I was filling every minute of my day with something to do, leaving zero time to spend on my own meaningful occupations or additional quality time with my family. When we truly examine how we are spending every single minute of our day, it puts into perspective what we actually want to spend time on.

To start tracking your time, try this method:

1. On a piece of paper or using a notes app on your phone, track every single thing you do and how much time it takes. You can do this for two days in a row on a weekday or weekend. The goal is to determine the value of the things you do to see what truly needs to be done, as opposed to what you want to accomplish.

2. Make a list of "daily intentions." Rate the importance of each intention (e.g., one hour of "me" time could be a top priority and decluttering your closet would be a low priority, etc.). This will help you sort out what's preferred and what is truly necessary and how important each one is to supporting your overall mental, physical, and emotional well-being. This also helps you incorporate all aspects of your wants and needs into your days as best as you can.

3. After you have completed your daily intentions lists, assess what occupations (activities) are meaningful to you, which intentions must occur, and how to make ongoing adjustments to ensure you are using the time you have to meet your needs.

4. Now begin to implement your daily intentions and assess how the new flow of your day is going. Check in

with yourself at the end of each day and jot down what worked well and what still needs adjustment. Your daily intentions are not meant to be stagnant; rather, they are more of a guide. It may even be helpful to project your new daily schedule onto a calendar to get an idea of how much time each task will take you.

Trigger Technique

Task analysis is the act of breaking down the steps to any task and considering the cognitive, physical, and social factors (and any other aspects) that go into completing that task. For example, think about the steps involved in brushing your teeth. This would include taking the toothbrush out, putting toothpaste on the toothbrush, and then brushing your teeth.

Now, think about how much energy it *actually* takes to brush your teeth. Think about the coordination, balance, and cognition involved in completing this simple task. How much effort will it take? When you're trying to reorganize the things in your life and create some type of balance, think about what's most important to you and how much effort will be needed to complete these tasks successfully and realistically.

KEEP IN MIND

- Remember, true balance does not exist, but you can make your time more intentional and meaningful. My good friends Alexis and Brock talk about the concept of balance in an episode of the *Occupied* podcast (see page 148). Even though this podcast is focused on how disability, disease, or illness impact engagement in every-day activities, its insights are applicable to disruptions in the lives of parents.

- Listen to yourself, your body, and your emotions. Listen to your inner advocate screaming at you to take a break. Remember to block out time in your schedule to do absolutely nothing, to be more present with your family, or anything else you want to focus your energy on. Having a calendar dedicated to just your daily intentions can help you to assess and manage your time to feel a sense of balance.

- If we keep pushing off trying to balance our life and motherhood expectations day to day, it will create more stress for our future selves. Something will always pop up at some point, and there is no way to prepare for every transition or change in your schedule. In the moments when you find yourself saying, "I just need to wait until XYZ," replace that with, "What can I do now to get me to XYZ with more balance?"

CHAPTER 21

Absorbing Big Transitions and Change

Betty was adjusting to becoming a first-time mom. Her son, Tom, was just shy of a month old. She wanted to take a break from her job and focus on motherhood, but being a mom was a bigger change than Betty had anticipated. Her husband, Dave, only had a few days of paternity leave left, and then he would have to return to work. Betty was becoming increasingly anxious knowing she would be home alone with their son. It had been hard enough for both of them to get Tom on a schedule. They had spent the last two weeks trying to prepare as best as they could, and Betty was finally starting to find some relief.

Betty and Dave finally felt like they had gotten a solid routine down for Tom. One morning they woke up, eager to repeat the same routine they had been working on for the past several days, and Tom hated every aspect of it. He was going through a growth spurt, and his preferences were changing daily. He cried at things he had been happy doing the day before, he didn't respond to the bouncing and swaying that typically soothed him, and he woke up prematurely from his naps, which added to his overall fussiness. Betty turned to Dave in confusion. They had just gotten into a groove, and suddenly that routine was nonexistent. They were exhausted. On top of everything else, Dave was set to go back to work the next day.

Tom was up on and off throughout the night, and Betty barely slept. Morning came. Dave left for work, and Betty's eyes were filled with tears as her anxiety soared. This would be her first time alone with Tom since he was born. Even though she was overwhelmed with anxiety, she knew she had to try her best to adjust to yet another transition.

Motherhood brings physical, mental, environmental, and situational changes that all come with their own set of emotions. You are healing from the transformation your body went through to carry and birth a child; your hormones and emotions are all over the place; your environment has shifted to incorporate a new baby. And now you must add the role of motherhood and all the mental load that comes with it. I promise, it may not get easier, but you will find your flow.

STRATEGY SESSION

Change can create a surplus of negative emotions, leaving you drained, stressed, irritated, and angry. It may seem like there is a constant flux of transitions, and establishing a routine or feeling "normal again" seem out of reach. It will not feel this way forever. The more tools you have in your tool kit to support you in these moments, the better you will be able to respond when it feels like any balance is out of reach.

The following techniques will help support you during this tumultuous time of big transitions and change.

Establish a Workable Daily Routine

Routines help support balance and promote healthy development. They provide consistent times for meals, sleep, and play, which lessen any uncertainties a child might feel when changes occur. Routines do not have to be rigid; in fact, you should think of routines as interchangeable and flexible. Write down a general organization for the day (e.g., breakfast, play, nap, etc.). Plan your daily routine, knowing that some days will be consistent while others will change drastically. That's just how life works. But establishing a daily routine will provide a loose framework to help you guide your day and give your child an idea of what to expect.

Let It Go

Allow for the negative emotions that linger to feel like clouds in the sky. So often, mothers will hold on to these negative emotions, punishing themselves for not being able to function better during these transitioning times. Acknowledge these feelings, but rather than holding on to them, pause, sit with your emotions, and then send them on their way, like clouds passing in the sky.

Just like when we talked about managing expectations in part 3 (page 68), think about what you've been holding on to. What have you been trying to figure out how to make work that you just need to release? Use positive self-talk to honor where you are right now. Let go of the feeling that you can't adjust to these new transitions, because you can. Whatever is holding you back, let it go.

Don't Try to Be a Superhero

New mothers often feel they need to be "superheroes" or "have it all," and these false expectations minimize how intense the transition to motherhood actually is. You don't *have to* be "super mom" or have everything in your life running smoothly. This is unrealistic and will leave you feeling emotionally drained and like a failure for no reason. Accept that there will be uncertainty and change. Focus on what you can control and go from there.

Reconnect with Your Body

There is a common phrase I've heard many mothers say before, myself included: "When will I get my body back?" The truth is, your body never left. It evolved, reshaped, and provided a nourishing environment for your child to grow. Your body literally grew a life! I used to feel guilt, shame, and embarrassment when I looked at my C-section scar and stretch marks. In time, I realized that my scar came from safely carrying and delivering my son into this world. Establish a new connection with your body and honor all the transitions it went through in bringing your child safely to you.

Trigger Technique

To help ground you when transitions become overwhelming, try this square breathing exercise.

1. Picture a square in your mind and focus on the bottom left corner.

2. Slowly exhale. As you breathe in for a count of four, imagine traveling up the left side of the square. Hold at the top for a count of four, then exhale.

3. Take a deep breath in for a count of four as you travel across the top to the right side of the square. Pause and hold for four seconds once you get to the second corner, then exhale.

4. As you go back down, breathe for another count of four, pause, and repeat back to the left bottom corner. Pause again, hold your breath for four seconds, and exhale completely out.

KEEP IN MIND

- Becoming a first-time mom is unlike any other time in your life, full of transitions and big changes. Sometimes it'll feel like once you have gotten a schedule down with your baby, it changes the next day. Allow your schedule—and your expectations—to be fluid. This can help keep triggers at bay.

- Don't play the comparison game. Your social media feed is most likely filled with other moms who look like they have it all together, with prepregnancy waistlines, thriving careers, and infants who nap. Remember, just because no one is posting about their triggers doesn't mean they don't have them. You are being the best mom you can be by showing up every day for your child.

- Change can elicit fear and anxiety, as it interrupts the consistency from your premotherhood routine, which was far more controlled. Use the things that are within your control to help you maintain a sense of consistency, while navigating the many new transitions you are encountering day to day.

CHAPTER 22

Dealing with In-Laws and Extended Family

Dottie dreaded family gatherings. Her husband Ken's family was always commenting on her parenting style, offering unsolicited advice at almost every interaction, suggesting she could be doing something differently or that she spoiled her child too much.

Dottie would get an upset stomach the night before family gatherings and stay up late cleaning the house so it was perfect. She tried to anticipate and minimize the judgments from Ken's family as much as she could, but it never seemed like enough. Ken tried to interject at times when he could hear his mother giving the "If it were up to me" speeches again; however, sometimes even he was met with the same responses.

Even Ken's brothers and their wives put down Dottie's parenting style. They thought she was not firm enough with her son. Dottie had a much more conscious parenting approach—an intentional, gentle parenting method that embraces a child's emotions and uses coregulation to nurture the parent-child relationship—but when she was around Ken's family, they made her second-guess all her parenting decisions.

One weekend, they were set to have a family barbecue at their house. Dottie had been role-playing scenarios all week and practicing her intentional responses in preparation of Ken's family's comments. At the barbecue, Dottie's son began having a meltdown. Dottie paused, lowered the volume of her voice, and was present for her son, staying available to give him whatever he needed. Ken's brother made a comment to Dottie during this moment expressing that if it were his kid, he would just tell him to move on and get over it. Dottie looked at Ken's brother and said, "I appreciate your opinion, but this works for us." As this response threw Ken's brother off, Dottie recognized that his opinion did not impact Dottie's ability to do what she knew was best for her son.

Everyone is going to have an opinion as to how to raise your child. This is when you need to learn how to stay grounded and confident in your parenting abilities, because no one knows your child better than you. The techniques and strategies found within this book can help you build your confidence and listen to your intuition and your inner advocate, especially during these types of interactions.

Setting boundaries can be challenging, but they are necessary to preserve your mental health and to ensure that your energy is not being drained by those around you. It's important to keep in mind that you may not agree on every opinion from others in your life, but trying to facilitate respectful conversations while remaining grounded with your own opinions should always be at the forefront of your mind. Let's explore some ways to help you support that.

STRATEGY SESSION

Boundaries are necessary to preserve your overall mental well-being. It can be very hard to keep your cool at family gatherings when you are subjected to negative-patterned family responses. Be prepared for pushback or defensive responses when setting boundaries, especially for the first time. This often happens when someone is seeing the situation through their own lens rather than considering someone else's perspective. Here are some suggestions on how to set—and stick to—boundaries when this occurs:

Shift the focus back to you. When others offer unsolicited parenting advice you don't agree with, respond with a simple "I" response. Beginning your sentence with an "I"—sticking only to your own feelings—can immediately set the tone of the conversation and keep it as neutral as possible. Instead of feeling pressured to lash out or adjust your thinking, just make an "I" statement. For example, you can say, "I appreciate what you are saying, but I feel at this time, XYZ is working just fine."

Use your tools. Make sure you fill your tool kit with all the strategies you have found to help you, so you can channel them during these moments. Try to anticipate the reactions others may have when you set boundaries. Role play various scenarios to help you implement these boundaries in the moment.

Think prevention rather than reaction. Read more about setting boundaries in chapter 12 (page 87).

Before you go, prepare your strategies. If you're finding it difficult to identify your triggers and supporting strategies, make a chart with three columns. In the first column, write down each trigger. The second column should ask the question, "Why is this a trigger to me?" The third column should ask, "What do I need to support myself when the trigger arises?" Answering these questions while you are in a calm state of mind will help you understand your triggers and pair them with a technique, such as a breathing exercise or a simple pause, to use in the moment.

Don't react, anticipate. Try to anticipate the reactions that others may have when you choose to stand your ground as you set new boundaries. Think back to previous interactions you have had with each person with whom you are trying to set boundaries and note how that person has responded in stressful situations. This will help you frame your tone, body language, and dialogue so you remain respectful while standing your ground and setting necessary boundaries. This is another preventive way to help you choose individual strategies to implement based on who the interaction is with and what the context of the situation could be.

Trigger Technique

Once you've identified your triggers (page 145), you can begin
to practice ways to establish boundaries. Ask a friend or your
partner to practice with you. Make sure you practice with
someone who can provide you with a safe space for managing
difficult emotions; when trying to establish these boundaries,
you are most likely going to be met with pushback. Practice
does not make perfect, but it can help you become more confident and mindful in the moment when holding boundaries in
real-life interactions.

KEEP IN MIND

- Two families and friend circles are merging. There may be many different values, cultures, mindsets, and parenting styles involved. Try reframing opinion-oriented conversations toward neutral topics, positive comments, and factual statements, trying as best as you can to leave emotion out of the context of the conversation.

- Consistency is key. The more you are consistent in your actions, your values, your beliefs, and your parenting style, the more grounded you will appear and the better you will be able to manage interactions with others.

- Remember, you cannot change people, but you can control your responses to people during triggering situations.

- You are Mom. You know your child best. There will be an excessive amount of unsolicited advice thrown at you during your motherhood journey. Make sure to channel all of your techniques during these moments to remain calm, stay grounded, and remember to never lose faith in yourself as a mother.

Resources

21-Day Habit Tracker from the Petite Planner: ThePetitePlanner.com/21-free-printable-habit-trackers

Danielle Delorenzo Consulting Company, LLC: DanielleDelorenzo.com

DBT Skills Training by Marsha M. Linehan: Surviving CPTSD .files.wordpress.com/2018/01/dbt_skills_training_handouts _and_worksheets_-_linehan_marsha_srg_.pdf

InsightTimer.com/incorporate_mindfulness/guided -meditations/finding-your-anchor-3

"Is Occupational Balance BS? ft Alexis Joelle" Brock Cook; Occupied Podcast: OccupiedPodcast.com/038

"Meditation for Managing Expectations" by Jessy Coleman: InsightTimer.com/jessycyoga/guided-meditations /meditation-for-managing-expectations

Mindfulness In Motion, Inc.: TheMIMProject.com

NeuroClastic (neurodiversity resources): Neuroclastic.com

"What Do You See" Chart: DanielleDelorenzo.com/wp-content /uploads/2021/05/What-do-you-see-chart-for-book.pdf

"What Your Need to Know About a Sensory Meltdown" by Laura Petix, *The OT Butterfly* (a pediatric occupational therapist who specializes in helping parents understand and support their child's sensory needs): TheOTButterfly.com /sensory-meltdown-triggers/social-emotional-skills

"Your 8 Senses" from the STAR Institute: SensoryHealth .org/basic/your-8-senses

The Zones of Regulation: ZonesOfRegulation.com/index.html

Instagram pages for parents raising autistic or neurodivergent children:

@afriendforlillybug

@autienelle

@disabilityreframed

@fidgets.and.fries

@lifeinautismworld

@maisiesoetantyo

@mornings.with.an.ot.mom

@neurodiversity_ot

@nurturung_neurodiversity

@theneurodiverseot

@unmasked

References

PART 1

"Breastfeeding Facts." Centers for Disease Control and Prevention, September 28, 2020. CDC.gov/breastfeeding/data/facts.html.

Bryant, Miranda. "Maternity Leave: US Policy Is Worst on List of the World's Richest Countries." *The Guardian*, January 27, 2020. TheGuardian.com/us-news/2020/jan/27/maternity-leave-us -policy-worst-worlds-richest-countries.

Iyengar, Udita, Sohye Kim, Sheila Martinez, Peter Fonagy, and Lane Strathearn. "Unresolved Trauma in Mothers: Intergenerational Effects and the Role of Reorganization." *Frontiers in Psychology* 5 (2014): 966. NCBI.nlm.nih.gov/pmc/articles/PMC4150444.

Kabat-Zinn, J. "Mindfulness-based Interventions in Context: Past, Present, and Future." *Clinical Psychology: Science and Practice* 10, no. 2 (2003): 144–156.

Muharrar, Aisha, writer. *Parks and Recreation*. Season 3, episode 8, "Camping." Directed by Rob Schrab. Aired March 24, 2011.

"National Resources for Families." Nurse-Family Partnership. Accessed May 18, 2020. NurseFamilyPartnership.org /national-resources-for-moms.

Oribhabor, Geraldine I., Maxine L. Nelson, Keri-Ann R. Buchanan-Peart, and Ivan Cancarevic. "A Mother's Cry: A Race to Eliminate the Influence of Racial Disparities on Maternal Morbidity and Mortality Rates Among Black Women in America." *Cureus* 12, no. 7 (2020): e9207. NCBI.nlm.nih.gov/pmc/articles/PMC7366037.

PART 2

Cherry, Kendra. "The Fight-or-Flight Response Prepares Your Body to Take Action." Verywell Mind, August 18, 2019. VeryWellMind .com/what-is-the-fight-or-flight-response-2795194.

Robinson, Lawrence, Melinda Smith, and Jeanne Segal. "Laughter Is the Best Medicine." HelpGuide. Accessed May 3, 2021. HelpGuide.org/articles/mental-health/laughter-is-the-best -medicine.htm.

Spector, Nicole. "Smiling Can Trick Your Brain into Happiness—and Boost Your Health." Better by *Today*, January 10, 2018. NBCNews.com/better/health/smiling-can-trick-your-brain -happiness-boost-your-health-ncna822591.

PART 3

"31 Free Printable Habit Tracker Templates for Your 2021 Goals." Develop Good Habits, November 3, 2020. DevelopGoodHabits .com/habit-tracker-template.

Ackerman, Courtney E. "9 Self-Compassion Exercises & Worksheets for Increasing Compassion." PositivePsychology.com, March 5, 2021. PositivePsychology.com/self-compassion-exercises -worksheets.

American Occupation Therapy Association. "Areas of Occupation" chart. *The American Journal of Occupational Therapy*, June 30, 2016. AOTA.org/~/media/Corporate/Files/Advocacy /Federal/coding/OT-Practice-Framework-Table-1-Occupations.pdf

Birndorf, Catherine. "Managing Expectations—and Emotions—as a New Mother." *Goop*, May 1, 2019. Goop.com/wellness /parenthood/new-mother-emotional-health.

"Cognitive Behavior Therapy: Learn the Skills to Unpack Emotional Baggage." Foundations Counseling, LLC, August 16, 2017. FoundationsCounselingLLC.com/blog/cognitive-behavior -therapy-unpacking-emotional-baggage.php.

Fletcher, Jenna. "4-7-8 Breathing: How It Works, Benefits, and Uses." Medical News Today. MediLexicon International, 2019. MedicalNewsToday.com/articles/324417#about.

"FREE Printable Habit Tracker PDF: The Ultimate Habit Tracker Guide." Teal Notes, February 2, 2021. TealNotes.com/free-printable -bullet-journal-habit-tracker-template.

Goldstein-Schu, Carly. "5 Healing Shame Exercises to Help You Show Up More Fully." Estes Therapy, October 5, 2020. EstesTherapy.com /healing-shame-exercises.

Jewell, Tim. "What Is Diaphragmatic Breathing?" Healthline, September 28, 2018. Healthline.com/health/diaphragmatic-breathing.

Lindholm, Marika. "Don't Let 'Mom Guilt' Make You a Worse Parent." *Psychology Today*, February 22, 2019. PsychologyToday.com/us/blog/more-women-s-work/201902/don-t-let-mom-guilt-make-you-worse-parent.

Linehan, Marsha M. *DBT Skills Training Handouts and Worksheets, Second Edition*. New York: The Guilford Press, 2015. SurvivingCPTSD.files.wordpress.com/2018/01/dbt_skills_training_handouts_and_worksheets_-_linehan_marsha_srg_.pdf.

Mills, J., T. Wand, and J. A. Fraser. "On Self-Compassion and Self-Care in Nursing: Selfish or Essential for Compassionate Care?" *International Journal of Nursing Studies* 52 (2015): 791–793.

Schure, M. B., J. Christopher, and S. Christopher. "Mind-body Medicine and the Art of Self-Care: Teaching Mindfulness to Counseling Students through Yoga, Meditation, and Qigong." *Journal of Counseling & Development* 86 (2008): 47–56.

Tucker, Judith Stadtman. "Motherhood, Shame, and Society: Interview with Brené Brown, author of 'Women & Shame.'" The Mothers Movement Online. Accessed May 8, 2021. MothersMovement.org/features/bbrown_int/bbrown_int_1.htm.

"Your 8 Senses." STAR Institute. Accessed May 8, 2021. SensoryHealth.org/basic/your-8-senses.

PART 4

Cook, Brock. "Is Occupational Balance BS? ft. Alexis Joelle." *Occupied*. Podcast audio. May 21, 2019. OccupiedPodcast.com/038.

Wilson, Sylvia A., and Gregg Landry. *Task Analysis: An Individual, Group, and Population Approach*, 3rd Ed. Library.aota.org/Task_Analysis_3e/34.

Index

Acknowledgments

Chris, you are my best friend and an amazing father. I love you. Thank you for your endless support! To my parents, Mary Anne and Frank, thank you for always believing in me every step of the way. Thank you to my family and friends who have been a constant support in all aspects of my life. Susan Lutfi, thank you for giving me the opportunity to be a published author and bring my dreams to reality. And to my editor, Samantha Holland, you were the first to call me an author. Your wisdom and guidance during this process has set my foundation as a writer. I will appreciate you forever.

About the Author

Danielle Delorenzo, MSOT, OTR/L (she/her), is a pediatric occupational therapist, business owner, professor, writer, and mother to an amazing neurodivergent little boy. She has a master's degree in occupational therapy and postgraduate studies in infant mental health, and she is pursuing a post-professional doctorate degree in occupational therapy. Danielle created the blog *Mornings with an OT Mom* and is cofounder of mindfulness in mOTion, Inc. Her mission is to empower, uplift, and educate anyone interested in all things occupational therapy, early intervention, and education. Find her at DanielleDelorenzo.com or on Instagram at @Mornings.with.an.OT.Mom.

CPSIA information can be obtained
at www.ICGtesting.com
Printed in the USA
JSHW011919140821
17871JS00004B/10

Truman Capote—
Enfant Terrible

Truman Capote—
Enfant Terrible

ROBERT EMMET LONG

continuum

NEW YORK • LONDON

2008

The Continuum International Publishing Group Inc
80 Maiden Lane, New York, NY 10038

The Continuum International Publishing Group Ltd
The Tower Building, 11 York Road, London SE1 7NX

www.continuumbooks.com

Printed in the United States of America on 50% postconsumer waste recycled paper.

Library of Congress Cataloging-in-Publication Data

Long, Robert Emmet.
    Truman Capote, enfant terrible / Robert Emmet Long.
        p. cm.
    Includes bibliographical references and index.
    ISBN-13: 978-0-8264-2763-2 (alk. paper)
    ISBN-10: 0-8264-2763-4 (alk. paper) 1. Capote, Truman, 1924-1984. 2. Novelists, American--20th century--Biography. I. Title.

PS3505.A59Z685 2008
813'.54--dc22
[B]
                                2008004957

For Carolyn, with love

Contents

Preface and Acknowledgments

I first became aware of Truman Capote when I was a high school senior in an upstate New York town, and happened upon a paperback edition of *Other Voices, Other Rooms*. I was amazed by the contents of the book, and by the bizarre jacket photograph of the author. A year or so later I almost met Capote. I was then a student at Columbia College, and noticing that he would be giving a reading at the YMHA, I went to see and hear him. The moment he began reading in that strangest of voices, the audience—or some of it—broke out into disbelieving laughter. Capote paid no attention and continued to read, and within a few minutes the laughter subsided and was replaced by a kind of awed silence and absorption in what was being read. At the end Capote received a huge ovation.

Inspired by the reading, and with the confidence of my eighteen years that Capote would be happy to see me, I finessed my way backstage to offer my congratulations. He was standing alone behind the curtain, and when he saw me he looked startled; his eyes grew wide with terror. Then the strangest thing happened: as if some magic wand had been waved, in a split second he disappeared! At a later time (but also in New York) I was with a friend—a Southerner, as it happened—in a Greenwich Village bar. At some point the friend said to me, "Oh, there's Truman Capote." But when I looked to the doorway where he had been standing, he once again had vanished. Like a phantom.

On another, later occasion, I was at a party in New York honoring the filmmakers Ismail Merchant and James Ivory; among the guests, and next to me in a buffet line, was Gerald Clarke, then writing his biography of Capote. We talked a bit about the book and the progress he was making with it; and I prepared to hear all manner of things behind the scenes when he was lured away by his female companion, and my approach to Capote through his authorized biographer proved yet another phantom experience.

Yet it was after I moved back upstate that I had my closest near encounter with Capote. A new family moved into a Victorian house across the park from where I lived, and before long we became friends. As it happened, my newfound friend, Mary Aswell Doll, was the daughter of Mary Louise Aswell, a prominent editor in New York who had a generation earlier helped discover Capote and befriended him. It was at her summer house on Cape Cod that he had finished writing *Other Voices, Other Rooms*. Over dinners and barbecues, incidents involving Capote were recalled (one about his taking her to a school dance, and of his being no taller than she was). I was getting very close, if not close enough.

More time has passed since then, and even though I never did have my meeting with Capote, I have at last, in preparing this book, come face-to-face with him.

* * * * *

I am indebted to the New York Public Library's Humanities and Social Science Library, where on five different occasions I made use of the Truman Capote Papers for my research, and to the New York Public Library for the Performing Arts at Lincoln Center—for its elaborate clipping files and its Theatre on Film and Tape Archive. I am grateful, too, to the Library of Congress in Washington, D.C., which vies with the New York Public Library for possessing the largest Capote collection in America. In addition, I am grateful to Alan U. Schwartz, Capote's lawyer and friend, with whom I spoke on numerous occasions. Gerald Clarke's splendid and indispensable *Capote: A Biography* provided a treasury of information and insight; and George Plimpton's *Truman Capote*, a collection of memories from early childhood on by those who knew Capote, was a pleasure to read and savor. It goes without saying that I read all of Capote's work and the principal literature about him. My thanks to all.

Chapter One

The Early Years: Engaging Two Worlds

Of the Southern writers who came to public attention in the middle of the twentieth century, Truman Capote was the most unlike the others, the most resistant to being typed as a "local writer." A polished and detached observer, he was ultimately placeless; like his character Holly Golightly in *Breakfast at Tiffany's*, he was always "traveling," unwilling or unable to put down roots. He was born in a New Orleans hospital in 1924, and spent the early part of his childhood in Monroeville, Alabama, a town with fewer than a thousand inhabitants that was not near any big city. In one respect, at least, this setting served him well, for in works like *The Grass Harp* and "A Christmas Memory" he was able to create his own fictional world based in the South.

His surname was not originally Capote, but Persons—his mother, Lillie Mae Faulk, having married Archulus Persons in 1923 when she was barely more than sixteen and he twenty-six. Five feet tall with dark blond hair, she was a local beauty who lacked maturity and had married "Arch" Persons for the money she thought he had. He belonged to a respected Alabama family that had produced lawyers and judges, but Arch was an empty suit—a man who dressed smartly and talked big, but in the end spent time in prison. Lillie Mae learned on her honeymoon that he did not have anything like the means she imagined. The marriage was an on-again, off-again affair. Lillie Mae lived for a time with her Faulk relatives in Monroeville, but the marriage officially lasted for six years, during which time the couple were reunited intermittently. During one of these reunions, Lillie Mae became pregnant. Capote was born in a New Orleans hospital, his infancy spent in a New Orleans hotel suite where he was conspicuously neglected by his mother.

Virtually a child herself, Lillie Mae hadn't the least idea of how to bring up her infant son. She had no trouble attracting men, with whom she spent much of her time, while her child remained locked in their suite, sometimes in a dark closet. Fearing that he had been abandoned, Truman would begin screaming at the top of his lungs. Lillie Mae instructed the hotel management to ignore his wild screams, which they did, and he would continue screaming for hours. He was abandoned, literally, when Lillie Mae left him with her relatives while she went to New York to pursue a dream of mingling in café society. The Faulks, who lived in a substantial white frame house on South Alabama Avenue in Monroeville, consisted of three unmarried women and their reclusive, unmarried brother Bud. Jennie Faulk was the prosperous, dominant one; her sister Callie kept the books at Jennie's dry goods store; and a distant relative, Nanny Rumbley Faulk, or "Sook," as she was known, was a woman of a shy and childlike nature who had no well-defined function in the family, which Capote would later describe as "Southern Gothic."

Sook, memorialized by Capote in "A Christmas Memory," adored Truman and loved nothing better than playing games with him in the attic of the big house. They liked to find oddments in trunks and create make-believe costumes. According to Capote's Aunt, Capote "was almost unnatural in its intensity." In her loneliness she desperately clung to the small boy. Perhaps she sensed in Truman a kindred spirit. They were both forgotten people, Sook by her sisters and brother, Truman by his parents. Both were outsiders—Sook because her childlike mind kept her apart from the adult world; and Truman because his pretty looks, delicate build, and girlish tenderness offended other people's notions of how a "real boy" ought to look and act. Sook loved to sort through the collection of old clothes to dress Truman up; "putting a bonnet on his head, slipping faded white arm-length gloves on his hands, wrapping a feathered boa around his neck," Sook would exclaim, "'[D]on't you look like an elegant lady ready for the ball!'"

In his loneliness, Truman did have a close friend apart from Sook—Nelle Harper Lee, who later, writing under the name Harper Lee, would become the author of the best-selling novel *To Kill a Mockingbird* (1960). They were, in fact, about the same age and lived next door to each other in Monroeville. Their friendship began at once and lasted a lifetime. Lee's biographer, Charles Shields, observes that "from the start they recognized in each other 'an apartness,' as Capote later expressed it, and they both loved reading. When Lee's lawyer father gave them an old Underwood typewriter, they began writing original stories together. She was also his protector. In their childhood Truman was beaten up, and she rescued him from the other boys. By the time she was seven years, she was a fearsome stomach puncher, foot-stamper, and hair-puller. . . . Once some boys tried to challenge her . . . each ended up face down . . . crying 'Uncle!'"

In *Other Voices, Other Rooms*, Capote would model the tomboy Idabel after Lee, and in turn Lee drew on Capote for her character Dill in *To Kill a Mockingbird*. In the 1950s Lee would join Capote on trips to Kansas, where she helped to secure the cooperation of the towns-people for Capote's nonfiction novel *In Cold Blood*.

The lonely childhoods of Truman and Nelle were connected by their estrangement from their mothers. Nelle's mother had a bipolar condi-tion causing mood swings that disqualified her from serving as a model for her daughter, who thus adopted a masculine identity. Truman's troubled relationship with his mother also had consequences, for she left him with a lifelong sense of abandonment; she did not show him the love she should have, and she was repelled by his effeminacy. Even from the beginning, he fought back, refusing to be other than who he was; there was deadly warfare between them.

Capote was not the only notable creative writer of recent times who became locked in years of conflict with his mother. One sees this, for example, in the playwright Edward Albee and his well-to-do step-mother, who in the end disinherited him. That relationship is reflected in the formidable mother figure in Albee's *Three Tall Women* (1994), and it is spelled out in full in Mel Gussow's revealing biography of Albee, *A Singular Journey* (1999). But not even Albee's strenuous ex-perience can eclipse the lastingly destructive relationship of Lillie Mae Persons and her son Truman. In his Monroeville years Truman had already been convinced that he would be a writer, and he spent many hours recording his impressions and his ideas for fiction. This juvenile writing was locked away in a trunk on the upper floor of the Faulk house, and he would allow no one to see its contents. But his mother, perhaps under the influence of alcohol, set fire to the trunk; it was as if she were destroying everything for which he stood. Years later he would say that his mother was "the single worst person in my life."

Jack Dunphy, Capote's longtime companion, has written in *Dear Genius: A Memoir of My Life with Truman Capote*, that even late his life,

> Capote would talk to his mother in his sleep, demanding [to know] why she had not taken him with her, why she had left him behind to haunt the post office for news of her to enliven his life in the small town of Monroeville. It was the commencement of her life-long determination to dominate a spirit she no more understood than she did the turnings of the moon. . . . She was forever trying to make him over, make a man of him. That she did not really want him, and never had, was only to surface with her later on, when drink bared her secret most soul, not only to herself but to Truman as well. . . . He confessed how he had almost pushed her out the window of the Park Avenue apartment once when she was drunk. He never said that he hated her but he did all the same. He despised and feared her somewhat as well.

Dunphy goes on to describe essential differences between mother and son:

> She would have liked to sit on him and smother him and subdue him utterly, as some animals, motivated by jealousy and competitiveness, do to their young. Truman was an exotic, and she had no connection with him, really, except in the mere biological sense. He did not love her, but he wanted her to love him. I don't think that [she] was ever in love in her life. She struck me as being all for herself, whereas Truman possessed the gift of selflessness. He was not like other sons. He was better. He was this instrument, this finely tuned thing made of nerves that helped him catch the nuances of things and recover them.

After shuffling him around for six years, Lillie Mae left Truman with the relatives in Monroeville for good in 1930. In 1931 she moved to New York City, where she eventually found restaurant work. It was here that she re-encountered Joseph Capote, a Cuban immigrant she had originally met in New Orleans in 1925. Before long they were married. She shed her countrified name of Lillie Mae and became Nina; and Truman, now adopted by her husband, became Truman Capote. In the 1930s Nina and Joe Capote lived it up; they traveled abroad and vacationed at the best American resorts. They had a house in Brooklyn at first, then moved to an attractive apartment on

Manhattan's Riverside Drive in 1933. Truman, now a fourth grader, was enrolled at the exclusive Trinity School.

There his high-strung nerves made him a problem case; as a school administrator of the time relates in Gerald Clarke's biography *Capote*, "'There were problems at home, and his mother would call to talk about his temper tantrums, which I gather were not uncommon. The year he entered I witnessed one such incident myself. He was lying on his back in the hallway, kicking his feet like a child of two. He was obviously on the verge of hysterics.'" Clarke adds, "Like many disturbed children he was a sleepwalker: on more than one occasion he suddenly woke up to find himself in pajamas in the lobby of his apartment building."

Nina took him to psychiatrists in an attempt to have him remade as a "normal boy," and when this did not work, she sent him to St. John's, a military academy up the Hudson River in Ossining, New York, where she left him to his fate as the smallest and prettiest boy in the school. When Truman's year there proved a complete disaster, Nina enrolled him again at the Trinity School, where he was as obstinate and difficult as ever. In 1939 the Capotes left New York to live in the wealthy community of Greenwich, Connecticut. Thomas Flanagan, a classmate at Greenwich High School who would himself later become a distinguished novelist, has provided a revealing glimpse of him at this time; Capote, he notes in Clarke's biography, was "'full of energy and self-confidence, and quite flamboyant, a show-off. He had a sense of himself as a special person, a fact that he was under no impulse to conceal from other people.'" This sense of being a special person was shared by Capote's English teacher, Catherine Wood, who catered to him in and out of the classroom. Impressed by the stories he was writing, she invited him to her home for dinner and predicted that he would one day be famous.

Capote also found a new friend and confidante at the school in Phoebe Pierce, an attractive girl who shared his passion for writing. They had in common, too, that they had absent fathers (Pierce's father died when she was sixteen) and mothers who were alcoholics. Nina Capote would begin her scotch drinking in the afternoon, drinking that sometimes led to rages. Pierce's mother was not only an alcoholic but also mentally ill. In the loneliness of their lives, Capote and Pierce banded together, and on Sunday nights they would take off for Manhattan to immerse themselves in its nightlife. They would begin by visiting the jazz clubs that flourished along Fifty-second Street, and around midnight would drop in at the Stork Club and El Morocco, then make a mad dash for the last train back to Greenwich.

By 1942 the Capotes were back in New York in an apartment at Park Avenue and Eighty-seventh Street, and Truman was attending the Franklin School, a private school on Manhattan's West Side. Phoebe Pierce was attending Barnard College, but by then Capote had found some other girls as companions—Carol Marcus, Oona O'Neill, and Gloria Vanderbilt, who were all close friends; they belonged to a circle of debutantes and to café society. His friendship with them came about when he met Eleanor Marcus. She introduced him to her sister Carol, and Carol was so struck by him that she introduced him to her best friends—O'Neill and Vanderbilt. Each has since written her own memoir, in which Capote appears; and the three women are treated together in another book, Aram Saroyan's composite biography *Trio: Portrait of an Intimate Friendship* (1985).

Oona O'Neill had exceptional credentials as the daughter of the great American playwright Eugene O'Neill and the future wife of one of the greatest figures in film history, Charlie Chaplin. In 1942 she was attending the Brearley School for girls. At the end of her senior year she was admitted to Vassar College, but instead of going she decided to devote herself to the city's glamorous nightlife. A celebrity at an early age, she became associated in the public mind with the Stork Club, and the famous columnist Walter Winchell, among others, wrote about her comings and goings; in 1942 she received the title Debutante of the Year. Carol Marcus (who would later marry the playwright William Saroyan, and then the actor Walter Matthau), was at the Dalton School that year, and there met Oona O'Neill in a dance class; the two immediately became close friends. They met Gloria Vanderbilt, the third member of their group, at a private party on Long Island. Vanderbilt had been famous at the age of ten as the "poor little rich girl," the object of a custody battle that made front-page international news. Wherever she went in her adolescence in the 1940s, her fame preceded her. The three women would claim later that they were a composite model for Capote's character Holly Golightly in *Breakfast at Tiffany's,* for like them she had plunged into Manhattan nightlife; but Holly was a little-known bird of passage rather than a partying debutante with a well-defined place in society.

In this period in which he was befriended by a clutch of rich girls, Capote was hired as a copyboy by the *New Yorker* magazine. He was a very odd-looking office boy, whose appearance—at eighteen he looked hardly more than twelve—drew stares. *New Yorker* editor William Shawn has remarked in Clarke's biography that Capote was "'like a small boy, almost like a child.'" He carried himself, however, with the utmost confidence and panache. He had lunch delivered to him not from a neighborhood delicatessen but from fashionable restaurants like the "21" Club. Once again he forged an alliance with a woman—in this case with the *New Yorker*'s exacting and feared office manager Daise Terry, who soon gave him a coveted assignment as copyboy for the art department. His job was to sort through unsolicited cartoons and ideas and send the more promising ones to the art director for a final selection. Given to embellishing his life, Capote would later have people believe that he acted more as a quasi-editor than as a lowly copyboy. His most thankless job was to lead the nearly blind James Thurber through the city to his assignations with women, which involved sitting in an adjacent room and overhearing the graceless sounds of sex acts.

He also clashed with Robert Frost when the renowned poet was giving a reading at the summer 1944 Breadloaf Writer's Conference in Vermont. Capote had either claimed to be representing the *New Yorker* or had somehow given that impression. Sitting in the front row of the audience, he bent down to rub his ankle and then discovered that he could not get up. In this awkwardly frozen position he hobbled as discreetly as possible up the aisle. Seeing Capote, whom he believed to be the representative of the *New Yorker*, leaving in the middle of the reading, the poet flew into a rage, slammed down his book, and refused to continue. When word of this absurd incident reached the *New Yorker*, Capote was promptly fired.

Capote then asked for and received money from his stepfather that enabled him to return to Monroeville to write fiction. Later he returned to New York to be near the magazines in which he was hoping to place his short stories. He was fortunate in that short stories appearing in the glossy women's magazines paid well and could even launch a career—a condition that does not exist today. He made the most of his opportunities, and was especially effective in winning over women who were highly placed editors. Carmel Snow, who was such a person, is described by Clarke as "another in the succession of middle-aged women who clasped him to their bosoms and caused heads to turn wherever they went with him. She was the famous editor, a perfectionist who was seen only in Balenciaga; he was the stripling writer, more than thirty-five years her junior, whose only distinction in dress was the long Bronzini scarf that fluttered after him. . . . A more curious and singular pair could scarcely be pictured. . . ."

But the closest and most enduring friendship that Capote had with a female editor was with Mary Louise Aswell, the fiction editor of *Harper's Bazaar*. It is impossible to read his letters to "Mary Lou" without being conscious of her as an ideal mother figure to him, the diametrical opposite of the actual mother he had in Nina Capote. This is not to say that Capote did not find these sorts of friendships satisfying in their own right, and they were clearly of benefit to his career: Aswell published his early fiction in *Harper's Bazaar*, and introduced him to people who could be helpful to him.

It was at her apartment in the autumn of 1945 that Capote first met Leo Lerman, an articulate and sociable gay man who made it a practice to know everyone in the arts. His apartment at Ninety-fourth Street and Lexington Avenue, only a block from Capote's, was a gathering place for composers, novelists, poets, stage actors, film stars, and dancers. According to Lerman's obituary in the August 23, 1994, *New York Times*, Maria Callas, Marlene Dietrich, Marcel Duchamp, William Faulkner, and Evelyn Waugh all paid visits. Lerman was in an ideal position for entrée into this sociocultural scene in New York as the features editor at *Vogue* and editor in chief at *Vanity Fair*. In addition, he wrote frequently on theater, dance, music, art, movies, and books for a variety of publications, including the *New York Times*.

Capote was welcomed into Lerman's circle at a precocious age, and it would be hard to imagine that he wasn't affected by the importance of such achievement and fame. Lerman kept a diary that has been published recently as a lengthy book, *The Grand Surprise: The Journals of of Leo Lerman*, and Capote is often mentioned in it. It is revealing to see young Capote through his host's eyes. In a 1946 entry he remarks, "Truman lacks all education. He is remarkably astute in contemporary letters—mostly fiction—but of the past [he knows] almost nothing." Two years later, after the publication of *Other Voices, Other Rooms*, Lerman calls Capote "excessively immature and selfish . . . a great mythomaniac, and his myth now enlarges." The acid nature of these comments was perhaps due to Capote's condescending sketch of him as "Hilary" in *Local Color* (which was first published in the 1940s in glossy magazines, then later collected in book form in 1950) and his remark to Lerman that he would "soon outgrow" him. "Truman cannot help betrayal," Lerman writes in a 1948 entry, "it is in him and something he cannot control." Yet their friendship, with all its reservations, did continue through the years. With his gift for conversation and wit, and his ability to fascinate, Truman made new and invaluable contacts. Indeed, it was at Lerman's apartment that Capote met his life partner Jack Dunphy.

Dunphy was a very different sort of person from Capote. Older by ten years and ruggedly good-looking, he was the eldest of six children in an Irish family that had settled in Philadelphia. He had ambitions to become a dancer, at first, and then a writer. He married Joan McCracken, with whom he danced in *Oklahoma!* McCracken, commonly remembered as the "girl who falls down" in the musical, was a rising star until her career was cut short by a heart condition that took her life at an early age. When Dunphy returned from the service during World War II, he broke up with McCracken, began to explore the homosexual side of his nature, and published a novel—*John Fury*, about the poor Irish in Philadelphia—that was favorably reviewed. Capote and Dunphy were together for years, but Dunphy was not someone to whom affection came easily. He shunned the people Capote socialized with, and could be rude, cold, and distant. His temperament, Dunphy said, was "hyperborean." His writing, which never had the widespread appeal of Capote's, was idiosyncratic; his book *Dear Genius*, supposedly about their years together, has little to say about their relationship.

* * * * * *

In the spring of 1946 Capote received an appointment to spend close to a year at Yaddo, the artists' colony at Saratoga Springs in upstate New York. The novelist Marguerite Young, who was at Yaddo at that time, recalls vividly in Clarke's biography what the young Capote was like: "'I remember him as being absolutely enthralling that summer, high-spirited, generous, loving. We all thought he was a genius.'" Katherine Anne Porter, a writer he admired and learned from, and John Malcolm Brinnin, who would later publish a memoir of his friendship with Capote, were also at Yaddo at this time. Significantly, as it turned out, the highly regarded literature professor Newton Arvin was also there, working on what was to be his prize-winning biography of

Herman Melville. Capote and Arvin became lovers almost immediately (his relationship with Dunphy understood that they were both free to roam) and Arvin began to mentor him in American and European literature, introducing him to the works of Nathaniel Hawthorne and Marcel Proust. Capote would later sit in the back of Arvin's classes at Smith College, and was a member of a private seminar at Arvin's Prospect Street apartment in Northampton, Massachusetts. Lerman, in one of his diary entries, has said that he thought "Truman was less physically amorous of Newton than he was overwhelmed by his prodigious intellectuality and [response to] all things aesthetic and his position in academe. Newton reads to him every day [from] *The Odyssey* or *The Iliad* in Greek." Capote once said of their relationship that "Newton was my Harvard." He was more than that; he was also a father figure of striking contrast to Arch Persons.

Arvin introduced Capote to academic colleagues—Daniel Aaron, Granville Hicks, Louis Kronenberger, Harry Levin, F. O. Matthiessen, Lionel and Diana Trilling, and Edmund Wilson. In Clarke's biography, Aaron sums up the impression the boyish Capote made on these people: "'I remember his [Arvin's] talking about Truman even before I met him: this marvelous boy, this genius, this incredible figure who was wildly uneducated and yet had this gift.'" By the late 1940s this "marvelous boy" was being invited everywhere. Bennett Cerf, at Random House, was fascinated by him, and invited him to his brownstone on East Sixty-second Street in Manhattan and to his country estate in Mt. Kisco. Cerf's wife Phyllis tells an amusing story about one of his visits: "I first met Truman at a dinner party Bennett and I were having. The doorbell rang and the butler came in and said, 'Are you expecting a child?' Bennett said, 'Yes, that's Truman Capote!'"

What launched Capote as an enfant terrible was his first novel, *Other Voices, Other Rooms*, and in particular the eye-popping photograph of him reclining on a Victorian sofa as he stares at the viewer with a strange—some have said erotic—fixity. It was the most dramatic arrival on the literary scene since, eight years earlier in 1940, Carson McCullers had published her first novel, *The Heart Is a Lonely Hunter*, and became world famous. McCullers's physical appearance, like Capote's, was also widely commented on; she, too, looked like a child. As it happened, their careers would become closely intertwined. Both were from the South and published their acclaimed first novels in the same decade of the 1940s—she at the beginning, he near the end; and they had a number of shared preoccupations. Loneliness is the great provenance of McCullers's imagination. It is ubiquitous and inescapable. Capote does not possess the same depth of sadness, the peculiar somberness as McCullers; his touch is lighter, more charming and flamboyant, and his interests and canvases more varied, but there is no doubt that his characters, like hers, are forever outsiders. Both were fascinated by the lives of children, by doomed wistful yearning, and conflicted sexuality. McCullers named the Southern Gothic movement and exemplified it; Capote sprang from it and went on to become a writer who was identified with it, but with an intermixture of worldliness and classicism.

McCullers and Capote were, in fact, friends, and she opened doors that helped to make his career possible. They were not twins, but they were like cousins. McCullers published her first novel at the age of twenty-three, making her a prodigy. Critics and the general public were amazed that a work of such penetration and maturity as *The Heart Is a Lonely Hunter* could have been written by one so young. She looked no more than sixteen at the time. Lula Carson Smith from Columbus, Georgia, who would later become Carson McCullers came to New York in 1934 with the aspiration of becoming a writer. She enrolled in a creative writing course at Columbia University taught by Whit Burnett, who also edited *Story* magazine, which published her story "Wunderkind" in 1936. It took her only a few years after that to become a literary celebrity, her picture on the cover of national magazines. In 1945, in a replay of sudden early success, Capote, at age twenty-one, appeared at the offices of *Mademoiselle* in an attempt to interest them in publishing one of his short stories. George Davis, the magazine's editor, turned it down. But the story, and Capote himself, impressed Davis's assistant, Rita Smith, who was Carson McCullers's sister. Surmising that McCullers and Capote would hit it off, she arranged to have them meet. When they did, they immediately became friends.

McCulllers went out of her way to promote Capote's career. Together with her sister, she found him an agent in Marion Ives. She also wrote a strong letter of recommendation to Robert Linscott, a senior editor at Random House who had been her own editor; her intervention secured Capote's adoption by a major publishing house. Further, she arranged for him to join her at Yaddo, where all of his expenses would be paid and he would be free to write. As Clarke explains in *Capote*, to be accepted at Yaddo, McCullers told him, he had only to ask; she would pull all the strings. Elizabeth Ames, the director, was one of her best friends. Before he knew it, Capote was accepted, and he and McCullers spent the spring together at the artists' colony. They were the closest of friends; it was said that they were like brother and sister.

Yet as time went on the relationship soured. Newton Arvin had been her dearest friend at Yaddo, but now Capote claimed him as his own; and he used material from her fiction. Thereafter McCullers regarded him as an enemy; sometimes while giving a lecture she would suddenly burst into a denunciation of him. Her own life was full of difficulty and complaints. On coming to live in New York she had suffered a stroke on the subway, and subsequently had others, as well as developing a heart condition—all by the time she was thirty. Subject to depression, she drank to lift her spirits, but her increasing use of alcohol turned her into an alcoholic obsessed by herself and what she considered the amazing beauty of her writing. Gore Vidal, who knew her well, remarked that "an hour with a dentist without Novocain was like a minute with Carson McCullers."

During World War II, McCullers lived in a house at 7 Middagh Street in Brooklyn Heights with a group of other artists and writers. Tenants in this experiment in living included such figures as W. H. Auden, Jane and Paul Bowles, Benjamin Britten, Klaus and Erica Mann, and Richard Wright. The house became a crossroads of culture and new directions in art and letters. One visitor described it as "a household of 'Enfants Terribles.'" Some of the residents found McCullers hard to take, and Wright decided to move out to get away from her. Paul Bowles called her an "essentially childlike woman who could talk of nothing but herself."

McCullers and Capote crossed paths in later years when they were no longer friends. He once mentioned in a letter that he had seen her in Rome in a befogged alcoholic state. Eventually a severely disabled woman, she rarely left her house in Nyack, New York, where she died practically alone at the age of fifty. When McCullers was sinking inexorably into alcoholism, Capote was still enjoying heady success; and if there was a warning to him in her brilliantly youthful ascension to fame followed by a terrible fall, it was an unheeded one.

Chapter Two

Early Stories: "Miriam," "A Tree of Night," "The Headless Hawk," "Shut a Final Door," "Master Misery," and "Children on Their Birthdays"

"Miriam"

In "Miriam," a sixty-year-old widow living alone on the far east side of Manhattan—a woman mild and careful in her habits—suffers a psychic breakdown after encountering a strange and bold little girl named Miriam. Capote later spoke of the story as "a good stunt and nothing more," but his statement is belied by the tale's artistry and tonal perfection. "Miriam" belongs to a genre of horror story in which a character's whole equilibrium is overthrown by some impish being or object. A good example of the genre is the movie classic *Dead of Night*, released in 1945, the same year in which "Miriam" appeared in *Mademoiselle*. Michael Redgrave starred in the film as a ventriloquist who falls under the control of a demonic dummy. *Dead of Night* inspired other horror films of a similar type, including *Magic* (1978), in which Anthony Hopkins played a ventriloquist named Corky who is steadily driven mad by his evil dummy. The twist in "Miriam" is that in place of a malignant dummy's taking possession of its owner, Capote deals with an eerie child who takes possession of a vulnerable adult.

The principal character in Capote's story is a woman named Mrs. Miller, who goes out one wintry night to a neighborhood movie theater, where she is accosted by a peculiar little girl. The girl explains that although she has the price of a ticket, it wouldn't be sold to her because she is alone and unaccompanied by an adult. Would Mrs. Miller, she asks, buy the ticket for her?

She does this but at the same time wonders timidly if it is quite right; hasn't she become involved in breaking the law? In Capote's fiction, movie theaters are often associated with fantasy and escape, mystery and dreams; and Mrs. Miller's collusion with the child will turn her cautious life into a most disturbing dream.

It will become dreamlike through the agency of the little girl, Miriam, whom she has just helped, and with whom, as it happens, she shares the same first name. Miriam is unsettling because she does not seem at all like a child. She does not speak like a child, but like an adult. Her hair, "silver-white, like an albino's," flows down to her waist. Her eyes, "lacking any childlike quality whatsoever and, because of their large size" seem to "consume her small face." Strangely, she does not appear to have a last name, and it is never explained why she is out alone on such a cold, wintry night, or who her parents are. Soon this little girl will be the older woman's stalker.

One evening soon after their encounter at the movie theater, while sitting up in bed reading, Mrs. Miller hears her doorbell ring incessantly. When she goes to the door, she finds Miriam in the hallway wearing a white silk dress; reluctantly she allows her to come in. The child takes the upper hand immediately, and is soon going through Mrs. Miller's jewelry case in her bedroom bureau. She demands to be given a cameo brooch that had been given to Mrs. Miller by her husband, who died a few years earlier. He is never described or otherwise specified, making him seem rather unreal; when he is mentioned at all he is referred to as H. T. Miller, giving the impression of a certain distance that existed between husband and wife. Miriam's appropriation of the brooch has the effect of cutting the husband out of Mrs. Miller's life entirely and of leaving her more alone than ever. Not only does Miriam take Mrs. Miller's brooch, she also smashes a vase of paper roses, referring to them as "imitations." Mrs. Miller is left stunned, her eyes "stupidly concentrated on nothing," and her cheeks "mottled in red patches" as though a fierce slap had left permanent marks.

The next day Mrs. Miller has a strange dream with symbolic overtones. In it a small girl wearing a bridle gown and a wreath of leaves leads a procession down a mountain path while those who follow ask where she is taking them. A possible explanation of this vaguely pagan ceremony is that she is taking them to the netherworld. Miriam has a very pronounced association with the color white, beginning with the albino whiteness of her hair. In the dream she is called a "frostflower, shining and white," and she is, of course, all in white in her bridal gown. It is a dress in which she weds herself, so to speak, to Mrs. Miller as she leads the old woman to the land of the departed. Through this color symbolism, Miriam is also associated with the snow that falls on the city throughout the story. During a snow storm that lasts for days, Mrs. Miller loses track of time, a period of passivity and inertia in which the extinction of her identity begins to take hold. The ubiquity of snow in the story has a similar kind of all-embracing suggestiveness as it has in James Joyce's story "The Dead" (1904); and, as in Joyce's story, it is linked with death and finality.

A day after the incident with Miriam at her apartment, Mrs. Miller has an impulse to go shopping. She does not quite understand why this should be, or perhaps even why she should buy the almond cake and cherries that the girl Miriam had liked, but it is clear that she has already fallen under Miriam's spell and is carrying out her will. While doing her shopping along Lexington Avenue she becomes aware of footsteps following her. She glimpses the figure of an old man in a shabby brown coat (he is the sort of mysterious shabby old man who will appear two decades later in the plays of Harold Pinter), and ducks into a florist shop, where she buys six white roses (not paper ones). Through its window she sees him passing by, his eyes looking straight ahead, but just at the moment he passes he tips his hat as if to salute her as a comrade. During her next meeting with Mrs. Miller, Miriam reveals that she had lived earlier with an old man.

Their next meeting occurs in the late afternoon of that day. Miriam again rings Mrs. Miller's doorbell incessantly, and when Mrs. Miller finally opens the door she finds her sitting on a box, cradling in her arms a beautiful French doll with a powdered white wig. This doll that Miriam is "loving" is disturbing; beautiful as it is, it is also artificial and inanimate: "its idiot glass eyes [seek] solace in Miriam's." Mrs. Miller, an adult, in a reversal of roles, is to be comforted like an inanimate baby doll by a child who assumes complete power over her.

Tension continues to mount between Miriam and Mrs. Miller, but this final scene—in which Miriam has come, she announces, to live with Mrs. Miller—is in every sense climactic. It now begins to become clear that Miriam exists only in Mrs. Miller's mind. When she seeks help from the couple in the apartment on the floor below, the husband goes up to look around and can find no trace of Miriam or her belongings. Mrs. Miller is now revealed as a seriously schizophrenic woman, a divided personality whose stronger and bolder self is now destroying the defenses of her timid and sheltered self that has denied the depth of her loneliness and fear of approaching death.

Images of death and darkness now rise up. The living room of the apartment seems as "lifeless and petrified as a funeral parlor." Mrs. Miller sinks as if in a dream into a chair, and it seems to her that the room is "losing shape; it was dark and getting darker . . . she could not lift her hand to light a lamp." She makes a heroic effort to believe that she has regained control over herself, free of Miriam, but from her bedroom she hears the sound of bureau drawers being opened and closed, and then the murmur of a silk dress approaching nearer and nearer, and "swelling in intensity till the walls trembled with the vibration and the room was caving under a wave of whispers." Then Miriam's eyes stare directly into hers. "Miriam" is a story with a Gothic disintegration theme that Capote has put into a modern urban setting in which his quiet realism is just as striking as the Gothicism, and it is exquisitely handled all the way through. It is this that distinguishes it from horror tales: the literacy, the intricately tight writing, and the superb youthful confidence.

"A Tree of Night"

Published in *Harper's Bazaar* only a few months later, "A Tree of Night" has some important features in common with "Miriam." Both are explorations of the psyches of women who are essentially alone and victimized by mysterious strangers who make wholly unpredictable appearances in their lives, and both narratives have a dreamlike quality and a sense of hallucination. Kay in "A Tree of Night" is much younger and more out in the world than Mrs. Miller in "Miriam" yet she, too, is very vulnerable. Almost nothing is known about Kay; she is nineteen and a college student somewhere, but she has no last name, and no family—apart from a recently deceased uncle—are ever indicated. What happens in "Miriam" occurs largely in Mrs. Miller's modest-sized apartment in New York, while what occurs in "A Tree of Night" takes place in the confined space of the coach of a train traveling through some part of the South. This spatial confinement reinforces a sense of their lack of freedom. It is wintertime in both cases, and the frigid weather has a numbing effect on the protagonists, who can find no way out of the stressful situations in which they find themselves. The view from the window of the coach in "A Tree of Night" is a no-exit "wall of trees." The coach, moreover, has dim, old-fashioned lighting and red plush seats that are falling apart with age. It is a place of dank, unpleasant odors where passengers are slumped in the oblivion of sleep, and trash is scattered in the aisle. Its whole atmosphere reeks of deterioration and decay. It is here that Kay experiences her hallucinatory sense of dissolving reality.

"A Tree of Night" draws in part on an exploit of Capote's biological father, Arch Persons, who put together a tent show in which a man known as the Great Pasha is buried alive and then restored to life. Gerald Clarke gives a vivid account of this traveling attraction:

> Arch spied an elusive gold mine in the Great Pasha, otherwise known as Sam Goldberg from the Bronx. Goldberg, who wore a turban and a robe, made his living putting on a kind of grotesque variety act. His best trick, the gimmick that excited Arch so much, was his ability to survive burial. With the help of what was advertised as a secret Egyptian drug, he could retard his heartbeat to such an abnormally slow rate that he hardly needed to breathe; he could remain alive in an airtight coffin for up to five hours. Calling him the "World's Foremost Man of Mystery," Arch staged his Pasha Show . . . in half a dozen places. In Monroeville, people came to see it from a hundred miles around. . . .

Capote's concept for the story is that there would be a man who travels in the South with a buried-alive act like that of the Great Pasha (in his performances Capote's character even wears a Turkish turban like Arch's Pasha). He travels with a female companion who appears to be his wife, and they are together in an alcove in the crowded coach when Kay comes aboard and takes a seat—the only one available—next to them. It should be said immediately that the unsavory pair are a great conception, fully realized and pushed to the limits of bold imagining. They are convincingly real and yet fantastic, and are among the most memorable characters in the collection *A Tree of Night and Other Stories.*

One of the many peculiar things about them is that they have no names, always being referred to as simply the man and the woman. The woman, garishly dressed and gin-soaked, would be comical were she not so unnerving and ominous. With her very short chubby legs and unusually large—even huge—head she is freakish. She wears an oversized lavender hat with celluloid cherries sewn to the brim that flop about crazily whenever she bobs her head. Her manner toward Kay can change suddenly, from friendly to menacing ("Well, who asked you? Anybody ask you?"). There is a marvelous moment when she hoists up her skirt and "enthusiastically" blows her nose on the ragged hem of a petticoat, after which she rearranges her skirt "with considerable primness." She forces gin on Kay, and when Kay begs off the woman tells her she "wouldn't be so snotty if you knew who we was"; she has already told of her upbringing in a Texas family of wealth, which even included "Paris, France, clothes." Her pitiful pretensions are undercut at every turn by her crudeness, and by her weird manner and "dangerous smile." Stricken by fear, Kay is unable to act decisively.

Yet the man with her is stranger still. He is a deaf-mute who looks like a child "aged abruptly by some uncanny method." His vapid face has no expression. He reeks of cheap and disgusting perfume, and with another intimation of his resemblance to a child, he wears a Mickey Mouse wristwatch. Particular attention is called to his eyes, which are described as looking like a pair of "clouded milky-blue marbles" that despite their strangeness are also "oddly beautiful." The woman is known immediately by her vulgarity but the man is harder to make out, often seeming inscrutable.

The woman shows Kay a handbill for the "Lazarus" show they stage in tank towns throughout the region. In these performances, the man is placed in a tightly sealed coffin for an hour or more, and when it is opened he is still alive. In the New Testament, Jesus performed the miracle of resurrecting Lazarus from the dead; in Capote's story, on the other hand, the man is resurrected, so to speak, but the circumstances surrounding that event are a travesty of the spiritual life. As part of the act, the woman stands before the coffin wearing a black dress and a black veil as if in tearful mourning. The whole thing is tawdry, including the "lure," in which the man lies stiff and corpselike in the front display window of a local store, his face sprinkled with talcum powder, on the evening before the act is to be performed.

Yet if the man can mimic death by some kind of self-hypnosis, may he not also have a hypnotic effect on Kay? The way he looks at her makes her feel squeamish, yet she cannot take her eyes off him. He induces in her a feeling of absolute loathing, as in the horrific moment when he suddenly reaches out and gently strokes Kay's cheek. "Despite the breathtaking delicacy of this movement," Capote writes, "it was such a bold gesture Kay was at first too startled to know what to make of it. . . . He leaned forward till his queer eyes were near her own; the reek of his perfume was sickening." A motif of death pervades the story. Kay has just returned from the funeral of her uncle, and she cannot expunge from her mind the memory of his face as he lay in the casket. She even sees it superimposed on the face of the man on the train. This association unleashes the deepest fear of her childhood, of the "wizard man" lying in wait for her, of the "haunted limbs on a tree of night."

Accompanying these fears are insinuated fears of sexual molestation. Freudian symbols appear in the story—from phallic trees that are dark and threatening to the vaginal purse that Kay presses to her body as if in fear of the intentions of strangers. She has some reason to be wary of the deaf-mute, whose eyes are upon her. At a particularly eerie moment he takes what appears to be a shellacked peach seed from his pocket and balances it in the palm of his hand. He then looks directly across at Kay, opens his eyelids wide and begins to squeeze and caress the seed in "an indefinably obscene manner." She goes out to the open platform at the end of the car to get some fresh air, and has something like a nervous breakdown in which she whimpers softly "like an irritable child." Returning to her seat in the coach, she begins to lose consciousness. The imagery of surrender of her will as she looks into the man's face, and a warm laziness that comes over her, have strong sexual overtones; and when the extinction of her identity seems complete, in a wonderful last line, the woman has taken away her purse and "gently pulled the raincoat like a shroud above her head."

Exactly what does happen to Kay at the end is left open, increasing the mystery. A number of particulars within the story are left open also. What does it mean, for example, that Kay carries a green guitar left her by her uncle? Are the couple thieves, or are they soul-snatching devils? The artistry of the work is consistently impressive in the suggestive nature of its imagery. One thinks of the image of the man blowing smoke rings "that mounted upward like hollow eyes and expanded into nothing." The freezing temperature, which is felt as being ubiquitous, reinforces the idea of being drained of life, the fate of Kay. "A Tree of Night" is a Gothic fiction that coexists with a sharply observed realism, and is particularly striking in its creation of atmosphere, by which I mean the atmosphere of irrationality. It is preeminently modern, and all in all the best of Capote's early Gothic tales.

"The Headless Hawk"

Written in the same mid-1940s period as "Miriam" and "A Tree of Night," and related to them thematically, "The Headless Hawk" is unlike them in a number of other respects. Its principal character is a man named Vincent Waters who is employed at a New York art gallery, where he meets and becomes involved with a young woman who has no name, only the initials D. J. She appears at the art gallery one day with a painting she would like to sell if she can. The painting is a bizarre portrayal of a headless female figure in a robe of some kind seated on a vaudeville trunk; in one hand she holds a blue candle and in the other a miniature gold cage. Her severed head lies bleeding at her feet against the background of a darkening sky and the wings of a headless hawk. The waiflike elfin girl immediately intrigues Vincent, but she leaves suddenly when his attention is distracted, leaving behind the strange painting. He cannot get her out of his mind, and constantly finds himself looking for her in people he glimpses in the street. Eventually they meet again and become lovers, but the relationship does not last. In the end both of them are alone, guilt-ridden and seemingly doomed.

Of all of Capote's early stories, "The Headless Hawk" is the most reminiscent of the works of Edgar Allan Poe. It is suffused with a dreamlike atmosphere in which the protagonist is trapped within his own loneliness and aberration. To an extraordinary degree, Capote is concerned in the story with the unconscious, and the fear and dread felt by Vincent. Both he and D. J. believe that they "were born to be murdered." The tensions consuming them belong to Gothicism and specifically to Poe's ritualistic dream scenarios. In one of the story's Gothic dream passages, Capote describes a ball where Vincent sees an old man "with yellow-dyed hair, powdered cheeks, kewpie-doll lips"— and recognizes himself. Actually there are two selves, one young and handsome, the other old and disgusting. The "old and horrid" Vincent creeps on all fours, and climbs spiderlike onto the back of the young Vincent. He is appalled at the sordidness of his appearance at this elegant ball; then he notices that many of the other men also carry "malevolent semblances" of themselves. A lizardlike man "rides an albino-eyed Negro." The host appears and on the crook of his arm he supports "a massive headless hawk whose talons, latched to the wrist, draw blood." The hawk's wings unfurl as the host puts an old record on a worn-out, handle-wound phonograph that plays a tinny old waltz.

The host, with the hawk on his arm, moves among the grotesque dancers, who come to include former lovers, both female and male, that he has cast off. The hawk wheels above them, swoops down, claws foremost. The decadent waltz in effect heralds the death of love. Like Poe in his macabre tale "The Masque of the Red Death," Capote orchestrates his Gothic story with the formality of an elegant revelers' ball.

Capote's prose in the tale thrives on sudden odd or startling impressions: an umbrella "taps code-like" block after block; a young black man's open mouth is a "grinning display of tartar-coated teeth; scarlet lobsters "bask on a beach of flaked ice"; the bursting kernels of a popcorn machine "bounce like crazy moths"; a shirt button pops off and rolls along a carpet "like a pearl eye"; a pair of scissors rip through the canvas of a painting "like a ravening steel mouth." He is particularly partial to "as if" and "as though" constructions. A collision occurs so suddenly and loudly that it is as if "cotton plugs had been blasted from [Vincent's] ears"; D. J.'s eyes have an astonished or shocked look, as though, having at one time witnessed a terrible incident "they'd locked wide open." But Capote's most arresting images have a surrealistic quality: a "serpent of light" suddenly "blazes"; a woman wagging her finger seems "to break into separate pieces: a nose, a chin, a red, red eye." Sometimes Capote's conceits expand into surrealist fantasias: a butterfly "magnified on the ceiling, huge as a bird, and there were more: a flock of lilting winking yellow, whispering lonesomely, like surf sucking a shore. The wind from their wings blew the room into space."

The movement of the story is relatively uncomplicated; it begins in the present, drops back into the past, and near the end returns again to the present. The fabric of the story, however, has a daunting complexity and richness achieved through a large play of allusion, often involving iterative motifs and color symbolism. The color green (its connotations are teasingly unexplained) appears frequently and most noticeably in connection with D. J. She wears a green raincoat (Capote refers to the "green whisper of her raincoat"). She has "cat-green eyes," and carries a "green sack." Other motifs include heat, circles, and masks. The faces of passengers aboard a bus loom "like wave-riding masks." Other faces, too, are said to be like masks, and an Oriental mask is suspended from a ceiling cord in an antique shop. The terrible heat of New York at midsummer is persistent in the story—to the point of suggesting that the characters may be occupants of hell.

But the principal motif is water, implied even in the protagonist's name, Vincent Waters. Other Capote stories of the mid-1940s are set in New York during the snowfall and freezing temperatures of winter; the characters themselves seem to be freezing, their ability to act or to assert their will gradually draining from them. In "The Headless Hawk," on the other hand, it is not snow but rain and water that predominate. Vincent feels "as though he moved below the sea." Even city buses are "wave-riding;" and when Vincent spies D. J. in the doorway of a shop her "greenness" is "distorted wavy through the double glass." The wavy distortion in which characters are seen suggests that they are actually underwater. Vincent's quest for D. J. is like a descent into a dreamlike, watery underworld, a descent redolent of the Greek myth of Orpheus searching for his lost love Eurydice in Hades. Capote's story itself seems like a dream: his characters are as much dreaming their lives as living them.

In a work that is so much concerned with dreams and dreaming, it would be appropriate to speak of Sigmund Freud. "The Headless Hawk" taken in its entirety is all about Vincent's psychic state and his unfulfilling sexual partnerships. He has been as directionless as the headless hawk, and suffers from deep inner anxiety and fear; D. J. is the sum and essence of these failures. In certain ways they are twins: both believe that they have been born to be murdered; both have an ambiguous sexuality. The girl he pursues through the tale looks like a boy. Her close-cropped haircut is like a boy's. "The carefree bangs that fringe her forehead give her the kind of face "seen in paintings of medieval youths." As a girl who looks boyish, she is linked with Vincent, whose lovers have come from both sexes. Both have a fractured innocence, and are driven by some unnamed dread.

D. J. is a character who is never at rest, is always moving to another hard-to-find address, or is in flight to somewhere else. She appears late in the story in an illuminating scene set in a mental hospital. Previously she had spoken with fear in her voice of a person named Destronelli; but at the asylum the reader comes to know who this Destronelli is, or rather who he is not. He is responsible in her schizophrenic mind for the shattering of her innocence. Destronelli's name suggests a destroyer, and if he cannot be pinned down as a particular person, he is undoubtedly frightening as an idea. D. J. is the story's most realized character, being both a believable girl on the run and an abstraction. She must be understood as a projection of Vincent's own psyche; she is a doppelgänger, an other self. The ghostly double who haunts Poe's tales of the 1840s reappears a hundred years later in Capote's New York.

"The Headless Hawk" has avant-garde written all over it, but it has its roots in what D. H. Lawrence called classic American literature. That Capote's Gothic tale should be framed by a symbolic painting calls Nathaniel Hawthorne inevitably to mind; and the likeness is not lessened by Capote's theme of the violation of innocence. It also happens that at this same time Capote met Newton Arvin at the artists' colony Yaddo, and it was Arvin who told Capote that his sense of evil reminded him of Hawthorne's. There isn't much plot in Capote's story, but there is a great deal of metaphysical excitement, melodrama teased into exquisite art. It isn't a perfect work (it seems at times to be clotted with themes); but it is the key work pointing with certainty to Capote's famous first novel. It cannot be a coincidence that Capote wrote "The Headless Hawk" at Yaddo while having already begun *Other Voices, Other Rooms*.

"Shut a Final Door"

In "Master Misery" (1949) the character Oreilly uses the expression "round and round" to convey to Sylvia that there is no way out for him in his desperate life. He is merely moving in a circle from which he cannot break free. The same refrain appears in "Shut a Final Door" (1947). The protagonist's name this time isn't Oreilly but Walter Ranney, but they have the same trapped psychology. The name Ranney evokes a man in flight, and in this case it is from himself. His name is his life in capsule form, just as thirteen years later, John Updike's protagonist Rabbit Angstrom's name in *Rabbit Run* is his life story in essence.

Stylistically "Shut a Final Door" is noticeably different from the urban Gothicism of, say, "The Headless Hawk." Despite Walter's deepening desperation, the tone of Capote's writing in this story is more apt to be detached and observant (a female character is captured quickly in remarking that she has lipstick on her teeth and bulging eyes). There are even moments that seem cartoonish. Walter's social climbing includes weekends at Rosa Cooper's fashionable home on Long Island, where he hopes to make contacts that will advance his career. Her guests include Taylor Ovington, Joyce Randolph ("the starlet"), E. L. McEvoy, and "a dozen or so people whose names cast a considerable glare in his address book." Mingling the socially elite with gossip and backstabbing, "Shut a Final Door" is the germ or seed from which Capote's jaundiced vision in *Answered Prayers* will later take root.

Of all the early stories, "Shut a Final Door" seems the most self-referential. A purveyor of gossip and exploiter of friends and lovers, Walter is, if anything, an antihero; yet there is much in his background that reflects Capote himself. His relationship with his father, whom Capote never forgave for his unwillingness to take an interest in him or be part of his life and upbringing, looms in the background of Walter's tortured dream in which his father cruelly rejects him. On a train to Saratoga Walter falls asleep and has a dream in which his father appears prominently. In the dream Walter stands in a long, deserted street and, except for an approaching procession of slow, black funereal cars there are no signs of life: "[E]yes unseen observed his nakedness from every window, and he hailed frantically the first of the limousines; it stopped and a man, his father, invitingly held open the door. Daddy, he yelled, running forward, and the door slammed shut, mashing off his fingers, and his father, with a great belly laugh, leaned out the window to toss an enormous wreath of roses." In other cars were people who had entered in some way in his life and an unidentified woman with diamond eyes: "Each door opened, each closed, all laughed, all threw roses. The procession rolled smoothly away down the silent street. And with a terrible scream Walter fell among the mountain of roses: thorns tore wounds, and a sudden rain, a gray cloudburst, shattered the blooms, and washed pale blood bleeding over the leaves." The father's mashing off his son's fingers is clearly an act of castration, just as the thorns rending his flesh are a projection of the agonizing denial of the father's nurturing presence and love.

In his own life, as mentioned, Capote was denied the supportive love not only of his father but also, and more important, of his mother. No mother appears in the story to complement the father, but there is a mother character of a sort, and she is grotesque. On the train to Saratoga, on which Walter has his dream, an incident occurs that is as strange as a dream. A woman seated nearby notices Walter as he wakens, and he smiles at her sheepishly but she looks away. They then meet again at a hotel in Saratoga, and in its bar late at night and after many drinks they go up to her room. Unfortunately she is a woman with a distressingly deformed foot that makes it necessary for her to wear a giant shoe. She is in town for a convention of doctors who will be using her in their public discussion of her affliction. She and Walter were to have had sex, but Walter cannot go through with it.

The woman with the giant shoe, however, is understanding: "'Poor little boy,' she said, patting his back, 'My poor little boy: we're awfully alone in this world, aren't we?' And presently he went to sleep in her arms." The incident is the one really compassionate moment in the story, the point at which these two damaged individuals come together in a recognition of their loneliness. When the woman with the deformed foot calls him "my poor little boy," she becomes, in a bizarre way, Walter's mother.

That the woman should call Walter a "poor little boy" also turns a searchlight on his incapacities and exposes him sexually. One of the most distinctive features of "Shut a Final Door" is Capote's new willingness to introduce the subject of homosexuality in a large if still oblique way in his fiction. The character most apt to be detected as homosexual is Irving, "a sweet little Jewish boy" who is twenty-three but looks sixteen. His stature is so small that his feet cannot reach the bar stool's footrest but rather dangle doll-like in midair. It cannot be a coincidence that Irving should, like Capote, be in his early twenties and look years younger, and should be of the same height and physical stature. Walter meets Irving in a Greenwich Village bar and befriends him; and there is more than a hint that that they are both childlike and vulnerable. Walter is said to have sex with women, but his heterosexuality, though affirmed, is unfelt. It is more credible that he should have been briefly "involved with" the head of the advertising agency where he works. This chief executive, Kurt Kuhnhardt, a lean bachelor who lives on Sutton Place, has some Picassos on his walls, and South Sea Island masks, and has a "burly Danish youngster" as his houseboy. Anna Stimson, a woman Walter cultivates, puts it to him bluntly when she says, "You're a man in only one respect, sweetie."

Helen Garson has noted that "Shut a Final Door" is essentially about Walter's sexuality. "Walter's dream," she remarks, "signals an unconscious understanding of his sexual identity and his despair about this understanding. He is running from knowledge of his homosexual nature." This may be true as far as it goes, but what Walter is running from most of all is Capote's own traumatizing childhood, from the denial of love and acceptance by his parents. He is running from a lone-liness so profound and painful that he cannot escape it ever. Walter's experience takes him "round and round," as if he moved within a circle from which there is no exit. A circle, Capote writes, must have a center, and the circle's center in this case is New Orleans, where Capote was born and his suffering began.

Garson describes Walter's final destination at the New Orleans hotel as being Gothic, but surely this is an overstatement: it lacks Gothicism's horrific effects and paraphernalia. But if the final scene isn't Gothic, it is unquestionably theatrical. The mysterious ringing of the telephone (as if it were his conscience pursuing him) is theatrical. Walter's lying on the bed in the tremendous heat like a broken doll beneath the round-and-round movement of the overhead paddle wheel fan is theatrical, and might even suggest a sufferer in hell. Walter's last thoughts are fabulously theatrical: "Think of nothing things. Think of wind." The title of the story, "Shut a Final Door," signifies Walter's turning away from life. His burying his face in a tear-stained pillow links him with the women in "Miriam" and "A Tree of Night" whose personalities and identity dissolve before the reader's eyes.

When *Other Voices, Other Rooms* burst upon the world it seemed to come out of nowhere, an exotic work by a precocious author with a strangely childlike appearance. But the novel did not come out of nowhere. Capote began writing at a very early age, and in the short stories that led up to it there was some movement toward or anticipa-tion of the novel—and not least in "Shut a Final Door," which intro-duces the theme of a protagonist's struggle for selfhood in a work shadowed by homosexuality.

"Master Misery"

Published in *Mademoiselle* in the late 1940s, "Master Misery" has not been as highly regarded by Capote's critics as some of the other early stories; and it is true that one of the central characters, Mark Oreilly, is hard to accept as a believable figure. But "Master Misery" by no means fails completely. It is very much in the mainstream of Capote's writing about dreams and the characters who are immersed in them. The story's principal character is a young woman named Sylvia who leaves her hometown in Ohio, with its oppressively small, earthbound concerns, to live in New York, where she can find a higher plane of consciousness. But the work she finds there is pedestrian, too, and the couple she stays with, whom she knew from her hometown, are merely reminders of why she left for New York. With the onset of a snowy and frigid winter she sinks into depression and then desperation. At this point the story takes on the quality of fantasy.

She meets the man named Oreilly, who tells her of a Mr. Revercomb (*reve* is the French word for dream) who buys people's dreams. Sylvia leaves the apartment of the couple she had been staying with to live in a lonely room by herself; in time she is fired from her monotonous and meaningless job and has hardly any money left. At this point she goes to see this Revercomb; he buys dreams from her until she has no more left to sell, and she reaches a nadir of hope.

She has, however, one friend in Oreilly, a former clown, now without employment and addicted to drink. He, too, has sold his dreams away to Revercomb, a coldly impersonal figure who must live by consuming the souls and dreams of others. Sylvia and Oreilly are alike in their desolation, but they are alike also in that they are essentially children. As a child Sylvia has a menagerie of clown dolls in her bedroom, and she has never really outgrown them. It is implied that some of her reluctance to become fully adult has to do with a fear of sex. This fear is suggested at the beginning of the story when at dusk Sylvia decides to walk through Central Park, defying the well-meant but patronizing warnings of the couple from Ohio.

As two grinning boys appear on her path, fear and desire in her begin to mingle, a reaction expressed by Capote in partly surreal imagery: "[T]hey loomed in the dusk like menacing flames, and Sylvia, passing them, felt a burning all through her, quite as though she'd brushed fire. They turned and followed her past a deserted playground, one of them bumping a stick along an iron fence, the other whistling: these two sounds accumulated around her like the gathering roar of an oncoming engine, and when one of the boys, with a laugh, called 'Hey, whatsa hurry?' her mouth twisted for breath."

Sylvia has sexual dreams in which the phallic smokestack of a factory visible in the distance from her window keeps reappearing; and she even has a dream in which Revercomb puts his cold arms around her, with his lips close to her ear to draw her dreams from her.

Early in the story Estelle, the woman with whom she had stayed, tells Sylvia that she would not be so lonely if she were married; "there is nothing like lying in bed at night with a man's arms around you." By the end Sylvia and Oreilly, at the end of their ropes, momentarily experience happiness with each other. Sylvia sleeps with Oreilly's arms around her, and in that evening she comes to terms with adulthood and can confront fear. It's not a happy ending, since she and Oreilly will be going their separate ways in hardship, but in a way the experience has been their salvation. "Master Misery" is as bittersweet poetic fable that foreshadows others in Capote's later writing. In fact, the story is full of anticipations. The two characters of childlike innocence, Sylvia and Oreilly, exiles from a joylessly unfeeling world, look ahead to *The Grass Harp*; and Oreilly's compulsive dreaming and drifting, which he calls "traveling in the blue," is a prophecy of Holly Golightly in *Breakfast at Tiffany's*.

"Children on Their Birthdays"

Published serially at the end of the 1940s, "Children on Their Birthdays" belongs at least in part to Southern folk storytelling. In its isolated rural landscapes, its character types, and the type of its humor, it is a near relative to the tales of Eudora Welty. Its narrative strategy, too—the use of an anonymous spectator-narrator who belongs to the community he describes and can vouch for the veracity of the happenings he records—has Southern antecedents such as William Faulkner's "A Rose for Emily."

The central figure of "Children on Their Birthdays" is a ten-year-old girl named Lily Jane Bobbit who is always called Miss Bobbit, as if she were an adult. She arrives with her mother on a bus one day at a sparsely populated rural town in Alabama, and quickly becomes talked about. She seems not only like an adult but like an adult who knows how to manage things. "[S]he sassed along," Capote writes, "with a grown-up mince, one hand on her hip, the other supporting a spinsterish umbrella. Her mother, lugging two cardboard valises and a wind-up victrola, trailed in the background." Wherever she goes she takes command; although she meets resistance in some quarters, she wins everyone over by the end, even coming to be loved by the community. Perhaps the most amazing thing about Miss Bobbit is that one actually comes to think of her as an adult, forgetting her actual age of ten years. She is the most brilliant of Capote's early hybrids, those characters who are part child and part adult or part male and part female. Capote was something of a hybrid himself, and the complication seems to have had a peculiar attraction for him.

Garson makes a good observation about Miss Bobbit and her fantasy quality:

> Although she gets off the six o'clock bus, it is as if she simply materializes from another world. We learn almost nothing about her past life [and very little about her father now serving time in prison] . . . the secret longing to do whatever they want that children sometimes have is reinforced by the absence of a father figure. . . . She is what all children wish to be: free of parental restraint, free from attending school or church; free to criticize anything; free to make friends she wants; free to earn money as she chooses and to spend it as she prefers; free to do whatever she wants when she wants to do it. And, unlike a real child, who dreams impossible dreams, but does nothing to achieve them, Miss Bobbit employs all her considerable energy to make the dreams reality.

The key word here is *dreams*. Miss Bobbit is a Capote character because she is dream involved, as quite a number of his characters are. Her very existence feels like a dream.

Describing Miss Bobbit as "self-determined" and "totally "independent," Garson sees her as the forerunner of certain other characters yet to be created, not the least of whom are Idabel Tomkins in *Other Voices, Other Rooms* and Holly Golightly in *Breakfast at Tiffany's*. But if they are like her in being "self-determined," they are very much unlike Miss Bobbit in other respects. Idabel cannot enchant people as Miss Bobbit can. She is not imaginable as dancing alone in the moonlight like Miss Bobbit, or giving a sassy twirl to her parasol, or wearing makeup ("Whoever heard of a child wearing makeup!" Aunt El gasps), or inciting local boys to fight over her, or performing a rousing song-and-dance number in which her blue lace panties are glimpsed as she struts and sings, "If you don't like my peaches, stay away from my can o-ho o-ho" while local people in the audience go wild.

Holly Golightly, too, notes Garson, is "self-determined, but otherwise unlike Miss Bobbit." Holly sleeps around and is uncertain of her direction, while Miss Bobbit knows where she is going and who she is. Where Miss Bobbit really does have a kinship with Holly, is that they are both dreamers. They belong to a series of characters in Capote's fiction who speak of themselves, or explain themselves, in practically the same language. Oreilly, the unhappy clown in "Master Misery," tells Sylvia that he "travels in the blue"; Miss Bobbit, according to her father, "lives in the sky"; and Holly "travels in the sky." They are all Capotean dreamers.

Quite apart from being the germ for the character Holly, "Children on Their Birthdays" is a source for other writing of Capote's that would soon come into being. It is in some ways the workshop from which *The Grass Harp* came, and that novel, too, is set in a small rural community in the Deep South and is inhabited by the same kind of people with the same kind of manners. When Billy Bob in "Children on Their Birthdays" finds refuge and sanctuary in the branches of a tall pecan tree in the family's backyard, he foreshadows the treehouse conceit in *The Grass Harp*. Similarly, Manny Fox, the appropriately named con man in "Children on Their Birthdays" who skips town with the money he has purloined from the townspeople, is the forerunner of the absconding con artist Morris Ritz in *The Grass Harp*. And there are the children in the story, who are not so different from the children in *The Grass Harp*; both it and "Children on Their Birthdays" are fables of childhood.

Yet what is arresting in the story is not so much its foreshadowing of future work as the character of Miss Bobbit herself. In speaking of her sense of her relation to place, she makes an astonishing statement: "'I think always about somewhere else, somewhere else where everything is dancing, like people dancing in the streets, and everything is pretty, like children on their birthdays.'" The innocence of this statement is so radical that the reader doesn't quite know what to make of it. It makes one think vaguely of J. D. Salinger's *The Catcher in the Rye*, which was to appear in 1951, several years after the Capote story. What really makes Salinger's sixteen-year-old Holden Caulfield happy is a vision he has of saving children from falling off a cliff:

> I keep picturing all these little kids playing some game in this big field of rye and all. Thousands of little kids, and nobody's around . . . except me. And I'm standing on the edge of some crazy cliff. What I have to do, I have to catch everybody if they start to go over the cliff. . . . I have to come out from somewhere and *catch* them. That's all I do all day. I'd just be the catcher in the rye and all. I know it's crazy, but that's the only thing I'd really like to be. I know it's crazy.

As different as they are, Miss Bobbit and Holden Caulfield have the unique ability to dream their innocence in wildly eccentric ways.

Miss Bobbit arrives in a dry, parched season when dust hangs over the dirt highway, and brings refreshment to the lives of the townspeople, who later see her off with heaps of blooming yellow roses. She is associated with flowers throughout, as well as with the color yellow that at times seems to give the idea of a light, mellow happiness, like F. Scott Fitzgerald's "yellow cocktail music" in *The Great Gatsby*. Miss Bobbit (what a lively name) wears a lemon-colored party dress; elsewhere Capote boldly refers to "the sunflower yellow of her eyes," and at the end flowers and the color yellow are blended together. Aunt El's yellow Anne roses are blooming again, and young Billy Bob and Preacher Star, her acolytes as it were, hold out armfuls for her, their "flower-masked faces" like "yellow moons." "Children on Their Birthdays," like Capote's other writing, sparkles with imagery that at times has a darting, surrealist quality: Miss Bobbit's mother has "silent eyes," and when townspeople at the end call out warningly to Miss Bobbit their voices are like "lightning in the rain."

Miss Bobbit's associations are with germination and renewal, and she is also suggestive of art. She is by nature a performer, and "acts," as it were, in her everyday life. Most of all, she has a passion for music and dance. When she arrives at the town she brings her most prized possession, her wind-up victrola. At dusk she plays a recording of "The Court of Luxemborg" and dances to the music. Strips of gold-glittering tinsel in her hair shine in the gathering darkness to give her an "illuminated quality." For a long time, while standing on the tips of her toes, she holds her arms arched over her head. Then she begins to waltz around and around; even after onlookers leave for the night she continues to spin like a top, an impressive solitary figure dancing to the strains of music under the moonlight. The vignette endows her with mystery and stature. It is the stature of the artist who enriches, enlarges, and celebrates life.

Though a tale of apparent simplicity, "Children on Their Birthdays" is actually very sophisticated, and on one level is a parable of the artist—and of Capote as artist, in particular—who combines childlike innocence with adult experience and understanding. Miss Bobbit's innocence is stressed in the story's conclusion; when she is about to be run over by the bus, she is dressed in white, the traditional color of innocence in church symbolism. "She looked," Capote writes, "as though she were going to Communion, dressed in white and with a white parasol." At this moment of her death she becomes poignant as a girl whose purity is saved from corruption through an untimely death. In an odd way she has something in common with Henry James's eponymous character in *Daisy Miller*, a girl with a flower name whose destiny is to be forever young and innocent. "Children on Their Birthdays" is the jewel of the collection *A Tree of Night and Other Stories*, and a perfect illustration of Capote's blending of Southern folk writing with Jamesian classicism.

Chapter Three

Summer Crossing

During this period in which he was writing short stories, Capote made his first attempt at a novel; called *Summer Crossing*, it was eventually abandoned. For years the manuscript was presumed lost, but then it made a sudden and startling appearance in 2004 when Random House brought it out as a hardcover book.

Capote began writing the novel in 1943 while working for the *New Yorker*. After being fired by the magazine, he obtained money from his stepfather that enabled him to return to Monroeville, Alabama, where he felt he could write quietly and without interruption. But in December 1944, Capote remarks in *The Dogs Bark*, "I said good-night, locked myself in my room, tossed the manuscript of *Summer Crossing* into a bottom bureau drawer, collected several sharp pencils and a fresh pad of yellow lined paper, got into bed fully clothed, and with pathetic optimism, wrote: '*Other Voices, Other Rooms*—a novel by Truman Capote.'"

After *Other Voices* was published in 1948, and while living abroad, Capote resumed working on the cast-aside *Summer Crossing*. His letters of this time contain numerous allusions to his progress with the novel. As early as April 1949, he writes to Robert Linscott, his editor at Random House, "I have fine hopes for *Summer Crossing* and I feel alive and justified in doing it, but it makes me nervous all the time." A month later, in a less confident tone, he writes to his friend Andrew Lyndon, "My book has changed somewhat since I outlined it slightly to you. . . I do after all profess to some sort of style, and that is something I can only hope to improve upon, but the material and my own view toward it are different from anything I've attempted before. God, what a revolting mess it could be. And may."

Writing again to Linscott in May of that year, Capote seems both hopeful and uncertain: "When I finish a draft of it here before going home, then I will have it all polished by the first of the year, which means that you could publish it by the following June—that is, if you have a mind to. But we will see what happens—it is by far the most difficult thing I ever tried to do." By the end of August, Capote writes to Linscott that he is now "2/3rds the way through—at least in draft form—some of it I'm impressed with, some of it not, naturally. I think that it will run to about 80,000 words, rather longer than I expected— but then it has turned into quite a different, infinitely more complex novel than I originally proposed, and to pull it into shape will be a monumental effort." By 1950, when he began work on *The Grass Harp*, he decided to discontinue any further work on *Summer Crossing*. In 1953 he refers to it in the past tense to Mary Louise Aswell. "As for Summer Crossing," he remarks, "I tore it up long ago—anyway, it was never finished." The manuscript, as we now know, had never been destroyed. In later years he asked himself if it should be published after all, but he did not go back to it, and then the manuscript disappeared.

It reemerged in 2004 with a collection of newly found Capote material—letters, photographs, manuscripts—offered to Sotheby's for auction. With it came an account of how this trove of material became available that reads like fiction.

With the runaway success of *In Cold Blood*, Capote moved into a two-bedroom apartment at the United Nations Plaza, which at that time was considered the smartest address in New York. He then sent word to the superintendent of the building in Brooklyn Heights where he had had an apartment since 1950 and was now being kept for him by a house sitter, that any possessions of his that remained on the premises should be disposed of. These things, which included the manuscript of *Summer Crossing*, which was presumed to be lost, were brought out to the street for garbage pickup. The house sitter, however, felt that the manuscript and other memorabilia should not be trashed, and held them back. Upon the house sitter's death they went to his nephew, who sold them to Sotheby's, and have since been acquired by the New York Public Library as part of their extensive Truman Capote Papers collection.

The first impression *Summer Crossing* is likely to make is its boldness, since in its detailed social realism it is unlike anything Capote had been doing. It is set in New York, but it is not the New York of Capote's short stories, in which his characters have exiguous lives touched by hallucination. Instead the novel begins with a set of wealthy characters who tend to view New York as their playground. In its striking opening one meets Lamont McNeil, his wife Lucy, and their two daughters—Apple, married and in her midtwenties, and Grady, a debutant of seventeen who is soon to have her coming-out party. It is a beautiful early summer day, and the family is breakfasting at the Plaza Hotel. In Capote's wickedly observant treatment of these characters, one seems almost to be entering one of Edith Wharton's novels of New York society. Most striking of all is Capote's Jamesian prose: the weave of his long, drawn-out, and sinuous sentences leading to some sharp perception. He writes of his young heroine, Grady McNeil,

> [O]nce when she was fourteen she'd had a terrible and quite acute insight: her mother, she saw, loved her without really liking her; she had thought at first that this was because her mother considered her plain, more obstinate, less playful than Apple, but later, when it was apparent, and powerfully so to Apple, that Grady was finer looking by far, then she gave up reasoning about her mother's viewpoint: the answer of course, and at last she saw this too, was simply that in an instinctive sort of way, she'd never, not even as a very small girl, much liked her mother.

The mother-daughter conflict is emphasized at the beginning, and it occasions razor-sharp satire of the mother's superficiality:

> "Grady doesn't think me an idiot, surely not," said Mrs. McNeil, but a tone of weak conviction indicated doubt, and her eyes webbed by the spidery hat-veil she now lowered over her face, were deeply confused with the sting she always felt when confronted by what she considered Grady's contempt. . . . she had, provoked by Grady's inconsiderate aloofness, slapped her daughter fiercely. Whenever she'd known afterwards similar impulses she steadied her hands on some solid surface, for, at the time of the previous unrestraint, Grady, whose green estimating eyes were like scraps of sea, had stared her down, had stared through and turned a searchlight on the spoiled mirror of her vanities: because she was a limited woman, it was her first experience with a will-power harder than her own. "Surely not," she said, twinkling with artificial humor.

Capote drops back into Mrs. McNeil's past to make her the butt of his humor even further, for she is, indeed, a "limited woman" whose overriding passion is to stage a coming-out party for Grady that will be the envy of her social rivals. This will involve in particular the selection of a gown that will set Grady off to perfection—a garment "made in Paris: Dior or Fath, someone like that. . . . something in white watered silk." Stretching on her white gloves, she tells her daughter, "You will wear white silk and carry a bouquet of green orchids: it will catch a little the color of your eyes and your red hair. And we will have that orchestra the Bells had for Harriet."

The father is treated satirically as well. In a brief recall of the past, Lucy's father invites Lamont—a young man with a winning hand on Wall Street who speaks in a "poker voice"—to their home in South Carolina for a duck shoot, where her old grandmother finds him "manly," thus earning him in her eyes "the golden seal." The sharp-edged Grady is a stray in this world of Lucy's parents, whom she resents and rebels against. Her closest friend is a young man named Peter Bell, who belongs to a family who are friends of the McNeils and are on a social par with them; he is another stray, and when he first appears he has just been expelled from Harvard University. They have been friends from childhood, and he and Grady would make a good match except for the uncertainties of his sexuality (he tells Grady that being seen with her "makes a man of me"). In their growing up together, Grady had been the protective one. She is feminine but not passively feminine. Her mother named Grady after her stillborn son, and in a way she stands in his place: while growing up she was considered a tomboy.

Although the writing of *Summer Crossing* preceded *Other Voices* and is conspicuously different from it, there are some features that they have in common. The relationship of Grady and Peter has a certain affinity with that of Idabel and Joel Knox in *Other Voices*. In both cases they are misfits in their social environments, and although they are close they do not enter into a physical or sexual relationship; the girl in each case is the stronger of the two. These characters seem to derive from Capote's own childhood friendship with Nelle Harper Lee, a tomboy who defended him against schoolboy attackers. But there are other reflections, too, of Capote's personal life in *Summer Crossing*. The McNeils have a Fifth Avenue apartment in Manhattan, but also own a house in the wealthy community of Greenwich, Connecticut, where the Capotes lived during part of Truman's adolescence. Lucy McNeil is a woman from the South who has an overriding concern with moving in the right social circles, a trait that brings Nina Capote to mind; in addition, the veneration of "manliness" in Lucy's family seems an oblique slap at Nina as a homophobic mother. Like other works of Capote's, *Summer Crossing* has a self-referential subtext.

The most prominent feature in the design of the novel is perhaps Capote's shaping of particular scenes, an example of which would be the opening, with its echoes of F. Scott Fitzgerald, in which the McNeil family have breakfast at the Plaza Hotel shortly before the parents' departure on an ocean liner. The breakfast scene is self-contained and stands by itself rather like the first act of a play, and it has been beautifully executed. It immediately announces the wealth and glamour of New York: privilege and money, haves and have-nots. As the characters are introduced, one becomes aware of the tension underlying what might seem to a casual observer to be a scene of family cohesiveness. Capote's humor in this scene is both bold and suave. Grady's conventional older sister, Apple, for example, is characterized tersely in the remark that she "twitters."

In addition to the confidence of Capote's handling of his characters as the work begins, one is struck by the degree to which he is an accomplished imagist. He writes that as Grady looks out the window of the hotel dining room, "the dazzle of traffic heightened the June morning quiet of Central Park, and the sun, full of first summer, that drives the green crust of spring, plunged through the trees fronting the Plaza." One of the most striking features of the novel's early section is the "gorgeousness" of Capote's writing. One thinks of the moment when Grady is traveling in a taxi to see her parents off at the dock. The taxi, Capote notes, has a "sky-window roof," and this sets off a chain of striking images: "dove flights, clouds and towers tumbled upon them; the sun, shooting summer-tipped arrows, jingled the new penny color of Grady's cropped hair, and her skinny, nimble face, shaped with bones of fish-spine delicacy, was flushed by the honeyed blowing light."

In the opening section, particularly, attention is called to the estrangement between mother and daughter. The character to whom Grady is closest is Peter; and this is especially apparent in the scene in which they drink champagne as they see off Grady's parents on the Queen Mary. Grady is drawn to Peter because they are two of a kind—outsiders in relation to their homes, schools, and classmates. The friendship and the attitude that goes with it seems very much like the friendship of Capote and Phoebe Pierce in Greenwich, Connecticut as adolescent rebels who made romantic Sunday night excursions into the nightlife of Manhattan. The ocean liner scene is handled with a light touch, and ends with Lucy McNeil's fear that Grady has just slipped away from her—which, in fact, she has. She is now free to explore life for herself, including its darker sexual underside. Before long she will

meet Clyde Manzer, a young Jewish man from Brooklyn who served
in the army in the war and is now an open-air parking lot attendant.

The title, *Summer Crossing*, has a double meaning, referring both
to the McNeil parents' crossing the Atlantic and their daughter's crossing over, during a roasting summer in New York, from an upbringing
of wealth and leisure to an immersion in the soiled urban world of the
middle and lower classes. The early part has the flavor of social comedy; it has the feel of a fable about a privileged girl's coming of age.
But once Grady becomes involved with Manzer the tone of the work
changes, becoming a dark fable of the girl's descent into a world containing forces stronger than herself.

In another part of the novel, Capote constructs a scene that is suggestive and symbolic. It takes place at the Central Park Zoo, located
almost directly across Fifth Avenue from the McNeil penthouse—a
strategy by which a private world of wealth and a common public
world face one another and Grady's crossover from one sphere to another is pinpointed. What should be a pleasant outing is made to seem
ominous through Capote's evocation of the animals at feeding time:

> The cat house of a zoo has an ornery smell, an air prowled by sleep,
> mangy with old breath and dead desires. Comedy in a doleful key is the
> blowsy she-lion reclining in her cell like a movie queen of silent fame;
> and a hulking ludicrous sight her mate presents winking at the audience
> as if he could use a pair of bifocals. Somehow the leopard does not
> suffer; nor the panther; their swagger makes distinct claims upon the
> pulse, for not even the indignities of confinement can belittle the danger
> of their Asian eyes, those gold and ginger flowers blooming with a
> bristling courage in the dusk of captivity. At feeding time a cat house
> turns into a thunderous jungle, for the attendant, passing with blood-
> dyed hands among the cages, is sometimes slow, and his wards, jealous
> of one who has been fed first, scream down the roof, rattle the steel
> with roars of longing.

This evocation of animal hunger is immediately followed by Grady's
psychical and sexual submission to Clyde Manzer. She even goes so far
as to marry him and have him live with her in her parents' penthouse.
The descent of Grady into an alien world is explored further in her
introduction to the life of Clyde's family, who live at the end of a
subway line in Brooklyn. Grady envisions Brooklyn as an ominous
wasteland, and its "ghostly lonesome streets, the lowness of the land

stretching in a confusion of look-alike bungalows, of empty lots and silent vacancy" strike her as terrifying. She meets Clyde's mother and her young children in their working-class apartment, which conveys a feeling of enclosure and constriction; and she meets Clyde's friends, whose names—Mink, Bubble, and Gump—have the effect of dehumanizing them.

Grady's attraction to Clyde in the first place comes from how he seems to epitomize a romantic life that is totally different from the one she has known with her parents. Grady is not an entirely sympathetic character; among other things, she is self-centered and headstrong. She also looks for romance in the wrong places—namely, at the movie theaters in the dim Times Square area, which hold a dark mystery for her. Manzer is an extension of that alluring mystery; but the romance of an ethnic underclass can be very unlovely. In the Central Park Zoo scene, she carries a balloon that gets away from her when she is shoved by a group of rowdy schoolchildren, and there seems an implication that her reading of life is no surer than the balloon she has carried and lost. By the end of the story she is moving in the circle of Clyde and his friends, who have been hardened by life and are patrons of the nightclub domains of drink and drugs. Grady, like Gustave Flaubert's Madam Bovary, finds that romance can be a sequined squalor.

Summer Crossing is especially rich in Capote's prose artistry, which is consistent with the brilliance of his early stories. But the novel also has major flaws, both in characterization and plotting. At this early point in his career, Capote had only a sketchy knowledge of the rich (would the McNeil couple really have left their unpredictable seventeen-year-old daughter alone in New York while they traveled abroad?), and he had even less knowledge of the Jewish working class. Worst of all, Clyde, a major character, is never convincing. His attraction for Grady and his hold over her are not felt by the reader; and even the way he speaks at times seems all wrong. The McNeil parents are effectively portrayed in the early section, only to disappear from the novel completely. Peter Bell is interesting and plausible, but he, too, drops out of the narrative until the very end; his reappearance merely makes the reader conscious of the oddness of his lengthy absence. *Summer Crossing* is a seriously flawed but at times attractive novel that might have worked as a short story about a young woman's journey into fear, a theme Capote had been orchestrating in his early stories.

Chapter Four

Other Voices, Other Rooms

Although Capote's stories showed a remarkable versatility, his first novel, *Other Voices, Other Rooms*, could hardly have been predicted when it was published in 1948; the bold candor of its treatment of homosexuality made it an immediate succès de scandale. The book's timing was perfect, since it coincided with the publication of Alfred Kinsey's *Sexual Behavior in the Human Male*, which demonstrated with academic rigor the greater than assumed prevalence of homosexuality. The subject had been broached in a few American novels of the earlier 1940s, but it was implied or hinted at rather than being confronted, as Roger Austen points out in his pioneering study *Playing the Game*. But in 1948 it was confronted directly in two novels, Gore Vidal's *The City and the Pillar*, a closely observed depiction of the gay world as it currently existed, and Capote's *Other Voices, Other Rooms*. Appearing together at the same time, the books made Vidal and Capote rivals; but their novels, apart from the eyebrows they both raised, were nothing alike. Vidal wrote in a received tradition of naturalism, while Capote turned inward for his vision of phantasmagoric experience in the modern-day Deep South.

Influences on *Other Voices* go as far back as Nathaniel Hawthorne and Edgar Allan Poe. The novel has a certain kinship with "The Fall of the House of Usher" (1839), for like Roderick Usher, Capote's Cousin Randolph inhabits a house that is partly in ruins and is said to be sinking into the earth. Randolph is not only the master of the house but also an artist figure like Usher, with high-strung sensitivities that place him out of the mainstream of life. Randolph's estrangement is further emphasized by the remote and desolate landscape of his large home, Skully's Landing—sometimes called Skulls Landing. To a remarkable degree both Poe's story and Capote's novel are preoccupied with death.

Hawthorne's is an even stronger presence. His story "My Kinsman, Major Molineux" (1831) relates to *Other Voices* unmistakably in its having to do with a youth's search for a relative he has not yet seen but who holds his future in his hands. Hawthorne's story takes place on the eve of the American Revolution; the relative that young protagonist Robin journeys to meet is a representative of the British Crown. Robin travels alone from his simple country home to Boston to find his well-placed relative and potential benefactor Major Molineux, and in doing so is immersed in mystery and frustration. The long-anticipated meeting finally takes place by torchlight in the dead of night, as the major appears before him stripped naked, tarred and feathered, and foaming at the mouth as rebellious citizens exhibit him in a cart rumbling through the streets. The whole effect of the scene belongs to nightmare.

In *Other Voices* the plot line is similar. Young Joel Knox journeys alone to be united with the father that he has never known. His meeting with his father is delayed and involves a deepening sense of mystery; when they eventually do meet, Joel discovers that his father is one of the living dead—a man so paralyzed and brain damaged that he is only able to communicate by releasing a red tennis ball that tumbles down a flight of stairs to attract the attention of his caregivers on the first floor. What Hawthorne's story and Capote's novel both dramatize is the overthrow of the father figure, and the gaping void of loneliness and isolation that come in its wake.

The Hawthorne relation is reinforced by very specific incidents in Capote's novel. In "My Kinsman" Robin takes a cudgel with him on his journey, believing naively that it will ward off any harm, and in *Other Voices* Joel is given a sword that had belonged to Jesus Fever's father, believing that it will keep him safe. Striking, too, is the way that the young travelers are transported by individuals who guide them into territory having ominous associations. In "My Kinsman," a ferryman, evoked as a Charon figure who pilots the dead across the River Styx to the underworld, transports Robin to his destination. Joel is given a lift by a truck driver at Paradise Chapel to Noon City, and from there rides in Jesus Fever's mule-drawn wagon to the ominously named Skulls Landing. Capote's equivalent of the ferryman-guide is a grotesque woman named Roberta Velma Lacey, proprietress of R. V. Lacey's Princely Place, a dismal roadside restaurant. She is described inimitably by Capote as having "long ape-like arms that were covered with dark fuzz, and there was a wart on her chin, and decorating this wart was a single antenna-like hair. A peach silk blouse sagged under the weight of her enormous breasts. . . ." Feminine and masculine at once, she provides directions and transport that will lead Joel ultimately to the masculine-feminine Cousin Randolph.

But *Other Voices* is indebted most of all to the Southern Gothic writers (William Faulkner is a looming presence). As in their work, a number of characters who appear in the novel are deformed, grotesque, or freakish. The hundred-year-old Jesus Fever is described as being "a little pygmy" who moves slowly, "with the staccato movements of a mechanical doll." His sickle-curved posture makes him look as though his back is broken. When the end comes for him, "it was as if someone had been tickling his ribs, for he died in a spasm of desperate giggles."

His granddaughter is Missouri Fever, but she is known as Zoo because of her unusually long neck that makes people think of a giraffe. Her neck has been slashed by her psychotic husband Keg Brown, a member of a chain gang who cannot wait to escape so that he can return and do Zoo in for good. A friend and confidante of Joel's at the Landing, Zoo leaves for a new start in Washington, D.C., but en route is set upon, gang-raped by some men in a truck, and then tortured by their impotent boss who thrusts the lighted end of his cigar into her navel.

The brutal boss is reminiscent of Faulkner's Popeye in *Sanctuary*, but other Gothic characters in the novel, like Miss Wisteria, are very delicately sketched. Miss Wisteria appears late in the work when a carnival comes to Noon City. Human oddities and misfits, like the Duck Boy, who has feathers sprouting from his chest, are exhibited there. But no one can compare with Miss Wisteria. She is so tiny that when she was a child it was said that she could sit in her mother's sewing basket. She has queer little hands that flutter about "so that they seemed to have a separate life of their own, and she glanced at them now and again as if they deeply puzzled her; they were smaller than child's, these hands. . . ."

In a wildly inventive scene she rides the Ferris wheel with Joel just as a terrifying thunder and lightning storm breaks over the carnival grounds, and the Ferris wheel ride in the electric storm is projected by Capote as though it were a fevered dream or hallucination. In a rocking Ferris wheel high overhead, Joel looks down to see a phosphorescent figure, that of Randolph, making a claim on him and drawing him closer to him. In this dream sequence all the characters' erotic desires are stymied; Joel believes that he is in love with the tomboy Idabel

Thompkins, but she has fallen in love with Miss Wisteria. In a hallu-cinatory scene following the thunder and lighting sequence, Miss Wisteria calls out for Joel, searching for him with a flashlight in a house with a "jungle" of rooms, and "weeping because little boys must grow tall." This kind of circular thwarting and frustration is obviously reminiscent of the writing of Carson McCullers. There is no doubt that Capote has poached on her property, but there is also no doubt that he has transformed it into something idiosyncratically and uniquely his own.

The Gothic nature of the novel derives not only from passages like the hallucinatory Ferris wheel episode, but also in the distinctive land-scape, mood, and atmosphere Capote evokes so memorably. The region where the story is set is "lonesome country," where "there are luminous green logs that shine under the dark marsh water like drowned corpses." Death abounds in the swamp country just beyond Skulls Landing. A place where a colony of ants feed on dead dogs, it is for Joel ominous and threatening. *Other Voices* is an initiation novel with pronounced mythic dimensions, and in some sense it is a search for the grail—a search for true knowledge, the finding of one's true self.

The novel's Gothicism, which highlights the search, belongs not merely to the present but also to the past, to which the novel returns at various times. The ruins of the Cloud Hotel, located part way be-tween Noon City and the Landing, are disquieting reminders of the past. It had once been very fashionable, with a grand ballroom and a lake that adjoined the building known as Cloud Lake; the hotel and its lake had been a magnet for well-to-do tourists. People came even from far off in their best finery to share in the glamour of the ballroom dances and to refresh themselves in Cloud Lake. Then one day people began dying in the lake and the patronage of the hotel dwindled to nothing. Mrs. Jimmy Bob Cloud, the owner of the hotel, was heart-broken, went to St. Louis where she rented a room, poured kerosene all over the bed, lay down in it, and struck a match. Capote remarks with a Gothic flourish that now "snakes slithering across the strings made night-songs on the ballroom's decaying piano." Joel "realized suddenly that this was not a hotel; indeed, had never been: this was the place folks come when they went off the face of the earth, when they died but were not dead." The fantastic Cloud Hotel is a foreshadowing for Joel of Skully's Landing.

The Landing is a decaying relic of the past, and those who inhabit it are marginalized themselves. They consist of Cousin Randolph Lee; Edward Sansom, Joel's long-absent father; Miss Amy, a disagreeable woman who became Sansom's second wife following his return to the Landing; Jesus Fever, an ancient family retainer; Zoo, Fever's granddaughter; and Joel Knox, the house's youngest and latest arrival. Joel, who has now reached the age of puberty, was raised in New Orleans where, following his mother's death, he went to live with her sister, Aunt Ellen, and her family. When a letter, supposedly from Joel's father, Ed Sansom, asks to have the boy come to live at the Landing with him and gives assurances of providing for Joel's education and well-being, Aunt Ellen, after some hesitation, agrees to the arrangement. Joel is then sent off alone to this strange and almost inaccessible house, and the question thereafter is what will happen to a boy as impressionable and vulnerable as Joel once there.

The presiding presence in the house is Randolph, a languid, effeminate man in his thirties who speaks of the plight of the artist and the homosexual. Over his pajamas he wears a seersucker kimono with butterfly sleeves and tooled leather sandals that reveal his manicured toenails. He has yellow curls that fall over his forehead and he dabs his hair with lemon cologne. He is a pastiche character who quotes from Henry James on the "madness of art" and remarks that "all children are morbid; it's their one saving grace" as if he were Oscar Wilde. One could say that Randolph is all caricature and nothing else, but he is actually quite a memorable figure. It is he who holds the sometimes wandering book together and is a more interesting character than Joel. The boldness with which he has been imagined is apparent in the episode in which Joel is standing in the ruins of the garden adjoining the house and looks up to see the figure of a "lady" in an upper floor window. The "queer lady," as Joel will later describe her, has just pushed aside the curtains, and is smiling down at Joel as if in greeting or approval. She has white hair "like the wig of a character from history: a towering pale pompadour with fat dribbling curls." Joel's discovery of this apparition in the window provides a dramatic close to chapter 2, almost as if it were the second act of a play; and it lends mystery and suspense that will be sustained throughout the rest of the novel.

One learns more about Randolph later as the narrative drops back into a time in the past when he was involved with a young woman named Dolores, and then in love with a swarthy, mustached prize-fighter named Pepe Alvarez. To Pepe, even after he has been beaten and rejected by him, Randolph is totally in thrall. Before the worst happens, the three of them came to live for a time in New Orleans. Looking back at the costume ball they attended and the feminine costume he wore, Randolph remarks, "I am a Countess and my king is Louis XVI; I have silver hair and satin slippers, a green mask, am wrapped in pistachio and pink: . . . before the mirror this horrifies me, and then pleases to rapture, for I am very beautiful, and later, when the waltz begins, Pepe, who does not know, begs a dance, and I, oh sly Cinderella, smile beneath my mask thinking: Ah, if I were really me!" Randolph may seem like a fool in this scene, but he is a modernist fool; he knows that desire is blocked, that everyone wears a mask to disguise his loneliness.

Joel's discovering his father, Ed Sansom, in his absolute isolation and loneliness, is easily the most pitiful moment in the novel. On a table by Sansom's bed stands an illuminated globe of frosted glass depicting Venetian scenes of gondoliers and young lovers drifting past romantic palaces, and a milk glass nude suspending a tiny silver mirror. Reflected in this mirror is a pair of eyes, which belong to Sansom and reveal in a terrifying way his utter helplessness. They are always open and staring, even in sleep. How different this glimpse of Sansom is from the depictions in frosted glass next to him of the carefree lovers in Venetian gondolas. The view of the lovers is pointedly cruel, since it was in Europe that Randolph was part of a love triangle with Dolores and Pepe Alvarez and, in a delirium, shot Sansom, Pepe's manager.

But if Sansom is a victim, so is Randolph. He is shown naked in bed next to a pile of bluejay feathers, a paste pot, and a sheet of cardboard. Dipping the bluejay feathers into the paste, he arranges them on the cardboard to give the effect of a living bird. What the scene actually suggests is Randolph's distance from life—from what is living, real, and free. Indeed, in one of the ways he is presented, he seems like a vampire, bent on possessing Joel and stealing his soul. In the Ferris wheel episode, Joel feels Randolph's presence as if he were a "[v]ine from the Landing's garden" that "had stretched for miles to entwine his wrists" and frustrate his plan to escape from the Landing with Idabel. He seems here like Gilbert Osmond in Henry James's *The Portrait of a Lady*, who seeks to bring Isabel Archer wholly under his domination and control.

Yet, in other passages Randolph seems only too fallible and hence more sympathetic. He is powerless and seems to be moving in circles, like Walter Ranney in "Shut a Final Door," a man entrapped within himself. Randolph mails letters to Pepe addressed to ports of call in practically every part of the globe, because without the possibility of human contact he has no hope at all. Ironically it is young Joel who counsels the older man. "Everything," he tells him, "will be all right."

Early in the work Capote alludes to Hans Christian Andersen's fairy tale "The Snow Queen." Joel recalls that Kay, the boy in the tale, is spirited off to the Snow Queen's palace, where everything is cold and has turned to ice. Arriving at the Landing, Joel fears that he, too, may suffer a similar fate but unlike Kay will have no one to come to his rescue. The theme of the fairy tale is the saving power of love in a world lacking human warmth and connection. In a number of the early stories, characters live in an almost fated isolation from one another, but in *Other Voices* Capote reaches out toward at least some amelioration of absolute loneliness. Randolph and Joel are in need of each other, and in time they grow closer together. Joel is in effect an abandoned child; his mother is dead and his father is so grotesquely maimed that he is unable to function as a parent whatsoever. Randolph will become the father he does not have; in a curious way he will be both father and mother to the boy. Joel, in turn, will bring youth, innocence, and comfort to the spiritually ailing Randolph.

The spiritual weather of the back country of Alabama where Joel has been cast is a cause for depression. Can there be any doubt that what he finds at the Landing is a fallen and death-haunted world? The novel's biblical epigraph from Jeremiah is a prophetic warning of imminent undoing and destruction. "The heart," the epigraph reads, "is deceitful above all things, and desperately wicked. Who can know it?" The corruption of the Jewish nation's faith and spiritual ideals, Jeremiah tells us, will bring a fearful fall and ruin. In *Other Voices*, the fall has already occurred: the Landing, which lies partly in ruins, is a token of a broken world. The slashing of Zoo's throat by Keg Brown and later her rape and torture by men on a truck when she attempts to leave the Landing for a new life is testimony to how fallen this world is.

The Cloud Hotel that Joel visits with Randolph late in the work is another reminder of beauty turned to decay and overtaken by death. Here they talk to the black "gnome" Little Sunshine, who lives in the hotel amid its wreckage. His quarters beyond the cobweb-strewn ball-room and in what had once been Mrs. Cloud's private apartment are "two simply furnished, spacious rooms, both beautifully clean . . . the evident pride he took in these quarters increased the charm of their surprise, and when he closed the door, he made nonexistent the ruin surrounding them." The decayed hotel provides Capote with scene painting that is full of tone, atmosphere, and poetry as he re-creates the heyday of gala balls together with the building's present state where "the diabolic tongue of a cuckoo bird, protruding out of a wall-clock, mutely proclaimed an hour forty years before. . . . where a fallen chandelier jeweled the dust, and weather-ripped draperies lay bunched on the waltz-waved floor like curtsying ladies."

The scene is also made memorable by another death, that of Jesus Fever's mule, John Brown. The mule has been tied to a spittoon on a balcony overlooking the lobby, but it becomes excited, and as if insane with terror goes careening through the balcony railing; on his way down his reins become entangled with a beam, twisting about his neck so that he is seen swinging in midair above the lobby, his big lamplike eyes staring into death's face. It is an image that might be found in a surrealist painting.

But if *Other Voices* is Gothic, it is also personal, for Capote, like Joel, was an "abandoned" child. Like Joel he went to live in a large house in a remote section of rural Alabama. Like Joel, neither his mother nor his father were present to help him grow up. And like Joel, he was a pretty boy considered to be effeminate who came to consciousness of his homosexuality at an early age. Capote said that many of the people he knew at that time are in the novel in some guise or other. Idabel was inspired by Harper Lee, and Capote remarked in an interview that the inspiration for Randolph came from two men he had noticed in New Orleans: one a seaman, the other a reclusive man who spent much of his time in an upstairs room and smoked menthol cigarettes. But except for the smallest externals, neither of these men could have provided anything like the model for Randolph. There was someone in his life at that time, however, who may well have affected his conception of the Randolph and Joel relationship. This was Newton Arvin, Capote's lover and mentor, and the person to whom *Other Voices* is dedicated. Arvin did not have any personal resemblance to Randolph, but he was like him in being a cultured homosexual man much concerned with the arts who adopted young Capote as Randolph adopted Joel. Their relationship was something of an idyll for both of them, and offered relief from their loneliness. Randolph and Joel by the end are offered a similar experience. Joel's recognition of his sexual identity is part of the growth of his consciousness in a larger sense; Capote clearly implies in the closing lines that his choice to ally himself with Randolph is a step toward maturity. Joel is putting his fear and dread behind him and entering a happier phase of his life.

Randolph appears in the window again at the end dressed as the beautiful lady of Louis XVI's court. In responding to Randolph's beckoning, and glancing back for a moment at the boy he had once been, Joel is affirming what Randolph stands for—a feminine as well as a masculine self, imagination and culture. Capote's view of life in *Other Voices* is extremely bleak, but he does finally allow his "innocent" characters at least a small ray of love and pleasure.

When *Other Voices* was published, it caused a sensation, and was controversial certainly for its subject matter (the *Library Journal* warned libraries against stocking it). Some reviewers objected to what they considered the clotted obscurity of its symbolism; others believed that he had produced "a bushel full of Southern decadence." Diana Trilling, in her review in *The Nation*, faulted Capote for his lack of "artistic moral fable." Writing in the portentous style for which she was known, she attacked Capote for having Joel yield to the seductions of Randolph rather than resisting them so as to make possible "more normal satisfactions." The majority of the reviews, however, were strongly positive, and expressed their conviction that a major young American writer had just arrived. Jacques Barzun concluded in *Harper's* magazine that Capote was destined "for the higher places of literary creation."

Other Voices, Other Rooms isn't a perfect work. Its symbolism can be too dense, and the episodic nature of the narrative loses momentum as it seems to wander back and forth between scenes with Joel and Idabel and the adult happenings at the Landing. Joel's reminiscent experiences with his chum Sammy Silverstein back in New Orleans are never convincing. But all in all, it is a breathtaking first novel, written with a rare gift for storytelling and for the creation of atmosphere and mood; and it has at its command a mesmerizing prose. It lives a long time—some say forever—in the reader's imagination.

Chapter Five

Early 1950s Reportage, Theater, and Films: *Local Color, The Grass Harp,* "House of Flowers," and *Beat the Devil*

In 1948, in the wake of the publication of *Other Voices, Other Rooms*, Truman Capote and Jack Dunphy traveled abroad, stopping first in England, where Capote's reputation as a wunderkind had preceded him. He was soon being introduced around to Noël Coward, W. Somerset Maugham, and other English writers, and narrowly missed meeting his favorite English novelist, E. M. Forster. Gerald Clarke, in his biography *Capote*, comments that "Even the English, who were accustomed to eccentric characters, were surprised by him." Lord David Cecil said Capote "'looked like a child, and talked like a very sophisticated, agreeable grown-up person.'" A strange thing about Capote, however, was that as sophisticated as he undoubtedly was, he could also be breathtakingly uninformed; he thought, for instance, that Oxford and Cambridge were not separate universities but a single one referred to by either one name or the other.

One of these English notables to whom he was introduced was Cecil Beaton, who became a longtime close friend. Beaton was twenty years older than Capote and already well established as a fashion and portrait photographer; an arbiter of taste, he was the photographer of choice of the royal family. In addition to that, he was a scenic designer for the ballet, and for theater and films. In the 1950s he would provide the sets and costumes for *My Fair Lady* and the costume designs for *Gigi*. Beaton was known, too, as a conversationalist, and he kept a diary in which he recorded his observations on the passing parade of English social life. Six volumes of the diaries would eventually be published, and in them he frequently comments on his American friend Truman Capote.

From the beginning, he was awed by Capote as a prodigy whose "interests encompass the world." In one diary entry he remarks, "I feel anxious that Truman may not survive to make old bones. I am slightly scared that someone who lives so intensely may be packing in a short span more than many people are capable of enjoying or experiencing in a long lifetime." He adds that Capote "is frightened or awed by nobody: he has courage." Elsewhere he notes that Capote was "avid for gossip," a trait the two men shared, for they were alike in certain ways. Both were ambitious to move in high society.

Everything about Beaton suggested that he belonged to upper-middle- or upper-class British life, but he didn't have this kind of background at all. Capote was struck by this and wrote about it. "There are very few people," he commented, "who are total self-creations and certainly he is one, because nothing in his background could in any way lead one to suppose that this person would emerge out of the cocoon of middle-class life." Capote, too, was a self-created person: Monroeville, Alabama, was a very unlikely training ground for the style-conscious social life that he cultivated. Beaton and Capote reinforced each other, but being older and more experienced Beaton must be presumed to have played the mentor role. Because he had access to the royal family, he could and did arrange for Capote to have dinner with the Queen Mother. The story of the dinner has been related in the following way by Gerard Clarke: "Truman had yet another conquest. After Cecil had escorted the guest of honor to the car, she pulled down the window and said she thought Mr. Capote quite wonderful, so talented, so wise, so funny. 'Yes, he's a genius, M'am,' Cecil . . . replied."

Beaton's photographs of beautiful women sometimes reveal him in the background, and it is almost as if he were merging with his image of them; this suggestion of androgyny would have been understood by Capote. It is true that Beaton was fascinated by Greta Garbo and wanted to marry her (Diana Souhami explores their relationship in her book *Greta and Cecil*); but what enthralled Beaton most in the beauty of Garbo's "perfect" face was its suggestion of sexual ambivalence. It was, as it were, the subversive element in Beaton's fixation with Garbo.

* * * * * *

After a brief but eventful stay in London, Capote and Dunphy went on to Paris, where the French publisher Gallimard was bringing out *Other Voices* and publicity about it was intense. The famous photograph on the back of the book's jacket excited the French, who were eager to meet Capote in person. Natalie Barney, one of the reigning hostesses in Paris, introduced him to Colette, Gertrude Stein, and others. Albert Camus, at Gallimard, was Capote's French editor, and they became acquainted, Capote later telling a skeptical world that they went to bed together.

Local Color

During this early period, when he divided his time between New York and Europe, Capote published a number of travel pieces in glossy magazines like *Harper's Bazaar* and *Vogue* that were collected in his third book, *Local Color*. Written in the late 1940s and 1950, the articles were about places he had lived in or visited, and the earliest ones have to do with American cities. The first piece, on New Orleans, is a snapshot-sized profile of a single individual, a black guitarist and blues singer named Shotgun who performs in a "Negro café." It is a Saturday night and the room seems to "float" in cigarette smoke. He sings of his life that has been immersed in strong drink and buxom women with whom he has fathered more children than he can count. His "black crazy face" glistens with sweat as he strums his guitar, and his stamping foot becomes the "heartbeat" of the room. His voice cries *"I want a big fat mama with the meat shakin' on her, yes!"* A single individual comes to evoke the sensuality and nocturnal life of a city, a people, and a place.

The never-identified yet strangely styled narrator of the piece on New York City is of course Capote. The city's local color, making it different from anywhere else, contributes to New York's being a "monumental machine" that consumes dreams and devours illusions. In this way the sketch overlaps with Capote's story "Master Misery." He describes New York as a place to hide, to lose or discover oneself, "to make a dream." The narrator tells of brushing against Greta Garbo in an antique shop and then of sitting next to her in a movie theater. He speaks of the metropolis as a magnet that draws the "talented untalented" who are "neurotically feeding on the fringes of the New York scene." Part of that art scene is revealed in the parties hosted by the narrator's friend "Hilary," who is unquestionably Leo Lerman. It was

Lerman's practice to host gatherings at his apartment while sitting up in bed; famous writers and film stars would mingle with circus freaks and college professors to create the effect of a very off-beat glamour. The New York sketch also provides Capote with an opportunity to try out or polish brilliant images, as when he writes that the midafternoon heat of the city "closed in like a hand over a murder victim's mouth."

In the sketch of Brooklyn, he explores this outer borough's uniqueness in terms of the social stigma of being a Brooklynite, an individual whose dialect, appearance, and manners are a national joke. He is intrigued by its long rows of look-alike buildings and broad, silent, vacant avenues. In this case the travel sketch provides notes for Capote's fictional writing in progress, since it corresponds to the ambiance of Brooklyn in the second half of the novel *Summer Crossing*, which belongs roughly to the same period.

A travel piece set abroad, "To Europe," concerns Capote's travels in Italy, and is an account of a journey he took aboard a train going from Italy to Switzerland. Also aboard the train and seated directly across from him were two white-haired Italian ladies who were without luggage but had a parrot in a cage that was covered by a silk shawl. During the ride the ladies remained silent, but the parrot would at times burst into "demented" and "unearthly" laughter, at which the ladies would smile at each other. When they came to the Swiss border, customs officials appeared and went directly to the parrot's cage, which, when they removed the silk cover, toppled over to reveal a cache of heroin in its feeding tray. The parrot in the meantime flew out of the cage, laughing wildly as it careened about the compartment and out an opened window. The elderly ladies, seemingly unconcerned about the discovery of the heroin, cry from the window for the bird to return to them as its flat silhouette is seen against a "cold Northern moon." Beautifully written in Capote's best lapidary style, the sketch could as easily be a work of fiction; it could be compared to one of Maugham's observant tales of strangers encountered in the course of travel.

Two sketches of 1950, "Ischia" and "Tangier," comment on locations that Capote knew firsthand, colorful settings with an element of the grotesque about them. In "Tangier" he reveals that he is well informed about the Casbah—an international crossroads of illicit activities from prostitution to drug smuggling. A shameless gossip himself, he is also well-informed about all the talk that goes on, and the variegated makeup of the society that flourishes there.

But the most charming of the European pieces is "A Ride through Spain," in which Capote, as narrator-passenger aboard a badly deteriorated and slow-moving Spanish train, makes a fool of himself. Hearing a burst of gunfire as they are passing through a region rumored to be unsafe, he cries "Bandits!". The passengers then panic, some falling on the floor. It soon comes out, however, that what happened was that an old man stealing a ride by clinging to the rear of the train lost his hold, and that a soldier seeing him fall, fired his machine gun to signal the engineer to stop the train. A "dark dusty" woman seated across from Capote glares at him and mocks "*Bandidos.*" The train starts up, moving so slowly that "butterflies flew in and out of the windows."

At the end, calm has been restored in the placid image of the butterflies that are so much at odds with frayed nerves and panic. One laughs, or smiles, at the narrator but he is not the only figure treated humorously. The woman who glares at Capote is described as an "overstuffed, dusty woman with sluggish disapproving eyes and a faint mustache," and the younger woman who accompanies her has the "scrappy features of a prizefighter." Most amusing of all is that the elder woman removes a lunchtime fish from between her breasts and begins to eat it "with glum relish." "A Ride through Spain" is similar to a vignette that Capote will later write, "A House on the Heights," in which he presents himself as a nervous coward. Both are alleged to be factual but have the feel and artistry of fiction; and this ambivalence points to a direction that Capote's writing would later be taking.

The Grass Harp

As fine as these short pieces were, Capote needed a second novel to consolidate his position among the leading young postwar American writers. This he found in *The Grass Harp*, which, as American a novel as can be imagined, was actually conceived and written at the Fontana Vecchia, a villa in Taormina, Italy. It was published to general acclaim in 1951. As in *Other Voices*, its main character is a boy similar to the childhood Capote. Collin Fenwick is bereft of his mother and father at an early age, and has come to live with his father's relatives, the Talbos. Theirs is a house of women—Verena and Dolly Talbo, and their black (purporting to be Indian) factotum Catherine Creek. These characters are all inspired by Capote's Faulk family relatives, with whom he lived as a youth. Callie and Jennie Faulk provided a composite model for

Verena, the town's richest citizen; and Sook Faulk, the odd member of the household who collected herbs in the woods and dispensed a home-brewed medication for dropsy, was the model for Dolly. A woman named Anna Stabler, who lived in a tin-covered shack behind the Faulk home and was befriended by Sook, suggested the character of Catherine Creek.

Even the attic of the Faulk house, from which the young Truman Persons could eavesdrop on the rooms below through the spaces between the flooring planks, appears in the novel as Collin's bedroom. Most of all, the backyard China tree that became a retreat for Capote and Nelle Harper Lee, a haven where they could tell and write stories, becomes in the novel the tree house where the innocent characters stage their rebellion against their surroundings. The tree house conceit is at the very heart of *The Grass Harp*.

Other Voices and *The Grass Harp* are both drawn from Capote's own experience, and are accounts of a young boy's coming of age in the prewar South, but in terms of style and intention the two works could hardly be farther apart. *Other Voices* is relentlessly driven by nightmare, while *The Grass Harp* is genial and playful. What pervades it most of all is the spirit of comedy—the comedy, as the character Judge Cool puts it, of "five fools in a tree." The work might be described as a comic pastoral, for much of it takes place in the nature that lies just beyond the vested interests of the community. It might also be considered a romantic comedy inasmuch as it involves courtship of a sort and ends with at least one marriage. It is romantic, too, in introducing a little world of wonder in the woods where the novel's little people seek a purer sense of their selfhood. *The Grass Harp* isn't the only work by an American writer to have sent a protagonist up a tree to escape the falsities and meanness of life; William Saroyan, in the largely forgotten play *Sweeney in the Trees* (1940), had already done this. Capote's novel, however, has what Saroyan's play does not—the ability to draw its audience fully into a dream.

Romantic largeness in the adventure of its unheroic characters is evoked in part through a repeated comparison of the tree house to watercraft. The tree house floor, for instance, is likened to a raft "floating in the sea of leaves," and it is remarked that "it was as though we floated through the afternoon on the raft in the tree." Elsewhere Capote writes that the China tree "swayed like immense oars dipping into a sea rolling and chilled by the far far stars." Perhaps the most telling line of all occurs when the reader is told that "Dolly knew and made me know, that [the tree house] was a ship, that to sit up there was to sail along the cloudy coastline of every dream."

In *The Grass Harp* nature tends to have connotations that are romantic and beneficent. It is endowed with aesthetic richness at various points, and certainly when the field of tall grass turns to a brilliant red with the change of seasons from summer to autumn. The wind blowing through the tall grass has, as it were, the effect of music, and it is even said that it can remember the past and tell its stories, as if it possessed the powers of creativity. In this background of nature the characters can be distinguished one from the other. Dolly is a misfit in the Talbo house; she finds acceptance in the serenity of the woods. Verena, on the other hand, has dedicated her life to the accumulation of wealth, and her attitude toward nature is exploitative. Morris Ritz (aptly named) is associated not with nature but the city, and like Verena he is concerned with how much money he can acquire. The self-righteous townspeople who stage a raid on the tree house in order to bring the mavericks who gather there under the control of town values, turn out in the midst of nature to be bumbling clowns; and one of them, in the midst of the fracas they create, shoots Riley Henderson, a young nonconformist who is most at home in nature.

It can be charged that Capote's conception of his characters is too black and white, too diagrammatic. But the novel, after all, is a comedy, and comedy does thrive on strongly typed and often contrasting characters. The solid citizens who march solemnly and stiffly through the woods to evict the group in the tree house are all comic figures. The sheriff, Junius Candle, an appointee of Verena's, has "a brutal jaw and the bashful eyes of a card sharp." The Reverend Buster is a nervous little man who walks behind his wife, and rubs his hands together with the effect of "the dry scraping feelers of an insect." His wife has a small vicious head, high hunched shoulders and a vast body. Capote refers to the procession of these characters as "a distinguished party." Opposed to them are characters who are not yet adults, and adults who are in some way childlike and have been put upon by others—Dolly by her sister and Judge Cool by his arrogant sons. Add to them the nonconformist evangelist Sister Ida, whose ministry includes the adoption of fifteen orphaned children (among them the child evangelist little Homer Honey) who help to defend the besieged characters in their tree house redoubt.

Like many classic comic works, *The Grass Harp* reaches a point of resolution where conflicts and disharmonies are reconciled. The characters began their adventure in the tree house to learn who they really are, and by the end of the novel things fall into place. Riley Henderson renounces his wild ways, marries Maude Rierdan, and settles down to become a prosperous businessman and a pillar of the community. After losing Maude, Collin follows the practical path and goes off to law school, becoming part of the conforming establishment; but one has the sense that he will always be an outsider. Dolly and Judge Cool have a rather shy and touching romance, but in the end Dolly turns down Judge Cool's offer of marriage to stay with her repentant sister Verena, who needs her; Dolly will never again experience nights of romance. Judge Cool is the most poignant at the end; he remains at Miss Bell's rooming house where, a sharply dressed and sturdy figure with an Indian rose in his lapel, he can do no better than to spend time with men "who talk and spit and wait." Off at the edges of the novel, another note is quietly sounded—the intimation of homosexuality in Collin, who idolizes the roughneck Riley Henderson, and Verena, who mourns for the fun-loving girl she had once doted on but who married and moved away. Looked at more closely, however, the apparent happy ending is not really happy: Capote's comic novel ends, finally, in resignation. The characters' destinies are not quite what any of them might have foreseen, but they do, at last, have a sense of who they are: the tree house dreamers have all fallen out of their dreams.

The Grass Harp was favorably reviewed when it was published, and it attracted the interest of the Broadway producer Arnold Saint-Subber, who traveled to Taormina to urge Capote to write a stage adaptation of the work; his offer opened up new possibilities for income at a time when Capote was still struggling to make his way. Working with intense concentration, Capote managed to complete a draft of the play in a year's time. He was personally involved in the selection of a production team, and was particularly eager to have Peter Brook, the twenty-six-year-old phenomenon of the British theater, as director. He also wanted Virgil Thomson to write the production's incidental music and his friend Cecil Beaton to do the set designs and costumes. Both Capote and Saint-Subber wanted the celebrated silent film stars Lillian and Dorothy Gish for the roles of Dolly and Verena Talbo, respectively, and they obtained the sisters' interest.

Yet when Brook decided not to commit to the play, a series of un-ravelings began. Robert Lewis, who had worked largely in the musical theater, replaced Brook as director, and rather than casting the Gish sisters, who would have been perfect as the Talbo sisters, he chose Mildred Natwick and a little-known actress named Ruth Nelson. *The Grass Harp* opened in New York on March 27, 1952. Apart from a glowing review from Brooks Atkinson (who called the play "effortless and beautiful" in the *New York Times*) reviewers found the work charming but without much dramatic intensity.

The play has had its own devoted following, however. Within a year of its opening on Broadway, José Quintero revived it at the Circle in the Square theater in Greenwich Village; and it has been staged from time to time in regional theater, including a production of it as a musical that starred Barbara Cook. In 1952 the *Kraft Television Theatre* presented a streamlined version of it for NBC television. In 1995 *The Grass Harp* was made into a movie that was produced and directed by Charles Matthau. His father, Walter Matthau, appears in the film as Judge Cool. Jack Lemmon, Matthau's foil from many earlier films, plays Matthau's bête noire Morris Ritz. Other well-known actors appear in the film as well—Sissy Spacek, playing against type as the hard-edged Verena, and Nell Carter as Catherine Creek. Included, too, are Charles Durning, Roddy McDowall, Piper Laurie, and Mary Steenburgen. Despite this impressive cast and respectful reviews, however, the movie is too subdued to leave a really deep impression.

"House of Flowers"

In the early 1950s Capote became further involved in the performing arts. He was approached once again by Saint-Subber, who was interested in his recent short story "House of Flowers": would he be interested in adapting the work as a musical play for Broadway? Despite the difficulties they had had in turning *The Grass Harp* into a stage play, Capote agreed for a second time to collaborate with Saint-Subber and set to work. Much of the writing was done in the Italian fishing village of Portofino; but Capote and Jack Dunphy found time to travel to Switzerland and Paris before returning to America, where Capote met again with Saint-Subber and continued his work on the musical.

Capote's short story "House of Flowers," written in 1950, evolved from his travel sketch "Haiti" (1948), which was included in the collection *Local Color*. The travel piece was occasioned by his stay on the island, and is another instance of how the notes he took on particular places and their customs could affect his fiction. Haiti offered promising material in, for instance, the bizarre wakes he witnessed at which mourners clawed the air, beat their heads on the ground, and joined in eerie communal mourning. Other exotica included the omnipresence of scampering chameleons and the rituals performed by a young *houngan*, or voodoo priest. But the most relevant section of the sketch "Haiti" deals with the island's nightlife, which is almost nonexistent except for a row of brothels set among foliage along Bizonton Road. One of these establishments is called The Paradise, while others have the names of flowers, giving the appearance of respectability. The girls sit out on the front porch in rocking chairs, "fanning themselves with cardboard pictures of Jesus."

The most pertinent passage in "Haiti," however, is this one:

> This is R's story. A few days ago he went out into the country to sketch, suddenly coming onto the bottom of a hill, he saw a tall, slant-eyed, ragged girl. She was tied to the trunk of a tree, wire and rope binding her there. At first, because she laughed at him, he thought it was a joke, but when he tried to let her loose several children appeared and began to poke at him with sticks; he asked why the girl was tied to the tree, but they giggled and shouted and would not give an answer. Presently an old man joined them; he was carrying a gourd filled with water. When R asked about the girl the old man, tears misting his eyes, said: "She is bad, monsieur, there is no use she is so bad," and shook his head.

Capote's short story "House of Flowers" transforms this account into a delicate and delightful work of art that has the quality of a fairy tale. The incorrigible girl in the travel sketch becomes the innocent child Ottilie, the youngest of the girls at a house called the Champs Elysèes. But Ottilie, who unlike the others is from the high hill country rather than Port-au-Prince, belongs to a world apart. She is described as a "delightful dreaming child surrounded by old, uglier sisters." A child and dreamer, she has an affinity with certain earlier characters in Capote's fiction. She is even a little like Miss Bobbit in "Children on Their Birthdays," who is real in a way yet seems to belong to a dream.

The fairy-tale dimension of the story is reinforced by the fact that neither Ottilie nor the young man she marries (who is also from the hills) is corrupted by the city. His name is Royal, an apt name for a fairy-tale prince; and just as striking, his surname is Bonaparte. Handsome and unspoiled, he is played off against a wealthy gentleman with a yacht named Mr. Jamison who would like to have Ottilie for himself, but unlike Royal, does not offer love.

In many ways Royal is ideally suited for Ottilie, for he is light-footed and magical. He wears no shoes, and "his golden feet were slender and airy, and the prints they left were like the track of a delicate animal." Ottilie and Royal go to live in his house in the hills, which is described as a "house of flowers" for the wisteria lilacs that shelter it and make it a cool and balmy retreat from the rest of the world. Then another character enters upon the scene—Royal's witchlike grandmother, Old Bonaparte, who is "bowlegged as a dwarf and bald as a buzzard." Old Bonaparte seeks to remove Ottilie from her grandson's life by poisoning her food and casting voodoo spells on her, but the innocent girl actually outwits her. Near the story's end, Ottilie is temporarily tied to a tree as punishment for bringing about the grandmother's death; this public humiliation shields her from evil spells Old Bonaparte might be able to cast on her from beyond the grave.

In the last lines, Ottilie, hearing Royal coming up the hill to the house, strikes a dramatic pose: "seen from a distance, it would look as though she had come to some violent, pitiful end." Royal begins running toward her, while she thinks, "This will give him a good scare." Ottilie, who can neither read nor write, might seem like the most vulnerable of the characters yet has a way of surpassing all the others. She exists in Port-au-Prince in an ambiance of Caribbean sensuality, yet is both pure and fulfilled, unsoiled in her innocence.

Capote had some very wispy material to work with in adapting "House of Flowers" for the stage, and in order to make the story effective as drama he had to make many changes. Instead of having the house of flowers refer to Royal's house in the high hills, he now has it refer to Madame Fleur's house of prostitution, where the girls who work there have the names of flowers, such as Tulip, Gladiola, and Violet. Ottilie lives there, too, but it is made clear that she is a virgin and not one of the regular girls. Another brothel is introduced that is in competition with Madame Fleuer's.

The original staging of the play *House of Flowers* has a history that is little short of amazing. From the beginning it looked as if it would be a major Broadway musical. The great Harold Arlen, who had written such legendary songs as "Stormy Weather" and "Over the Rainbow," would be supplying the musical score, with Capote providing the lyrics as well as the book. Peter Brook, the wunderkind of the British theater, had decided against directing *The Grass Harp* but now agreed, after heavy persuasion from Arlen and Capote, to direct *House of Flowers*. George Balanchine, a towering, internationally acclaimed figure in the world of dance, agreed to choreograph the show. Oliver Messel, Britain's most acclaimed theatrical designer, agreed to do the sets and costumes.

The production, which was to have an all-black cast, was blessed with outstanding dancers, including a young Geoffrey Holder, Carmen De Lavallade, Alvin Ailey, and Arthur Mitchell, the last two of which would go on to lead their own distinguished companies. Young Pearl Bailey was given the important role of Madame Fleur, and Juanita Hall (who leapt to fame as Bloody Mary in *South Pacific*) would play her rival Madame Tango. Ottilie would be played by the eighteen-year-old Diahann Carroll, who as an actress and singer would later become a household name in America.

With such an array of talent, it was almost inconceivable that the show could falter, but it did. It was the first time that Brook had directed a musical, and he made mistake upon mistake. His reputation was so formidable, however, that no one stood up to him. He alienated his African American performers by claiming that he was not prejudiced (groans were heard), and referring to them thereafter as "you people." He had no idea of how to direct the show's star, Pearl Bailey, although she begged for his help. George Balanchine knew every movement of classical dance but was unfamiliar with the mambo, the dance that was to energize the show. He excused himself during the Philadelphia tryouts and was replaced by Herbert Ross, who also took over from Brook as director. Although the show had a favorable reception in Philadelphia, the director's constant demands for revision only made the production worse. When it opened in New York on December 30, 1954, it was praised, but rather faintly. It ran for 165 performances, or about four months, which was not bad but far from being a resounding success. Like *The Grass Harp*, it attracted a cult following that raved about Harold Arlen's songs, like "Two Ladies in de Shade of de Banana Tree," and Oliver Messel's colorful sets.

In 1968 *House of Flowers* was revived off Broadway with Josephine Premice, the most prominent calypso dancer in America, in the leading role of Madame Fleur. Most recently it was revived again (in February 2008) in concert form as part of New York's City Center's *Encores!* series, with Tonya Pinkins and Armelia McQueen as the competing brothel madames and the very talented Kathleen Marshall as both choreographer and director.

Beat the Devil

While Capote and Dunphy were spending the summer in Rome, Capote was asked to do some screenwriting by no less a figure than David O. Selznick, the producer of such films as *Gone with the Wind* (1930) and *Rebecca* (1940). His new film, *Stazione Termini* (directed by Vittorio De Sica, 1953; released in America as *Indiscretion of an American Wife*), featured Selznick's wife Jennifer Jones as an American tourist and Montgomery Clift as her young Italian lover. Capote was hired to polish the script (replacing Carson McCullers), but the work he did on the film was merely marginal. He did, however, impress Selznick, who before long recommended him to John Huston for his new picture. It would turn out to be the most eccentric film Huston would ever make.

Beat the Devil was adapted from the early 1950s novel of the same name by Claud Cockburn, using the pseudonym James Helvick after being blacklisted during the McCarthy era. Huston wasn't satisfied with his screenplay, however, and commissioned Peter Viertel and Anthony Veiller to submit a new one, which he also rejected. They had envisioned the story as a work of international intrigue and melodrama, without any of the playfulness that Huston was really looking for. He had scheduled the shooting to begin in a matter of days, and still had no script; confronted by this crisis he contacted Selznick, who was also in Rome making *Stazione Termini*. Selznick, notes Clarke, responded by recommending Capote, also in Rome; he worked quickly, Selznick explained, and—most important—was "'one of the freshest and *most original* and most exciting writing talents of our time.'"

They soon met, and Capote agreed to write the screenplay; it was a collaboration that turned out to be a wild adventure, with the script improvised on the spot from day to day. Capote would stay up all night writing and appear the next morning in a bleary-eyed and haggard state to hand out the latest pages of dialogue to the actors, who did not realize that there was no completed script in place. The final product looks as if it had been improvised, and in fact it had, but that is part of its peculiar charm: things in the film seem to keep happening spontaneously. Charlie Chaplin loved the film's offbeat comedy, and there are actually Chaplinesque moments in it. In one, Robert Morley, Humphrey Bogart, and Huston himself are backseat passengers in a vehicle speeding down a steep mountain road; when it hits rough spots they are bounced in unison out of their seats, their heads striking the ceiling. They then resume their rather formal, dignified positions on the seat, only to be bounced in unison again from their seats. But the odd appeal of the picture involves more than pratfalls. Charles Champlin, for many years the chief movie critic for the *Los Angeles Times*, was so taken by the picture that he saw it thirty times.

Although *Beat the Devil* may seem to have thrown structure overboard, it is at least consistent as a sendup of Huston's earlier work, particularly his film adaptation of Dashiell Hammett's crime novel *The Maltese Falcon* (1941), in which a gang of inept international criminals compete for the possession of an ancient art object believed to be of fabulous value. Their pursuit of it, both together and separately, becomes an obsession blinding them from a recognition that their lofty quest is an illusion driven by greed. The characters all betray one another. Even Sam Spade, who has some conscience and standards, betrays his partner by having sex with his wife. In the end, the supposedly graillike quest implodes, leaving the criminals in possession of nothing real.

Beat the Devil was shot in black and white to reinforce its parody connection with Huston's film noir classic, and to emphasize it further Huston wanted to include Bogart, Sidney Greenstreet, and Peter Lorre as stars. Bogart and Lorre were available, but Greenstreet had recently died; recruited to take his place was the tall, overweight British character actor Robert Morley. In the film, the crooks are in pursuit not of an art object of priceless value but of a claim to priceless uranium deposits rumored to exist in British East Africa. In their eagerness to reach the African coast ahead of other claimants, to the uranium fields, they engage in various intrigues and experience spectacular setbacks. When the transportation they had counted on is unavailable, they board a steamer that is falling apart and explodes at sea (a reference to Huston's film *The African Queen*, 1951). All have to swim for their lives, and when they finally reach shore they are set upon by hostile Arabs.

In *The Maltese Falcon*, unfaithfulness is exemplified by a female character played by Mary Astor, who brings about the murder of her husband and, like the others, schemes to get hold of the falcon. In Capote's version of this theme of sex and duplicity, Billy Dannreuther (Bogart) is married to Maria Dannreuther (Gina Lollobrigida) but is really in love with Gwendolen Chelm (Jennifer Jones), who is married to Harry Chelm (Edward Underdown), who is really in love with Maria Dannreuther. The relationships are more complicated still, but this alone is enough to make one's head spin. One feels that it is Capote rather than Huston who has engineered this madness and is responsible for the "madly" witty comments the characters sometimes make.

Yet one is always conscious of Huston, too, and the recurring theme in his films of a quest that comes to nothing in the end—not only in *The Maltese Falcon* but also, for instance, in *The Treasure of the Sierra Madre* (1948). Indeed, both *Treasure* and *Beat the Devil* begin and end in the same way. *Treasure* begins with a crowd scene in a Mexican square and an execution, and it ends with another crowd scene and execution, only this time of the *bandidos* who have set upon the American prospectors. In a very similar way, *Beat the Devil* begins with an excited street scene and with a crowd of men surging toward the camera, and it ends with the same street scene but now with a clear close-up of Robert Morley and the other crooks in handcuffs at the front of the surging crowd.

Apart from the intrinsic interest of the film itself, *Beat the Devil* is remembered for the stories that are told about its making. Bogart was in an automobile accident that knocked out his front teeth, and Capote had a tooth so severely infected that he was rushed to a hospital where, although in pain, he continued working on the script. Other Bogart-Capote stories during the shooting of *Beat the Devil* are still talked about, particularly their arm wrestling incident. Bogart challenged Capote, whom he called "caposy," to oppose him in arm wrestling, and Capote not only agreed but also won the match. Incredulous, Bogart challenged him again, and again Capote put down Bogart's arm— and then another time after that.

Another story of Capote and Bogart on the set that is similar in some respects but also different has to do with Bogart's needling a young woman who was Capote's script assistant. Capote told Bogart to "step outside." When they did, he placed his foot behind the unsuspecting Bogart and shoved him backward so that he fell to the ground. Capote then leapt on him throwing blows while Bogart roared with laughter and refused to lay a hand on Capote. The two, in fact, became great friends. Bogart, notes Clarke, wrote to his wife Lauren Bacall, "'At first you can't believe [Capote], he's so odd, and then you want to carry him around with you always in your pocket.'" Even Huston, considered by many to be a homophobe, was immediately charmed by Capote, whom he called "an extraordinary little man who has courage and the determination of a lion."

In the mid-1950s, during all this work in the performing arts, Capote's mother died. By 1953 her life had already fallen apart; Joe Capote lost his job when the books were audited at the company he worked for and a hundred thousand dollars were found to be missing. The district attorney opened an inquiry that would lead by the end of the year to Joe's conviction and imprisonment at Sing Sing. Without the money they had previously had, and even with financial help from Truman, Nina and Joe had to make severe retrenchments—a horrifying humiliation that left Nina drinking more heavily than ever, and sunk in depression. By January of the following year, she committed suicide by swallowing a bottle of secobarbital. She was found on the floor, her arms reaching out as if she were attempting to cry for help. Capote flew to New York immediately to be at the funeral. Dead or alive, Nina's legacy would never leave him.

Chapter Six

The Mid- to Late 1950s: *The Muses Are Heard*, "The Duke in His Domain," *Observations*, *Breakfast at Tiffany's*, and *The Innocents*

The Muses Are Heard

In the early 1950s, Capote's reportage paid dividends when he was engaged by the *New Yorker* to accompany and comment on the Everyman Opera Company's trip to Russia, where it was to perform George Gershwin's opera *Porgy and Bess*. It would be the first American company to perform in Russia in over forty years; and coming especially at the height of the Cold War, it was considered an international event of some moment. The U.S. State Department was involved, anxious to prep the theatrical adventurers on what to expect and on the dos and don'ts of their own behavior. The size of the company and its entourage was considerably greater than might have been anticipated: it consisted of fifty-eight actors, seven backstage personnel, two conductors, assorted wives and office workers, six children and their schoolteacher, three journalists, two dogs, and one psychiatrist. Capote's lengthy piece, in two installments, on the meeting of American culture and Russian audiences was certain to attract attention, first in serial form and then as a book. The party crossed into East Berlin on December 19, 1955, and traveled eastward aboard a train called the Blue Express to Leningrad, where it expected to give its first performance of *Porgy and Bess* on January 10, 1956.

The Muses Are Heard (1956), Capote's observation of the people and places he encountered, is continually entertaining, if not respectful. He notes that Lenore Gershwin, wife of the lyricist for *Porgy and Bess*, wears too many diamonds too often, even on those occasions when they would seem inappropriate; and she calls everyone "darling." The wife of Robert Breen, the director and coproducer, is described as having maple-colored hair that is "worn upswept and held in place by huge pins that could serve as weapons." At a performance of the opera she dabs at her eyes "as though drying phantom tears."

Capote's dry, acidulous humor, however, can be seen in his depiction of the Russians. At a Christmas party he meets a man named Nervitsky, "a vain, once-handsome man with . . . a collapsing chin line" who wears makeup. Knowing no English, he tells Capote in French, "'*Je suis* Nervitsky. Le Bing Crosby de Russie.' His wife was startled that I had never heard of him. 'No? *Nervitsky?* The famous *crooner?*'" They are dispatched rather quickly, but another Russian who appears and reappears is more fully created. The man, Stefan Orlov, goes out of his way to meet Capote, although he is constantly harried by the fear of being too close to a Westerner in a country where people live under constant surveillance. Their meetings are furtive. He wants him to know that he himself is informed about Western writing and culture, although he is not; he is instead poorly informed and mixed up. "'Among your writers, the powerful one is A. J. Cronin,'" he says, "'But Sholokov is more powerful, yes?'"

Orlov wants to show Capote around Leningrad, but his ulterior motive is the hope of meeting Robert Breen's attractive assistant, Nancy Ryan. He has been under the impression that Capote and Miss Ryan are singers in the cast of *Porgy and Bess*. When Capote tells him he is a writer, Orlov becomes agitated and upset. Even so, Orlov takes him to a late night Leningrad bar, where the Russian drinks too much vodka and becomes incoherent: "'That's all I want. To dance with Nancy. Beautiful. A beautiful girl. You understand? Just to dance. Just to . . . Where is she?' His hand swept the table. Silverware clattered on the floor. 'Why isn't Nancy here? Why won't she sing for us?' With his head tilted back he sang 'Missouri woman on the Mississippi'. . . . His voice grew louder, he lapsed into Russian, a hollering still obscurely associated with the tune of 'St. Louis Blues.'"

Capote wrote later that he had envisioned *The Muses Are Heard* as a "brief comic novel," and that is the way it reads at times, but it is not entirely comic. There are passages in the Russian material that are darker than the rest of the book. One such episode occurs when Orlov asks Capote to meet him by a cathedral, and while he waits there he observes a Kafkaesque scene. Four heavy men in overcoats have backed a man against the cathedral wall and are pounding him with their fists, and then pound him with the full weight of their bodies, "like football players practicing on a dummy." Strangely, through all of this no one makes a sound. "It was," Capote writes, "like an episode from a silent film." Strangely, too, a well-dressed woman stands by not far away as if she were waiting for these men to finish a business conversation. The men are indifferent to Capote's presence as they pass by him to join the woman and drive off.

The man who has been beaten lies helplessly in the snow; unable to speak, he is like a "deaf-mute" attempting to communicate with his eyes." Then a taxi pulls up alongside the curb. Capote remarks, "The rear door opened, and Stefan Orlov called my name. Leaning in the door, I tried to explain what had just happened and ask him to help the man, but he was impatient, he didn't want to listen, he kept saying, 'Get in' . . . and at last, with a fury that shook me, 'You're an idiot!' he said, yanking me onto the seat. As the taxi swung in a U-turn, its headlights exposed the man sprawled on the sidewalk, his lifted hands plowing the air, like the claws of an insect cruelly tumbled on its back."

This whole episode reads like fiction; and elsewhere individuals encountered seem less observed by a journalist than delineated by a novelist. The *Muses Are Heard* is a benchmark work for Capote, for it is this work that opens the door to such later nonfiction projects as *In Cold Blood*.

Despite certain Russian passages, however, *The Muses Are Heard* is often humorous; it is a sly humor that can be lethal. Even though he seems to keep discreetly in the background, the book is really a star turn for Capote. One is always conscious of his powers of visualization and his elegant turns of phrase. He points out that the department stores in Leningrad all sell the same goods at the same price, and that the best restaurants are alike in being huge and dilapidated with an atmosphere about them of grandeur gone to seed. As to the cuisine, he notes that when peas are served they rattle on the plate "like gun shot."

But there are no grounds more fertile than that provided by the Astoria Hotel, which is alleged to be an upper-tier hotel but whose oversized rooms resemble a Victorian attic full of family discards all crammed into a tomb-dark, unventilated area. The hotel elevator is described as "an ancient bird cage that creaks on its cables." In what is the finest joke of all, the management has assigned the best rooms to the company's carpenters and stagehands and the worst rooms to the company's principal people. Herman Sartorius, a powerful New York financier who has come along with the company, has been assigned no room at all, nor has Lenore Gershwin, "who sat on her luggage in the lobby."

Confusion reaches a climax at the end when *Porgy and Bess* premieres in Leningrad. It is discovered at the last minute that the program notes in Russian explaining the plot to the audience are not yet available, which means that what happens on stage will be incomprehensible. A young interpreter for the Russian ministry named Sascha has to go out onto the stage to tell the audience what happens in the opera when he knows very well that they want no further delays, they want the opera to begin. "A sheaf of typewritten pages quivered in his hands," Capote remarks, "and his face, bloodlessly pallid, was drenched with sweat." The instant the audience saw that he was about to read them the plot, a mutiny broke out in the balcony, where rude voices started shouting for the opera to begin, and people stomped their feet while "Sascha went on reading, mumbling, as if he were whispering a prayer against the deafening tumult."

The first of the two acts were a mystery to the audience, which failed to applaud at the end of the numbers that in America had drawn stirring ovations. Nor was there any notice taken when the principal actor-singers came on stage. An ominous silence reigned. Capote tells of a particularly grotesque comic reaction by a member of the audience. After Crown has killed one of Porgy's neighbors, inhabitants of Catfish Row form a circle around the corpse. At this point an important Soviet dignitary is supposed to have turned to a correspondent and said, "Ah, now I see! They are going to eat him." The second act, however, was better understood; the response, if not of tidal-wave proportions, was at least respectful. The comedy of Capote's book's ending is that when the curtain falls, the journalists covering the event wire their papers that the opening night was an unparalleled triumph; one headline read, "LENINGRAD GOES WILD OVER PORGY AND BESS."

Racial issues do not enter into the book very much, although Capote does remark on the initial reaction of the welcoming party, made up of a hundred or more of Leningrad's leading theatrical agents, who "discovering that *Porgy* has a Negro cast look bewildered and . . . try to arrange their faces into an expression of more positive welcome." But one of the black performers, Earl Bruce Jackson, is a humor sketch too. A jive-talking extrovert, he wears a pair of gloves with holes along the fingers to reveal his rings. His rings are called attention to again when he is seen at the theater "lolling his hand over the edge of the box so that his jewelry, a ring on every finger, could be seen to advantage. In a thematic way, his rings recall Mrs. Gershwin's too prominently displayed diamonds. There is an almost universal undermining of people and their pretensions. The company head envisions lavish curtain calls for the production that never come. The production is meant to represent a breakthrough in Russian-American relations, but on opening night a thousand theatergoers cannot understand a thing of what is happening onstage. The book has in common with a novel that it has a shape and theme, and a farcical ending that is both inevitable and right.

It also shares with a novel an unusual care for and love of language. A Russian is described as having "a pushed-in, Pekingese face"; another is the "victim of a slightly receding chin." When their train stops in Warsaw in freezing weather, a gang of workmen come over to look in the windows: "One after another, distorted faces mashed themselves against the glass." Looking out the train window at the frozen Russian terrain, one saw that "[h]ere and there, like printing on paper, stretches of fir trees interrupted the whiteness [of the snowy fields]. Flights of crows seemed to skate on a sky hard and shining as ice." The ice forms in "lenses" on the train's windows, and gazing out one sees "merely spectral diffusions, as if your vision were deformed by cataracts." A man named Savchenko, a Russian military officer in charge of the *Porgy and Bess* tour, gave Capote's book its title via a Russian saying, "When the cannons are silent, the muses are heard." They can be heard distinctly in this work, which is sharp to the point of wickedness.

"The Duke in His Domain"

After the success of *The Muses Are Heard*, Capote was encouraged to write again about the entertainment world. He became interested in knowing something about the movie *Sayonara*, which was adapted from the novel by James Michener. Gerald Clarke notes in his biography *Capote* that, although set in Asia, "the subject was similar [to that of *The Muses Are Heard*]: another American company trying to open doors to an alien society. Set during the Korean War, the film was to have as its theme the cultural clash between Orient and Occident. This is a view worth noting, but I would think that Capote's real interest from the very beginning was less an interest in cultural collisions than in the movie's star, Marlon Brando. After all, in the mid-1950s there was no one in the performing arts more talked about, more imitated, and more exciting to the public than Brando; and a rare interview with him by Capote would be certain to attract attention—as the *New Yorker*, which commissioned Capote's Asian trip and the resulting profile "The Duke in His Domain" (1956), would surely have known.

When cocktail party rumors spread that Capote had it in for Brando and planned to interview him, Joshua Logan became alarmed. He was quite aware of how Capote had pulled the rug out from under the opera company that had brought *Porgy and Bess* to Russia, and he was determined to keep him away from Brando. Accompanied by Cecil Beaton, Capote flew to Kyoto in late January 1957, and while they were checking into their hotel they ran headlong into Joshua Logan. He sternly warned Capote to stay away from his star—and according to one source even shoved Capote through the front door of the hotel into the street. If true, this was a mistake; it merely increased Capote's determination to see Brando and win his cooperation. Capote wasn't a complete stranger to him; they had met earlier in New York, and had a friend in common in Sandy Campbell, a young actor and writer. For whatever reason, Brando disregarded Logan's warnings and agreed to see Capote. He later said that he didn't think his conversation with him was an interview; but if this is so, what did he think it was?

Brando's biographer Peter Manzo has described the interview vividly. When Capote arrived, he "lifted a bottle of Vodka nestled in his arm and placed it on the table. Marlon called room service for ice." "What an experience," Capote would later write in his diary, "and how he loved to talk—and *such* a vocabulary . . . very anxious to display all the long words he's learned. He talked nonstop, from seven fifteen until twelve thirty in the morning."

In the course of the interview, it appears that Brando would like to give the impression that he is the thinking man's matinee idol, but it is clear that he is out of his element. He also tells of the way he dominates those around him (like a "duke in his domain"), to bring them under his control. Yet even as he boasts of bringing others under his control, he falls under Capote's spell. He is unaware that Capote has told him of his personal sorrows only to get Brando to talk about his own. And Capote gets what he wants—an ample account of Brando's insecurities, and tales of a father who had shown no interest in him and an adored mother who became a slave to alcohol.

Brando isn't the only one in the sketch to be tripped up. Joshua Logan is depicted as being naively optimistic as he begins his various productions. "Logan's belief in whatever project he is engaged in," writes Capote, "approaches euphoric faith, protecting him, as it seems designed to do, from the nibbling nuisance of self-doubt." He has long been fascinated by the classic Kabuki theater, and he expects to make use of real Kabuki in *Sayonara*. What he has not foreseen is that the Shochiku film company, which controls the Kabuki theater as well as almost all performance media in Japan, will not necessarily accede to his wishes. "The ruler of the Shochiku empire," Capote remarks, "is a small, unsmiling eminence in his eighties, known as Mr. Otani" who soon derails Logan's hastily laid plans.

For one thing, Mr. Otani objected to Logan's casting the Mexican actor Richardo Montalban as a featured Kabuki performer, considering it an affront to the Japanese theater. Logan's misstep was exacerbated by his plan to use a genuine Kabuki star to substitute for Montalban in the dance sequences. A Japanese writer remarked that this "was much the same 'as asking Ethel Barrymore to be a stand-in.'" Despite priding himself on being authentic in his portrayal of Japan on the screen, Logan made other questionable choices in casting, notably in wanting Audrey Hepburn to play the Japanese girl with whom the Brando character falls in love. Hepburn refused even to consider the role, feeling that audiences would laugh at her in the part. As Logan's misjudgments begin to add up, he becomes a figure who is close to being comic.

Although it would seem to be written partly as a rebuff to Logan, the sketch of him is not at all embittered; Capote even seems to be having fun with him. The Logan sketch is actually more successful than the larger one of Brando that makes up the bulk of the article; the actor's failings as recorded by Capote all seem true enough, yet there is something that seems mean-spirited, particularly in the revelations of his mother's alcoholic degradation. It was a set up on the part of Capote, and despite his statement that Brando did not come off that badly, it was written to wound—and it did, haunting Brando for years. Logan and Brando are a matched set, both figures of vanity, but there is an animus in the portrayal of Brando that keeps it from being altogether delightful. Even the irony seems a bit heavy-handed and the imagery too obviously symbolic. We are made to see how lost and vulnerable young Brando is at the end of the article, when Capote sees a gigantic image of him in a billboard advertisement for *The Teahouse of the August Moon*. He is captured in a squatting position with the serene smile of a Buddha.

Curiously, immediately before this ending, with its straining for a classically "closed" effect, a passage appears that is totally unlike it in its openness as Capote wanders in a vast Asian city at night. The passage restores one's faith in Capote as a magician with language:

> There was no one at the desk, nor, outside, were there any taxis in view. Even at high noon the fancy crochet of Kyoto's streets had played me tricks; still, I set off through the marrow-chilling drizzle in what I hoped was a homeward direction. I'd never before been abroad so late in the city. It was quite a contrast to daytime, when the central parts of town, caroused by fiesta massiveness, jangle like the inside of a *pachinko* parlor, or to early evening—Kyoto's most exotic hours, for then, like night flowers, lanterns wreathe the side streets, and resplendent geishas, with their white ceramic faces and their ballooning lacquered wigs strewn with silver bells, their hobbled wiggle-walk, hurry among the shadows toward meticulously tasteful revelries. But at two in the morning these exquisite grotesques are gone, the cabarets are shuttered, only cats remained to keep me company, drunks and red-light ladies, the inevitable old beggar-bundles in doorways, and, briefly, a ragged street musician who followed me playing on a flute a medieval music.

Observations

As the 1950s flowed into the 1960s, Capote continued to be active on a number of fronts. In 1959 he published the book *Observations*, a collection of brief profiles of people affiliated in general with art or society whom he knew personally or had "observed." It was enhanced by his friend Richard Avedon's striking photographs. The profiles are of such individuals as Louis Armstrong, Coco Chanel, Charlie Chaplin, Jean Cocteau and André Gide, and W. Somerset Maugham, among others. Also included, however, is a piece called "A Gathering of Swans," in which Capote discusses what it is that makes a great female beauty, even in those cases in which the lady in question may be rather plain. "A Swan," Capote asserts, "is invariably the result of an adherence to some aesthetic system of thought, a code transposed into a self-portrait; what we see is the imaginary portrait precisely projected." The two reigning swans for Capote are Marella Agnnelli in Europe and Barbara ("Babe") Paley in America, both already his close friends as he moved ever further into fashionable society.

Observations verges on being a brilliant exercise, but it is eminently readable for the seductiveness of its prose. In a number of the sketches, Capote pays unusual attention to people's eyes. John Huston, for instance, has "warmly crinkled and ungentle eyes, eyes bored as sun bathing lizards." Richard Avedon, a subject as well as a collaborator, has deceptively normal eyes that are "energetic at seeing the concealed and seizing the spirit." In picturing Isak Dinesen's face, he misses no nuance; its "prisms glitter with intelligence and educated compassion," and her eyes, "smudges of kohl darkening the lids, deeply set, like velvet animals burrowed in a cave [do not] fall into the possession of ordinary women."

One profile that stamds out is that of Mae West. It is less studied or oblique than some of the others, and has a comic sense that bursts with life. The way that Capote builds slyly to the punch line is a testament to his comic timing. Approached by those who admire her, West is unsure of how to "be" when she isn't her theatrical self: "Removed from the protective reach of her hilarious creation, her sexless symbol of uninhibited sexuality, she was without defense: her long lashes fluttered like the feelers of a beetle on its back." Capote continues:

> [A]n intense young girl . . . approaching the actress, announced, "I saw *Diamond Lil* last week; it was wonderful."
> "Didja honey? Wheredja see it?"
> "At the Museum. The Modern Museum."
> And a dismayed Miss West, seeking shelter in the sassy drawl of her famous fabrication, inquired, "Just whaddya mean, honey? A *museum?*"

Breakfast at Tiffany's

The novella *Breakfast at Tiffany's* (1958) is not quite like any other work of Capote's. There is a quality of freshness to it, as if Capote were just at the beginning of his career or had commenced some new phase of it. Stanley Edgar Hyman has remarked that while Capote's early fiction concerns itself with the "inner world," his later fiction, exemplified by *The Grass Harp* and *Breakfast at Tiffany's* shifts his concern to the outer world, sometimes in a way almost sociological. *Breakfast at Tiffany's* in particular is a break from the past, for the patch of Manhattan that Capote seizes upon is evoked with a sharply focused realism. At the same time, the novel captures the mood and moment, the mise en scène of New York during the postwar years.

The bartender Joe Bell is a good example of Capote's merging of realism with comedy. He has been observed so keenly, so indelibly that his very presence brings to life his surroundings and the others who occupy them—his East Side bar, the Third Avenue el, the racetrack, the soldiers and sailors who now people the streets of Manhattan, the daring young women who now, throwing off repressions of the past, spend late nights clubbing. Joe Bell is as tremendously known by his speech as are the characters in John O'Hara's stories; his manner of speaking tells readers all they need to know about him—that he has a hard exterior surface and a tender heart. His speech establishes him as the quintessential New Yorker in touch with the rhythms and stresses of big-city life. (He seems always to be popping a Tums tablet for his sour stomach.) He is half in love with Holly Golightly, who has brightened his life. She has dazzled him.

Joe Bell qualifies as a great character of secondary stature; but so, too, does "Doc" Golightly, the horse doctor from Tulip, Texas, who married Holly when she was fourteen years old. With his halting manner, a sweat-stained hat, and flock of "churren" by his first wife, he is backcountry drabness itself. Yet he is a character of some decency and respectfulness, and in his different way he, too, has been dazzled by Holly. Like Joe Bell, he is an unpredictable character conception. When he finally finds her in New York and she explains to him why she cannot return with him to Tulip, he is big enough to let her go.

Other characters who comment in one way or another on Holly and her lifestyle in New York include Madame Sapphia Spanella, who lives in the same building as the narrator and Holly. She is a determined adversary, always ready to condemn Holly for having raucous parties in her apartment or for arriving home in the middle of the night with strange gentlemen. A delightful conception, Madame Spanella is an opera singer—a "husky coloratura" who goes roller skating in Central Park every afternoon. Although he scarcely appears in the novel, Sally Tomato manages to be as memorable as he is improbable. A mobster boss, he is serving time in Sing Sing Prison, where every Thursday Holly visits him, and he gives her—without her understanding what it is all about—an envelope containing coded messages to give to his lawyer.

There is an element of humor, indeed of farce, in characters like Madame Spanella and Sally Tomato; but some other characters have been conceived as grotesques. Mag Wildwood, whose name could have come out of a Thomas Hardy novel, is well over six feet tall and stammers compulsively. While standing upright in a drunken state at a party, she falls forward stiffly like a tree that has just been axed, landing on her face. Stranger still is O. J. Berman, the Hollywood actor's agent, who is introduced thus: "A creature answered the door. He smelled of cigars and Knize cologne. His shoes sported elevated heels; without these added inches, one might have taken him for a Little Person. His bald freckled head was dwarf-big: attached to it were a pair of pointed, truly elfin ears. He had Pekingese eyes, unpitying and slightly bulged. Tufts of hair sprouted from his ears, from his nose. . . . "

But even O. J. Berman pales beside Rusty Trawler, who is described as a "middle-aged child that had never shed its baby fat. . . . it was as if he had been born, then expanded, his skin remaining unlined as a blown-up balloon, and his mouth, though ready for squalls and tantrums, a spoiled, sweet puckering." These characters all gravitate to Holly and in their contrast accentuate her role as the novel's preeminent figure. Mag Wildwood and Holly are friends, at least for a time, and by pairing them off, Capote merely emphasizes all that Holly is and Mag is not. Holly is the person that others all talk about or are in love with.

Capote's playing off a marginal narrator-observer with a charismatic central character is strongly reminiscent of the alignment of characters in F. Scott Fitzgerald's *The Great Gatsby*. Like Nick Carraway in *Gatsby*, the narrator in *Breakfast at Tiffany's* is a mild and unheroic figure who happens to be the downstairs neighbor of the more imposing principal character. That Capote's narrator has no name is surely meant to indicate that he lacks a sense of identity. He is mild and repressed, while Holly is uninhibited.

Even the tone of the narrator's opening sentence—"I am always drawn back to places where I have lived, the houses and their neighborhoods"—could have been spoken by *Gatsby's* Nick Carraway, and it intimates that the novel will deal with some incidents or individuals that still survive strongly in his memory. Like Gatsby again, Capote's novel then drops back into the past in a long flashback about the growth of the narrator's friendship with the principal character. Notably, both *Gatsby* and *Breakfast at Tiffany's* are suffused with nostalgia.

Holly is Capote's most indelibly imagined character of the 1950s and, as mentioned earlier, a number of women were anxious to claim that they were the original model for Holly Golightly. Doris Lilly, Carole Marcus, Oona O'Neill, Phoebe Pierce, and Gloria Vanderbilt were all friends of Capote in the late 1940s and, like Holly, involved at an early age in Manhattan's nightclub life. One has the feeling that there was a model for Holly, but if so Capote never revealed her name. Gore Vidal, scornful as always of Capote, claimed that Holly was merely a redrawing of the character Sally Bowles in Christopher Isherwood's *Berlin Stories*. Holly, however, is more complicated and nuanced than Sally Bowles, and her conception involves different thematic ideas. Nevertheless, Capote would certainly have been aware of Sally Bowles.

A peculiar feature of Holly's background is that in certain respects it resembles the background of Capote's mother, who had come from a backcountry Southern region to immerse herself in the glamour of New York. Their first names, Lillie Mae and Lula Mae, are too similar for it to be mere coincidence. Moreover, they both changed their "country girl" names to names sounding less rural. It may seem strange that Capote should link Holly to his own mother Nina, especially since they are so different. But it would not be so strange if one posits that he is linking himself obliquely with Holly: both enjoyed the glamour of nightlife, but were also subject to bouts of anxiety, which Holly calls "the mean reds." The lives of both, moreover, were always in motion. During the 1950s Capote constantly moved back and forth between Europe and America, between one set of people and another, between writing fiction and writing for films and the theater. Holly's life is so much in motion that it is appropriate that the nameplate for her in the apartment building entranceway should read "*Miss Holiday Golightly, Traveling.*" When Holly and the nice but repressed young man who narrates the story exchange presents, she gives him a golden birdcage, while he gives her a St. Christopher's medal, which commemorates the patron saint of travelers.

Critics have sometimes referred to Holly as a prostitute, but in an interview Capote maintained that he never had that conception of her. She enjoyed nightlife, and the nightclubs where she met men who were only too happy to share her company; they might give her fifty dollars as "powder room change," but sex was not necessarily involved. Sometimes she met a man she really liked and wanted to be with, and they had sex—but not as a money-for-sex transaction. Perhaps the most memorable line about her in the novel occurs when O. J. Berman calls her a phony, and goes on to add, "'But on the other hand you're right. She isn't a phony because she's a *real* phony. She believes all this crap she believes.'" What Capote, through Berman, seems to be saying is that Holly is an innocent who lives naively, from the heart. She is a dreamer, a girl-woman waif who lives in a corrupt world without ever being, herself, corrupted.

A surprising thing happens later in the novel when she tells the narrator (and the reader) who she is. Her philosophy of life and love includes a ringing endorsement of gay marriage! A person, she says,

"ought to be able to marry men or women or—listen, if you came to me and wanted to hitch up with Man'o War, I'd respect your feeling. I'm serious. Love should be allowed. I'm all for it. . . . Good things only happen to you if you're good. Good? Honest is more what I mean. Not law-type honest—I'd rob a grave, I'd steal two bits off a dead man's eyes if I thought it would contribute to the day's enjoyment—but unto-thyself-type honest. Be anything but a coward, pretender and emotional crook, a whore. I'd rather have cancer than a dishonest heart."

Holly journeys through a compromised world in search of authenticity. Her name—Holiday, or Holly—can be understood in different ways. It proposes that life can be a holiday, something to be enjoyed. The connotations of her name are normally seen in this way. But name Holly also has other connotations, as the holly of Christmas decorations; and it might be noted that Christmas appears in the novel in a teasing context. The Japanese photographer Mr. Yunioshi comes across the wood carving bearing Holly's likeness in the African wilds of East Anglia on Christmas day of 1956. Christmas, however, is not the only religious allusion in the work; another is St. Christopher. The St. Christopher's medal given to Holly commemorates the martyr affiliated in some church annals with Christ, whose birth three centuries earlier offered the hope of love and truth in a corrupt world.

Breakfast at Tiffany's is raffish and humorous, but it has its complexities. By the end of the novel how is Holly to be regarded? Is she a saint or a fool in her endless pursuit of authentic love in a dishonest world? She becomes an enigma. She is not, however, an anomaly in Capote's fiction. Seen characteristically on the fire escape of the building, strumming a guitar and singing a ballad about wandering through the pastures of the sky, she thus takes her place among Capote's other guitar players, whose playing in one way or another is a meditation on desire.

The guitar is a key image in a short story of Capote's called "A Diamond Guitar," published eight years before *Breakfast at Tiffany's*. A sensitively written and evocative story with perhaps faint echoes of the work of Carson McCullers, it takes place at a prison farm, where a middle-aged man, a Mr. Schaeffer, is serving a life sentence. He has a solitary life until he is befriended by a new prisoner, an attractive young Mexican named Tico Feo. There are some homoerotic overtones to the friendship, without there being anything overtly sexual between them. Tico persuades Mr. Schaeffer to join him in a prison break and he agrees. Tico gets away, but Mr. Schaeffer injures his leg and can't go on; Tico abandons him to his fate. Later, in his austere prison farm existence, Mr. Schaeffer keeps Tico's guitar under his bed. At night his hand reaches down to the guitar "and his fingers drift across the strings: then, the world." In *Breakfast at Tiffany's*, Holly Golightly isn't another Mr. Schaeffer, but she does yearn for a perfection that cannot be realized; and for this reason there is an edge of sadness in Capote's often lighthearted fable.

In 1961 *Breakfast at Tiffany's* was made into a Hollywood film that starred Audrey Hepburn as Holly, George Peppard as the narrator (now called Paul Vaujak), and Buddy Ebson as Doc Golightly. It was directed by Blake Edwards and adapted for the screen by George Axelrod. In Axelrod's treatment, *Breakfast at Tiffany's* was stripped of the artistry that went into it, becoming a conventional romantic comedy of heterosexual love in the 1950s, with the male and female leads getting together at the end. What made it successful at the box office was the appeal of Audrey Hepburn, who was nominated for an Academy Award. The nostalgic and yearning musical score by Henry Mancini, which won an Oscar, included the Mancini/Johnny Mercer hit "Moon River." Hepburn carries the picture, but her fragile grace does not really fit the hillbilly-turned-Manhattan pub crawler Capote imagined. She is, however, a hundred times more engaging than the wooden Peppard.

Yet if there are some people who remember the film, flaws and all, with outright affection, no one can look back at the Broadway musical adaptation of *Breakfast at Tiffany's* without shuddering; it was one of the worst fiascos in modern theater history. It was the sharp-eyed, boldly mustached, and legendary producer David Merrick who conceived the idea of bringing *Breakfast at Tiffany's* to Broadway. He invested hundreds of thousands of his own money in the project, and recruited the cream of New York's theatrical talent for the venture. Abe Burrows, the force behind *Guys and Dolls* and *How to Succeed in Business Without Really Trying* and famous as an adapter and a peerless show doctor, was hired to write the adaptation and to direct. Oliver Smith, one of the most honored and prolific scenic designers in American history, would design the sets.

The cast would be led by Mary Tyler Moore and Richard Chamberlain, both having formidable followings from the popular television series in which they starred. By 1966 the show was in previews in Boston, where the highly touted show was beginning to fall apart. Burrows was physically and creatively exhausted from having taken on both the writing and directing and was unable to go on. Merrick brought in Edward Albee to do a new adaptation, and Joseph Anthony, a veteran of both straight dramas and musicals, to direct. Burrows had envisioned a stage Holly as a raffish figure who could give a Broadway audience of that time a jolt; but this seemed singularly inappropriate for an actress with such an extremely wholesome public image as Mary Tyler Moore. Albee's adaptation was more in line with the Holly of the novel, but it did not quite come together. Word spread quickly to New York that it was a disaster. Merrick closed the show before the previews had gone very far, and apologized publicly for the production. Capote himself had no part in it, but was clearly unhappy with the mess they had made of his novel.

The Innocents

Although Capote was absorbed at the time in writing *In Cold Blood*, he took off several weeks to write, with William Archibald, the film adaptation of *The Turn of the Screw*, Henry James's brilliant excursion into Gothicism. *The Innocents,* the theatrical title for James's story, had been produced originally on Broadway in 1950 as a stage play by Archibald, who in the same decade had also written an adaptation of James's *The Portrait of a Lady*. The play starred the gifted actress Beatrice Strait and won universal praise for its capturing of a difficult diabolic mood that was evoked by subjective rather than explicit deeds. As it happened, *The Turn of the Screw* was a tale Capote particularly admired. It is hard to say who deserves the greater credit for the film, Archibald or Capote, but there is no doubt that *The Innocents* (1961) is an artful and arresting work.

It was directed by Jack Clayton, who had worked on *Beat the Devil* and was instrumental in having Capote collaborate on this newer screenplay. Shot in an atmospheric black-and-white by cinematographer Freddie Francis, *The Innocents* starred Deborah Kerr and Michael Redgrave at their impeccable best. *Time* magazine, in a January 5, 1962, review, called attention to the "dangerous, intelligent darkness" of the picture, and to Kerr as an actress who "tunes herself like a violin string till she quivers exquisitely at the snapping point." Also fortunately cast are the two children, Miles (Martin Stephens) and Flora (Pamela Franklin), who are left practically alone in an isolated English country estate called Bly. The only other occupants of the estate are the housekeeper, Mrs. Grose, and the newly arrived governess Miss Giddens. Also present, however, are the ghostly previous governess and butler Peter Quint, who died mysteriously. It is intimated that they were involved in some sort of unspeakably evil relationship, and may now, Miss Giddens fears, be invading the souls of the children. Miles has recently been expelled from a private school for "corrupting" the other children, with no explanation as to what this corruption consisted of. Martin Stephens as Miles has remarkable film presence, and his character's way of calling Miss Giddens "my dear" makes one wonder if he isn't strangely and inappropriately mature. In a shocking close-up, he boldly and erotically kisses the governess on the lips.

Reviews of the movie were quite favorable, and in the course of time it has come to be regarded as a classic. In a lengthy piece in the summer 1962 *Film Quarterly*, Pauline Kael wrote that

> the dialogue has, at times, the same beauty and ambiguity as the images. I assume that Truman Capote, who is one of the finest prose stylists— as distinguished from writers—this country has ever produced, is responsible for some of these phrases. And the boy who plays Miles . . . is superb, not only visually, but in his poised and delicate enunciation of lines that are so beautiful they communicate a sense of the terror latent in such beauty. He is a true creation of Henry James—this writer with the children who are too beautiful to live. This beauty is what makes *The Innocents* the best ghost movie I have ever seen. It is an interpretation that honors its sources.

It is the best film Capote wrote or was involved in writing. It also has particular interest in that he wrote it at the same time he was writing *In Cold Blood*, another Gothic tale of innocence vanquished by evil.

Chapter Seven

In Cold Blood

Capote's account of a multiple murder in Kansas, *In Cold Blood*, raised the author to a new level in modern American writing. The book became a mammoth best-seller, at the same time impressing the critical establishment. In addition, Capote claimed that he had created a new literary genre in the "nonfiction novel." Actually, exploration of the interconnections of fact and fiction go far back; it can be witnessed, for instance, in Daniel Defoe's *A Journal of the Plague Year* (1722). In more modern times, the journalism of Rebecca West, and the memoirs of Isak Dinesen in *Out of Africa* (1937; one of Capote's favorite books) have had a strong novelistic quality; and Ernest Hemingway in *The Green Hills of Africa* (1935) even announced that his book was an attempt "to write an absolutely true book to see whether the shape of a country and the pattern of a month's action can, if truly presented, compete with a work of the imagination." Hemingway wrote his "true" book as he might a work of fiction, altering the chronology of events to create such vivid "fictional" effects as heightened suspense and a stronger, more emphatic climax. Other authors who have written journalism and reportage with the aesthetic heightening of fiction include James Agee, in *Let Us Now Praise Famous Men* (1941; a collaboration with photographer Walker Evans), and Joan Didion, in her books exploring the underside of the American dream in California, and more recently in *The Year of Magical Thinking* (2005). Capote's conception of *In Cold Blood* coincided with the emergence of the so-called new journalism being practiced by, among others, Norman Mailer.

As it happens, Capote and Mailer were exact contemporaries and published their first novels—*The Naked and the Dead* and *Other Voices, Other Rooms*—in 1948, in each case mostly to acclaim. During the 1950s and 1960s both wrote not only fiction but also reportage that had the immediacy and many of the qualities of fiction. They spent much of their lives in New York, and in fact lived for a time in the same Brooklyn Heights neighborhood. They were personal and temperamental opposites, Mailer always vaunting his manliness and Capote being openly and unapologetically gay. But they respected each other and were on friendly terms. Mailer has written a delightful account of meeting Capote one day in Brooklyn Heights and of their going to a nearby Irish bar neither had frequented before for a drink. Once inside, Mailer was alarmed to find that the working-class customers seated on stools along a brass rail were tough, unhappy looking Irishmen who turned to stare at them as they came in. "Truman," he remarks in George Plimpton's collection *Truman Capote*, "was wearing a little gabardine cape. He strolled in looking like a beautiful little faggot prince. It suddenly came over me: My God, what have I done? I've walked into this drunken den of sour male virtue with Truman! I walked behind him as if I had very little to do with him. . . . It took me half an hour for the adrenaline to come down." No fight broke out, but Mailer did have the shock of recognition of how much courage Capote had every day in just being his uncompromising self.

They were on friendly terms, but they were at times competitors. One night they appeared together on David Susskind's television show, and at first Mailer did all the talking, apparently having decided to bury Capote with all the weighty theories he was expounding. But when Capote did speak he was delightful. As George Plimpton reports in *Truman Capote: In Which Various Friends, Enemies, Acquaintances, and Detractors Recall His Turbulent Career*, Capote remarked that Jack Kerouac's work "isn't writing, it's only typing," and practically wiped Mailer off the screen. Mailer was under the impression that he had trumped Truman until the next morning, when friends called to say, "'Oh, man, did Truman murder you!'" His own sister told Mailer that he did well but that "'Truman was fascinating.'"

The reportage of Mailer and Capote tended to be self-centered, but each author was self-centered in different ways. Mailer immersed himself in the turmoil of public happenings, as in *The Armies of the Night* (1968), his account of the 1967 anti–Vietnam War protest march on the Pentagon in which he makes himself a main character. In Capote's reportage one always *feels* his presence even though at times he is a distanced observer, and he is likely to treat private, not public, experience. Mailer was almost hysterically prolific, while Capote's output was measured to the point of being sparse. Both were in love with language, and as prose stylists achieved their own striking effects. But they were opposites: Mailer was so much in love with words that he could not stop using them when at times it would be better if he had; Capote, on the other hand, was an admirer of Gustave Flaubert and felt that every word had to be right; he could craft sentences as if they were little works of art. Capote and Mailer each wrote a nonfiction novel, *In Cold Blood* (1966) and *The Executioner's Song* (1979) being considered their respective masterpieces. Each concerns a young man and his arrest, imprisonment, and execution. *The Executioner's Song* even seems a challenge to Capote. *The Executioner's Song* has powerful passages and narrative sweep, but is overwritten; it reaches a point at which it should have ended and then goes on for another hundred pages. *In Cold Blood* is more focused and creates a character in Perry Smith of such wounding that he cannot be forgotten. It is more questionable how deeply one feels about Mailer's Gary Gilmore.

The inspiration for *In Cold Blood* came to Capote when he was reading the November 16, 1959 issue of the *New York Times* and came across an article that caught his attention. It reported the macabre slaying of the Clutters, a family of four, by a person or persons unknown in the small, conservative community of Holcomb, Kansas. That this horror occurred in Finney County—where social life tended to be austere and attention was paid to the teachings of the Bible—intrigued Capote, who got in touch almost immediately with William Shawn at the *New Yorker* and proposed doing an essay-article on the impact of the fearful event on the townspeople of Holcomb. Shawn liked the idea and commissioned the article, but neither had as yet any inkling of how much larger an undertaking would be involved or of how many years would elapse during Capote's investigation of crime and punishment in America's heartland.

Before embarking by train for Kansas in mid-December of that year, Capote realized that getting to know the town and its people would be too much for one person, and brought along his longtime friend Harper Lee. She proved to be a fortunate choice: a trained observer, she provided him with an extra pair of eyes and ears. Most important, she entered into an immediate rapport with the local farmers and their wives, having lived for years in similar farming country in the South.

Upon Capote and Lee's arrival in Garden City, the capital of Finney County and not far from Holcomb, the townspeople were bewildered by Capote's flamboyant personal style, which included sporting a scarf that, tossed rakishly over one shoulder, trailed practically to the ground. His peculiar sounding voice was, for want of a better word, described by townspeople as "high-pitched." Snide comments were made about his fey manner; yet after a while—and largely through Lee's ingratiating effect on the locals—people began to change their minds about Capote. Fascinated by his conversation, they began to invite him to their homes for dinner. The real breakthrough occurred when Lee befriended the Southern-born wife of Alvin Dewey, who had been put in charge of the Clutter murder case for the Kansas Bureau of Investigation. Not at first, but as their friendship took hold, Dewey allowed Capote to have almost unlimited access to the two young men arrested for the murders. Without this access Capote's book could not have been written.

The fullest account of the Capote-Lee collaboration is found in Charles J. Shield's biography *Mockingbird: A Portrait of Harper Lee.* But the essence of it is that they had uncanny success as an interviewing team because they had retentive memories (townspeople relate that Capote could recall exactly what they said in a conversation with them a month or more earlier). Neither Capote nor Lee took notes or used tape recorders when they were interviewing people, feeling that their use would inhibit the people they were taking to. Instead they listened carefully and later compared what they had each been told; in this way, according to Capote, they arrived at a reasonably accurate account of what had been said.

Capote maintains that he taught himself a memorization technique that enabled him to recall what an individual told him to the point of 95% accuracy. It is important to note that he did not reveal to Dick Hickock and Perry Smith, the young men charged with the Clutter killings, that he memorized every word of their confidences to him. Transcripts of his interviews with them and with hundreds of others were so extensive, Capote told an interviewer, that "they filled a room."

Despite all the care and effort that went into the making of *In Cold Blood*, Capote's claims that every word in the novel was true have been disputed. Inaccuracies and distortions of various kinds later come to light in an article in *Esquire* and were anthologized in Irving Malin's *Truman Capote's* In Cold Blood: *A Critical Handbook* (1968). Some of the inaccuracies are of a minor nature, as when Capote puts the wrong people in the lead car returning Hickok and Smith from their capture in Las Vegas to Garden City. His depiction of Bobby Rupp,

Nancy Clutter's boyfriend and the last person to see her alive, is less an oversight, however, than a conscious distortion. "'He makes me out,'" Rupp told Phillip K. Tompkins in an interview included in Malin's book, "'to be some kind of great athletic star and really I was just an average small-town basketball player.'" Capote seems pretty clearly to be shading his description of Rupp so as to create an image of an ideal American teenage couple whose lives were shattered.

A more serious issue still concerns comments that Capote attributes to Josephine Meier, the wife of Garden City's undersheriff. In their imprisonment in the Garden City jail, Hickock and Smith were separated, Hickock occupying one of the facility's regular cells, while Smith was placed alone in a cell adjacent to Mrs. Meier's kitchen. She came to know him to some extent, and in a late-night conversation with her husband, according to Capote, remarks that Smith "wasn't the worst young man" she had met. Mrs. Meier, however, denies ever having said this. She also denies having made remarks about Smith that are attributed to her in a later passage. In this passage Smith is supposed to have broken down and sobbed. "'I heard him crying,'" Capote quotes Mrs. Meier as saying. "'Crying like a child. He'd never broke down before, shown any sign of it. He reached out his hand. He wanted me to hold his hand, and I do, I hold his hand, and all he said was, "I'm embraced by shame." I wanted to send for Father Goubeaux . . . but he just held my hand tighter.'"

Finally there is the issue of the last words spoken by Smith as he is about to be hanged. Capote has him speak out against capital punishment and referring specifically to the contribution he might have made to society had his life been spared. He then concludes by saying, "'It would be meaningless to apologize. Even inappropriate. But I do. I do apologize.'" It would not seem possible, however, for Capote to have heard these last words, since although a witness at the hanging, he was so distressed by it emotionally that he stepped back out of the range of hearing. On the other hand, standing only a few feet away from Smith at this critical moment was the editor of the *Garden City Telegraph*, and he was absolutely certain that Smith had not expressed contrition, had not apologized. Both of the passages just cited tend to make Smith more sympathetic to the reader, but they are actually questionable and make Capote's claim that everything in the novel was true seem questionable, too.

Yet even with its disputed passages, *In Cold Blood* is an impressive work. It was published to acclaim first in serialized form in the *New Yorker* and then, in 1966, as a book. There were, however, dissenters. Diana Trilling has compared it unfavorably to *Let Us Now Praise Famous Men*, Agee's account of the life of poor Appalachian sharecroppers in the Depression. Agee's book, she asserts in a piece included in Malin's *Critical Handbook*, is the superior work because it brings Agee himself to a point of self-examination and gives his "documentary" a dimension deeper than mere surface. Capote's method, she contends, is exactly the opposite, relying on surfaces alone and "abrogating the artist's right to emphasize or even to distort or suppress for his own purposes." It seems to me that Trilling has two blind eyes: she assumes that a factual documentary unmediated by declared personal involvement cannot rise to the qualities of fiction, and she assumes that Capote's account is all on the surface when his writing actually has texture and subtlety.

One aspect of *In Cold Blood* that none of the critics missed was Capote's incorporation of film technique. In Malin's *Handbook*, Stanley Kauffmann remarks that "he uses intercutting of different story strands, intense close ups, flashbacks, traveling shots, background detail, all as if he were fleshing out a scenario." The primary intercutting occurs between the daily life of the Clutters, unaware of what is about to befall them, and Hickock and Smith as they travel ever closer to their rendezvous with the Clutters and what will prove their own undoing. It is a movement back and forth between the haves and the have-nots. The Clutters are good churchgoing people, but as passive victims they do not exercise the same hold on the reader as do the doomed convicts Hickock and Smith.

The eighty intercut segments of the book help to sustain a mood of suspense; but mood is also evoked by landscape. Holcomb is located on the edge of the Kansas Bible Belt. It has a large number of mostly Protestant churches in its vicinity and it strongly discourages the use of alcohol. Herb Clutter, the very model of a man who is a stickler for restraint and self-denial makes a practice of firing any man who drinks or even smokes. His wife Bonnie has been brought up in a church environment too, but her health has broken down and she has become a nervous invalid. She sleeps in a bedroom apart from her husband's and has had to spend periods of time in rest homes. If the Clutter couple suggest the idea of repression, the landscape itself does not provoke any ideas of dancing in the street. It has no oases or rolling hills, but is flat as the eye can see, offering little refreshment for the eye.

"The land is flat," Capote writes, "and the views are awesomely extensive; horses, herds of cattle, a white cluster of grain elevators rising as gracefully as Greek temples are visible long before a traveler reaches them." The Holcomb version of Greek temples, exemplars of the highest ideals of a culture, are warehouses of grain, feed for their cattle, and an unexcited regimen of life that will be regular if austere. Explosive events are not usual in Holcomb, though they may happen. In 1957 in the nearby prairie state of Nebraska, two years before the occurrences in Holcomb, a young man named Charles Starkweather went on a murder spree. A youth with poor vision and misshapen legs, mocked as retarded and consigned to a job—evidently for life—of handling garbage, he shot his fourteen-year-old girlfriend's parents, and he and the girlfriend started on a wild journey of random killings across the heartland. In 1959, terror erupted in Holcomb.

Hickock and Smith do not go on a rampage of murder, but like Starkweather they are characters who have stepped outside the law. What is striking about them is that they have no stability: much of their lives are ruled merely by chance. Early in the book Smith is stepping off a bus in Kansas City; it is an appropriately captured moment, since he is always in motion, belonging nowhere. He is hoping to be reunited with a man named Willie-Jay, an ex-cellmate from the Kansas State Penitentiary; the chaplain's clerk, Willie-Jay was the only one in Smith's life to have taken an interest in him and wanted to help him. Ironically, he just missed him, Willie-Jay having left the terminal on another bus only five hours earlier. Smith then decides to look up Dick Hickock, another cellmate, a decision that will lead inevitably to the undoing of himself and others. When Hickock and Smith were cellmates they had talked of a robbery that they could carry off in Kansas. Each told the other a story influencing their future actions, and as chance would have it each of the stories was untrue. Wanting to impress Hickock, to score points with him, Smith spoke of his having killed "a nigger" with a chain. Hickock passed on to Smith what would turn out to be an erroneous story about a safe in the home of a well-to-do farmer named Clutter that they could rifle. The crime they would commit could come out of happenstance, missed opportunities, crossed wires, and falsehood.

Throughout the novel things continue to happen by chance. On the morning of the day of the murder, Clutter takes out a $40,000 life insurance policy with a double indemnity provision should he die of other than natural causes. The chances of his doing this at that time are mind boggling, but it is what he did. As Hickock and Smith travel toward Holcomb, they are about to procure black stockings worn by nuns with which to cover their faces during the robbery, but this goes awry, and because they want no witnesses to the crime they will now have to go through with the their talked-about murders after all. Hickock and Smith's arrest in Las Vegas when they have evidence on them of their presence at the murder scene is another instance of the ubiquity of blind chance in the novel. They had been spotted by the Las Vegas police, who could have arrested them immediately but decided to wait another ten minutes. In that time Smith appeared with a large box of his belongings, including a pair of boots whose imprint on the sole exactly matched the boot imprints found at the Clutter house.

In Cold Blood has the nature of a documentary, and F. W. Dupee (in Malin's *Critical Handbook*) has gone so far as to call it "the best documentary of an American crime ever written." It is full of subtleties that are not usual in documentaries, and it thrives on illusion and irony. Smith is influenced by Hickock because although he himself is dreamy, he sees Hickock as being completely practical and "totally masculine." Hickock's masculinity, however, is an illusion. When the testing time comes at the Clutter house, he cannot act, either by firing the gun or by wielding the knife. His manliness has been all talk, and Smith has to do the brutal killing for him. When they are captured in Las Vegas and grilled by the police separately, Hickock breaks down and sobs, "Perry did it. He killed them all." Hickock himself then went out into the corridor and fainted.

But Smith's mistaken conception of Hickock is not his only illusion. One of his prime illusions is that he will dive for sunken treasure, and scoop up handfuls of gold coins from long submerged Spanish galleons, even though his legs are so painfully maimed that he would not even be able to swim. Hickock, too, suffers from illusions. A major one, that the Clutter house contains a safe holding a large amount of money, is shattered when it turns out that there is no safe at all. Another is that he is "normal," despite his history of raping very young girls.

In Capote's novel, illusion and irony go hand in hand. Smith's favorite movie is *The Treasure of the Sierra Madre*, which he has seen at least eight times. He is struck particularly by Walter Huston's "old cuss" prospector, who reminds him of his father. Smith's fascination with the prospectors searching for gold in the mountains—indeed, his identification of himself with them—is ironic inasmuch as their quest ends ultimately in futility and death. His favorite movie is like a prophecy of what Smith's life is going to be.

The Clutters are also shown in multiple perspectives of irony. In his innocence of his impending gruesome fate, patriarch Herb Clutter looks over his apple orchard and reflects that with a little more rain "'this country could be Paradise—Eden on earth.'" On the eve of his terrifying helplessness and murder, he is told by a woman that he strikes her as someone who has never known fear and can talk his way out of anything. Even Clutter's wife Bonnie is depicted in terms of irony. A Bible is found at her bedside, in which a bookmark placed between two pages is embossed with the words "Take ye heed, watch and pray: for ye know not when the time is." These ironies add to an impression in the book that life is enigmatic and at times cruel beyond understanding.

Much of the imagination of *In Cold Blood* is Gothic. Capote's career began with Gothic stories and an exceedingly Gothic first novel. Although sometimes held in abeyance, Gothicism never entirely disappeared from his writing, and with *In Cold Blood* this element reappears powerfully, in a new form in a work remarkable for the breadth of its exacting realism. Gothicism has as one of its foremost components an element of fantasy, but *In Cold Blood* that fantasy has been socialized by being "true." The frisson behind the novel's familiarity with the everyday world can be summed up in Smith's confession of his murder of Herb Clutter: "'I didn't want to harm the man. I thought he was a very nice gentleman. Soft-spoken. I thought so right up to the moment I cut his throat.'"

One never forgets that Smith is the product of what one might call a Gothic family; his parents were the "Tex and Flo" of a rodeo act that eventually broke up, and with it their marriage. Smith's Cherokee mother turned to heavy drinking, finally choking to death on her own vomit, while his father was a luckless and at times abusive prospector in Alaska. Of the four children, all but one had doom-ridden lives. One of the girls, Fern, turned into an alcoholic like her mother and jumped from the window of a San Francisco hotel room. On the way down she struck a theater marquee, bounced off it and rolled under the wheels of a taxi. In the room from which she jumped the police found her shoes, a purse containing no money, and an empty whiskey bottle.

The fate of her brother Jimmy is even more grotesque. A sensitive young seaman, he married a young girl with a promiscuous past, only to become obsessed by the gnawing suspicion that she was betraying him at every turn with other men. His unrelenting accusations drove her to put a shotgun to her face and pull the trigger. He found her on the floor, put her on the bed and lay next to her for hours, then reloaded the shotgun and killed himself. Such were Smith's siblings.

Gothicism in the novel is also hinted at in the initial account of the Clutter murders by the fact that the murderer had placed a pillow under his victims' heads before shooting them in the face with a shotgun. Capote is a master at noting details that leap out at the reader. Hickock's left eye is called "serpentine" and seems to "warn of bitter sediment at the bottom of his nature." At the end, Alvin Dewey remembers his first meeting with Smith, who was "seated in the metal chair, his small booted feet not quite brushing the floor."

It is always Smith rather than Hickock who is the focal character in the book. In his July 3, 1966, *New York Review of Books* review of the book, Mailer called Smith "one of the great characters in American literature," and whether true or not it does suggest how strongly he imposes himself on the novel. *In Cold Blood* is in part about the two Americas, one confirmed in money and position, the other disaffected and dispossessed; in the course of the work they come into collision. Smith is like his father who can find no place for himself in life, a man who continually changes his address as he pursues a way to wealth in the old gold rush country of Alaska, and finds only futility. F. W. Dupee, in a perceptive observation in his *Critical Handbook* piece, notes that the father of Nancy Clutter and the father of Perry Smith "are each in his own place and each in his own way, embodiments of free enterprise and the pioneering spirit." The difference between them, however, is glaring: Clutter is, in a sense, the American dream achieved while "Tex" Smith remains sunk in poverty and bewildered failure. Smith's perception of Clutter as a father figure on the night of the crime appears to embrace both the love and hate he had for his own father.

As an outsider who comes into contact with a well-to-do family, only to commit murder and end on death row, Smith has something in common with Clyde Griffiths in Theodore Dreiser's novel *An American Tragedy*, which, like *In Cold Blood*, was based on an actual murder case. Dreiser went to great lengths to be faithful in his novel to the 1906 crime involving a young man named Chester Gillette. He collected all the newspaper accounts of the case, consulted the court proceedings of Gillette's trial, traveled to the upstate New York community of Cortland where the original events took place and to the Adirondack mountain lake where the murder was committed, and even went to see the electric chair used for Gillette's execution. However different they are otherwise, *An American Tragedy* and *In Cold Blood* are novels taken from life that have a documentary quality and refer to the American dream.

Although Smith comes from real life, he has much in common with the "freak" characters of Capote's early fiction. He is peculiar in his physical appearance: his chest and upper body are powerfully developed but his legs are short and stumpy. Only slightly over five feet tall, he is a "chunky, misshapen child-man" with dwarfish legs. His "tiny feet," Capote remarks, "would have neatly fitted into a delicate lady's dancing slippers; when he stood up, he was no taller than a twelve-year-old child." As a child he was a chronic bed-wetter, and he is still a bed-wetter as an adult. Hickock overhears him crying in his sleep.

His childhood is a history of misfortune. Yanked out of school by his alcoholic, itinerant father and kept from attending school beyond third grade, Smith spent part of his early years in a Catholic orphanage, where as a bed-wetter he was punished sadistically by a nun; his later life as a Salvation Army ward was equally miserable. At other times he lived in Alaska with his father, who took out his frustrations on him and finally locked him out in the snow to fend for himself. When Perry Smith turned sixteen he joined the Merchant Marine but had a hard time of it, just as he did later when he was in the army in Korea. Discharged from the army, he became a vagrant and a thief.

He spent time in prison in Missouri and Massachusetts before arriving in New York City's Times Square, where he worked at a cheap amusement arcade. After a while, however, he was spotted by the FBI as a prison breaker and remanded to the Kansas State Penitentiary. Here he shared a cell with Hickock and a new chapter of his disturbed career began. Different as they were, each had been injured in road accidents, suffering multiple broken bones and brain concussions, which required lengthy periods of rehabilitation; this left Smith an aspirin addict due to the excruciating pain he continued to feel in his legs.

What makes Smith a compelling character in part is that he contains so many contradictions. A victimizer of others, he is himself a victim. A young man capable of murder, he is also strangely gentle. He has aesthetic interests, is fond of drawing and plays the guitar and harmonica. An autodidact, he is always attempting to climb out of the ignorance and deprivation of his background, sometimes using long words that he has just learned instead of simpler ones that would serve him better. In sexual matters he tends to be a puritan, and rebukes Hickock for his failure to restrain his sexual impulses. At the same time Capote scatters insinuations that Smith's sexuality, if it were to be expressed, would be homosexual. Hickock calls him "honey," and Smith sketches Hickock in the nude.

As a teenager aboard a Merchant Marine ship, Smith was ganged up on by tough "queens," and his sergeant in the army put pressure on him to "roll over." Smith disapproves of "queer stuff" but he calls it to mind. He has "lotion soaked and scented hair" and "calloused but girlish hands." His speaking voice is like a whisper. When the police interview his Las Vegas landlady about Smith, she says, "'You oughta hear him talk. Big, long words coming at you in this kinda lispy, whispery voice. Quite a personality. What you got against a nice, little punk like that?'" In a way Smith is stranger than Cousin Randolph in *Other Voices, Other Rooms*; at least Randolph knew who he was.

The wonder of *In Cold Blood* is that although Capote limits himself to what was actually said and done, he envisions this as Capotean fiction. All of the themes of the earlier writing are in the novel. Capote's dreamer characters are in it—characters such as Holly Golightly in *Breakfast at Tiffany's* and Mr. Schaeffer in "A Diamond Guitar" who strum guitars, invoking an enchantment that is sought after but out of reach. Smith may be true to life, but he also comes out of Capote's workshop of fictional conceptions, for he is the dreamer of dreamers, the great one.

His dreams include finding gold in Alaska or sunken treasure aboard a Spanish galleon. He dreams, too, of being a famous cabaret entertainer with his name changed to Perry O'Parsons, singing and playing his guitar and other instruments before an applauding audience. His reverie can also become nightmarish: in a recurring dream he is being devoured by a huge snake just as a great yellow bird rescues him and flies with him to heaven. He is immersed in dreams, but apart from Hickock he has no friends, and no romantic partners, either male or female. He is an alienated man who hates his life.

In the later sections of the book, especially, Capote sees Smith as a victim. His trial is unfair to the point of being grotesque. People are accepted as jurors who clearly favor the death penalty. The grim and stony-faced Judge Tate dismisses objections that in any other court would have been deemed proper. The young men were not read their rights and did not have access to an attorney when they were interrogated by the Las Vegas police. Only a day before the trial began, the Clutter estate auction sale had been held, accompanied by a mammoth amount of statewide publicity certain to inflame opinion against Hickock and Smith, yet Judge Tate did not find this prejudicial. Two distinguished forensic psychiatrists submitted detailed reports that Hickock and Smith were mentally disturbed, but no mitigating circumstances were allowed by Judge Tate, who reminded the jury that the M'Naghten Rule was in effect in the state of Kansas. The rule required the death penalty if in perpetrating a capital crime the perpetrator knew the difference between right and wrong; in this very simplistic ruling, no other factors were relevant. Because of this narrow and "cold-blooded" (and now archaic) ruling, Hickock and Smith went to the gallows.

Capote was shattered by the hangings, partly because he had formed a close tie with Smith. The moment he saw Smith, according to Harper Lee, "he saw himself." They were the same height, and there were similarities in their backgrounds: both had mothers who were alcoholics and fathers who had abandoned them. Smith's case was even worse than Capote's, and he did not have Capote's gift for survival. But the very painful situation of childhood was shared; it was one that haunted Capote all of his life, and he relived it again in Smith; it would appear to be, more than anything, the reason for Capote's powerful portrayal of Smith, with its objectivity and its compassion. *In Cold Blood* is less "private" than any of the works that precede it, and Smith's story does have something to say about American society and the failure of love. Written with Capote's usual perception, it is also notable for the somber tone that moved Rebecca West, appropriately, to hail it in a 1966 *Harper's* magazine piece as "a grave and reverend book."

Chapter Eight

Late Capote: *Music for Chameleons, Answered Prayers*, and Other Writings

After *In Cold Blood*

In the mid-1960s much was happening in Capote's life. He had been a celebrity, but only with the book publication of *In Cold Blood* in 1966 did he also become rich. He moved from the basement portion of Oliver Smith's brownstone in Brooklyn Heights to an expensive, high-rise apartment in the United Nations Plaza. For months he was kept busy giving interviews and appearing on talk shows. *In Cold Blood* was made into a movie in 1967, only a year after the publication of the novel. Partly at Capote's urging, Richard Brooks was selected to write the screenplay and to direct; with Brooks directing, he felt, the harsh realism of the story would not be compromised. The film that resulted is unusually dark and has the lonely nighttime look of film noir, with characters photographed at times in dark silhouette.

The picture was shot on location, even to the point of using the actual scene of the murders and the highway route Dick Hickock and Perry Smith followed after their departure from the Clutter house in Kansas to their destination in Las Vegas. Even the cells in which the young men were interrogated are authentic. Capote was not involved in the writing of the script, although he did visit the set, where he came face-to-face with Robert Blake, the young and relatively unknown actor who could have been Perry's double.

Capote describes his initial meeting with Blake in his essay "Ghosts in Sunlight: The Filming of *In Cold Blood*," included in *The Dogs Bark*:

I had seen photographs of Robert Blake (Perry) and Scott Wilson (Dick) before they were selected for the roles. . . . despite their clear physical resemblance to the original pair, their photographs had not prepared me for the mesmerizing reality. Particularly Robert Blake.

The first time I saw him I thought a ghost had sauntered in out of the sunshine, slippery hair and sleepy-eyed. I couldn't accept the idea that this was someone pretending to be Perry, he was Perry. . . . Here were the familiar eyes placed in a familiar face, examining me with the detachment of a stranger. It was as though Perry had been resurrected but was suffering from amnesia and remembered me not at all.

In Cold Blood is a cinematic novel to an unusual degree. And like a mirror reflecting its source, Brooks transferred Capote's cinematic technique to cinema itself. The novel stays remarkably close to the novel throughout with the single exception that Brooks has introduced a reporter character (Paul Stewart, a veteran film noir actor) who follows the murder case from beginning to end and is clearly meant to suggest Capote. He seems to speak for Capote, especially in the scenes leading up to and immediately after the executions when he opposes the death penalty. This sequence makes the character seem a mere contrivance. *In Cold Blood,* the movie, had generally favorable reviews; it had every advantage, including an intelligent script and perfect casting, yet in Brooks's insistently low-key, depressed literalness it lacks the Capote touch that might have brought it to life.

That same year Capote ventured into writing for television. Described by Jack Gould in the *New York Times* as the "Professor Higgins of the jet set," he liked to advise and mold young women he was close to. In the 1960s he encouraged his friend Lee Radziwill to take up acting. With Thomas W. Phipps, he made an adaptation for television of Vera Casary's play *Laura,* which he felt would be ideal for Radziwill. Her beauty and international celebrity (she was, after all the sister of Jacqueline Kennedy and the wife of Prince Radziwill of Poland) would make up for her lack of any extensive formal training. Her appearance, he surmised, would be an event and attract an audience. *Laura* was broadcast in January of 1968 and featured, in addition to Radziwill, Arlene Francis, Farley Granger, George Sanders, and Robert Stack.

Reviews of the two-hour made-for-television movie were crushing, with Radziwill's performance singled out as a conspicuous disaster. She wore clothes beautifully, it was said in *Newsday,* but she could not "simulate any emotion." "Miss Bouvier," *Variety* commented, "is neither good nor bad, she is just not an actress." It was well-known and duly noted in the reviews that she was appearing as Capote's protege. "If Mr. Capote," the *New York Times* declared, "will extend the courtesy of helpful professionalism, she might advance in small parts and rather enjoy them. But it was an essentially cruel and selfish move to project her participation into the limelight of *Laura*, particularly since the early film, with Clifton Webb and Gene Tierney is available on late night movies for inevitable comparison." Radziwill's debut in *Laura* finished her acting career and cooled her friendship with Capote.

In the period of the late 1960s and early 1970s Capote was also involved in other media projects which, with an exception or two, are not remembered today. As a carryover from *In Cold Blood*, he made a television documentary called *Death Row, U.S.A.*, which was completed in 1968. With Leland Hayward as producer, it was to be broadcast on ABC. But the network executives changed their minds, deciding that the subject matter was too grim for a television audience. Capote spent a year on the project with nothing to show for his time and effort. Never seen by the public, the documentary presumably gathers dust in some ABC vault, waiting to be seen.

Unlike *Death Row, U.S.A.*, *The Glass House*, a ninety-minute made-for-television movie did reach its audience, being shown on CBS in February 1972. Capote didn't write it, but it was his idea and he contributed suggestions. Its credited writer was Tracy Keenan Wynn and it starred Alan Alda, Dean Jagger, Vic Morrow, Kristoffer Tabori, and Billy Dee Williams. It dramatized the dehumanizing conditions of life and death in a penitentiary.

Not all of these projects, however, were concerned with crime and punishment. During a trip to California in 1971, Capote was in conversation with Paramount Studios about his doing a screen adaptation of F. Scott Fitzgerald's *The Great Gatsby*. With its New York setting, lyricism, and brilliant craftsmanship, it seemed an ideal assignment for him. A screen version of *Gatsby* had been made earlier, in 1949, that starred Alan Ladd as Gatsby, Betty Field as Daisy Buchanan, and Shelly Winters as Myrtle Wilson, but it was two-dimensional and had quickly become dated; it was time for a new *Gatsby*. Jack Clayton, who had directed *The Innocents*, was to direct this modern *Gatsby*, and he proposed Capote as its screenwriter. After the meeting in California, Capote signed with the studio.

The screenplay proved more difficult, however, than Capote had expected: much of the novel consists of atmosphere rather than action, and abstraction rather than a particularized realism. When Capote submitted his screenplay to Paramount early in 1972 the studio rejected it and refused to pay the balance of his fee. Capote sued and was awarded the amount that had been agreed upon. Capote's screenplay (now part of the Truman Capote Collection at the New York Public Library) is polished and strongly visualized; but there is little of Capote himself in it. Fitzgerald's novel has been reproduced but not interpreted. A Paramount executive is supposed to have told Capote, "This is just like the book," to which Capote replied, "I was under the impression we were adapting the book." But the executive, after all, was right: Capote's adaptation had no cinematically transforming vision.

For one of his media adventures of this time he did no writing at all. In 1975 he was a featured actor in the movie *Murder by Death,* a comedy written by Neil Simon. The conceit is that six of the world's most renowned detectives—Charlie Chan, Nick and Nora Charles, Agatha Christie, Hercule Poirot, and Sam Spade—are invited to the country estate of a wealthy eccentric criminologist. He lives in a mansion that looks something like a castle and is enshrouded in fog. His guests all take their pratfalls as they match wits with him in unraveling a seemingly impenetrable mystery. The movie had an awesome cast that included James Coco, Peter Falk, Alec Guiness, Elsa Lanchester, David Niven, Peter Sellers, Maggie Smith, Nancy Walker, and Estelle Winwood. It was a movie that seemingly could not fail, yet it did.

Capote wasn't Simon's first choice for the part of the eccentric criminologist. It was Ray Stark, the producer, who particularly wanted Capote for the part and got his way. Capote himself was an eccentric known to millions of people from his appearances on TV—someone who, after the enormous success of *In Cold Blood,* was apt to be associated in the public mind with mystery and murder and would draw audiences. The trouble was that *Murder by Death* wasn't much of a movie, and Capote had no fizz as an actor. How could he compete with such great actors as Alec Guiness and Peter Sellers? Compared to others in the cast he seemed a bit uncomfortable. "For Truman," Simon remarks in George Plimpton's collection *Truman Capote,* "it was a lark. He didn't ask for rewrites or anything. But he was very ill at ease with the dialogue. He was a great raconteur; we all know how funny he can be on his own, but he got stuck when he had lines to say."

Yet this same period brought Capote a windfall of media success. In the mid-1960s the independent filmmakers Frank and Eleanor Perry, who had made a strong impression with their movie *David and Lisa* (1962), approached Capote with their idea of adapting several of his stories for television. He had turned down proposals like this before; but when he met the Perrys he felt that their adaptations would have intimacy and resonance, and he agreed to collaborate with them. The stories they decided on were "A Christmas Memory," "Miriam," and "Among the Paths to Eden." "A Christmas Memory" was the crown jewel of the anthology, but all of the teleplays were works of quality. Frank Perry directed them, and Capote and Eleanor Perry did the adaptations.

The teleplay *A Christmas Memory* had the particular advantage of having the superb Geraldine Page—who had given memorable performances in the Tennessee Williams plays *Summer and Smoke* and *Sweet Bird of Youth* before taking on the role of Sook here. (She had also starred in a teleplay of another of Capote's childhood stories, "The Thanksgiving Visitor," which had earned her an Emmy). *A Christmas Memory* was televised at Christmastime 1966 on ABC, to enormous success. It received the Peabody Award as the best television program of the year, as well as numerous international awards. It won an Emmy for Geraldine Page and another for Capote and Eleanor Perry for their adaptation. *Miriam* and *Among the Paths to Eden*, adapted by Capote and Eleanor Perry, also featured brilliant actresses—Mildred Natwick in *Miriam* and Maureen Stapleton in *Among the Paths to Eden*, a performance that won her an Emmy.

In combined theatrical release, *Trilogy* was selected for screening at the Cannes Film Festival in 1968 before opening in America. In 1969 it was also published in book form in a text that not only included the texts but also photographs and commentary by Capote and the Perrys. In his commentary, Capote notes that he wrote the stories at different times and under different circumstances: "'Miriam' was written when I was seventeen and was doing my first published stories; 'A Christmas Memory' appeared in 1956—I wrote the whole story during one January night in Hong Kong; 'Among the Paths to Eden' was the last short story I wrote before climbing into the ring for my five-year battle with *In Cold Blood*. . . . despite the dissimilarities of setting—Manhattan, a Queens cemetery, a farm in Alabama—they have a subject in common: loneliness, lovelessness, love, lack of love."

Music for Chameleons

During his late period Capote published two new collections of fiction and reportage. *The Dogs Bark: Public People and Private Places* (1973) was predominately retrospective, reprising classic pieces published earlier in *Local Color* and *Observations,* as well as *The Muses Are Heard* in its entirety. New material, however, appeared in *Music for Chameleons* (1980). Of these pieces in the collection, the longest by far (nearly a hundred pages) is "Handcarved Coffins," which is subtitled "A Nonfiction Account of an American Crime."

Some critics found it below the level of Capote's earlier writing; essentially a thriller, it nonetheless has literary merit. Set in a lonely and dispirited Texas town, a major character is a psychopath. Capote himself (present in the work but identified simply as "TC") is a kind of character-observer; he is a friend of Jake Pepper, an agent for the State Bureau of Investigation.

It seems that certain townspeople have been receiving small hand-carved coffins shortly before their sudden and horrible deaths. Robert Hawley Quinn, the big man of the area, comes under suspicion but nothing can be proved against him. Quinn is felt as a powerful figure, both mentally (he beats everyone in games of chess) and physically. Capote's descriptions of him are intimidating, combining as they do both intimations of barbaric strength and of civilized cunning. He is said to have "simianlike arms" that dangle to his knees, together with fingers that are "long, capable, oddly aristocratic." Capote writes of Quinn, "The grey eyes . . . betrayed him: his eyes were alert, suspicious, intelligent, merry with malice, complacently superior. He had a hospitable, fraudulently genial laugh and voice. But he was not a fraud. He was an idealist, an achiever; he set himself tasks, and his tasks were his cross, his religion, his identity; no, not a fraud—a fanatic."

Quinn is eerie in that no matter what suspicions point to him as the murderer, he is always elusive; his evil cannot be contained. He has different shapes and identities—among them a traveling evangelist preacher who, as the Reverend Snow, baptized Capote in his childhood. (Note the connotation of a lack of human feeling in the name Snow.) The to-the-edge-of-death baptism at the hands of the Reverend Snow had been terrifying; he had been held under water to the point of all but drowning. At a certain point in the narrative Capote makes the frightening recognition that these two figures with monosyllabic names are one and the same person. Quinn has the ability to enter into people's most disturbing dreams. "[O]ccasionally, while I slept," Capote writes, "he knocked at the door and entered my dreams, sometimes as himself, his grey eyes glittering behind the wire-framed spectacles, but now and then he appeared guised as the white-robed Reverend Snow." At such times he seems reminiscent of the fright figure who haunts Kay in "A Tree of Night"—the "wizard man."

As he has been elsewhere, Capote is a splendid observer and image maker in "Handcarved Coffins." He is particularly adept at capturing characters through his descriptions of their eyes. Quinn's wife Juanita has "bored onyx eyes." But the most memorable of these ocular images appears in a passage about Clem Anderson who, while driving in an open car struck a sharp and nearly invisible wire that had been stretched across the highway so that his head was sliced off neatly. His decapitated head then rolled down the road, "but didn't look dead, merely serene, and except for the jagged gash along the forehead, his face seemed as calm, as unmarked by violence as his innocent, pale Norwegian eyes." The most Gothic of the ocular images, however, appears in an earlier scene when a lawyer and his wife step into their car and are instantly attacked with unbelievable fury by rattlesnakes that have been injected with amphetamine. The couple are found with their swollen heads resembling "Halloween pumpkins painted green."

The most pitiful of the murders comes at the end, and is not witnessed but imagined. Adelaide ("Addie") Mason, on the eve of her marriage to Jake, goes for a swim in the river that has been a bone of contention between Quinn and his victims, who had diverted some of the water passing through Quinn's land and their own. There is no proof that Quinn murdered Addie in the water, but there is the strongest suspicion of it. The reader is left to imagine her helpless terror, not unlike the terror felt by Capote as he was held under water by the Reverend Snow. The theme and imagery of water run all through the story, culminating in the setting of the fought-over river in which the final murder is committed and the psychopathic Quinn's "holy mission" is completed. "Handcarved Coffins" may merely be a thriller with some implausible incidents, but in its craftsmanship more generally it does not stand outside the bounds of literature.

Among other stories, profiles, and sketches in *Music for Chameleons* is a Southern story, "Hospitality," that might have been written by Eudora Welty; and a New Orleans story, "Dazzle," that could only have been written by Capote. The protagonist in "Dazzle" is an eight-year-old boy who harbors a fearful secret until the end. Capote tantalizes the reader about what this secret can be, and there is the theft of some jewelry, and a witchlike woman Mrs. Ferguson who is believed by some to have magic powers. To her the boy eventually reveals his great secret: "'I want,'" he tells her, "'to be a girl.'" Mrs. Ferguson's reaction, the narrator remarks, "began as a peculiar noise, a strangled gurgling far back in her throat that bubbled into laughter. Her tiny lips stretched and widened; drunken laughter spilled out of her mouth like vomit, and it seemed to be spurting all over me—laughter that sounded like vomit smells.

"A Beautiful Child" is a profile of Marilyn Monroe, a personal friend of Capote's. There is quite a bit of humor in it in the way that Monroe speaks, a combination of salty language and innocence of heart, and it is this that makes her "a beautiful child." At another extreme is "Then It All Came Down," in which Capote interviews Robert Beausoleil, a central figure in the Charles Manson murders. The chilling thing about Beausoleil is his total absence of any moral sense even in his more mature years.

"Derring-do" is a high-spirited, extremely humorous piece of reportage about a bizarre experience of Capote's in California. It is an account of an all-points-bulletin search for Capote by the San Diego Sheriff's Office after he did not appear in court to give the contents of a confidential interview he had done with a prisoner on death row. The manic comedy of the piece heats up when the actress-singer Pearl Bailey and the performers in her troupe smuggle the fugitive Capote aboard a plane bound for New York that is under the tightest possible surveillance in anticipation of Capote's departure. With her exuberance and sass, Bailey gives a great performance, and Capote is uproariously amusing, particularly in the restroom scenario in which costumes are exchanged and a janitor suspects that indecency is afoot.

Another story in *Music for Chameleons,* "Mojave," was originally published in *Esquire* magazine in June 1975 and probably intended as a chapter in Capote's work-in-progress *Answered Prayers.* It isn't clear who decided not to include "Mojave" in *Answered Prayers,* but its focus *is* different from the other chapters—"Unspoiled Monsters," "Kate McCloud," and "La Côte Basque"—which also appeared in magazine form that year. Moreover, there is no reference whatsoever to P. B. Jones, Capote's alter ego who provides the narrative voice in *Answered Prayers.*

The spiritual weather of "Mojave" is suggested in its wasteland title and the sense the reader has of the vacancy of its characters, essentially two married couples who belong to markedly different backgrounds and do not enter into direct contact. George Schmidt, a masseur, is old and blind, while George Whitelaw is a young man not long out of Yale University and hitchhiking across the country. When Schmidt and Whitelaw meet in the desert, Schmidt tells the younger man of his marital woes. His wife, Ivory Hunter, had been a stripper at the Chicago World's Fair in 1932 and is now a faithless wife. In the trailer park where they live, she betrays him flagrantly, carrying on an affair with a Hispanic man. She draws all of Schmidt's money from the bank, and drives him out into the desert with her paramour concealed in the back seat; when Schmidt leaves the vehicle for a moment, they drive off, leaving him there—presumably to die.

It is interesting to note that the young Hispanic lover is named Freddy Feo, and he appears to be Tico Feo from Capote's earlier story "A Diamond Guitar." In the "Mojave" story he has, if anything, grown worse. Like Tico, Freddy has spent time in prison and plays a guitar that can draw people to him seductively. Picked up by the manager of the trailer park in a "fag bar," he beguiles both women and men. But the beauty of his playing is merely an imposture, like the "diamonds" on his guitar that are really paste. He is interested only in what he can get from people. But he is a side issue; it is the women who are the most treacherous, and use their sexuality to maim the men who love them. Schmidt compares women to snakes. "'The last thing that dies,'" he tells Whitelaw, "'is their tail.'"

"Mojave" is a two-tiered story, the second part concerned with the upper-class Sarah Whitelaw, George's wife. If Ivory is garish, Sarah is sophisticated and subtle. After two painful pregnancies, she no longer sleeps with her husband but has a secret affair with her former psychiatrist, Dr. Bentsen, described as being repulsive, physically and in all other respects. The detail that he wears thick socks while making love implies the numbness of his contact with his partner. She, in turn, derives no pleasure in having sex with him, but how demeaning to her husband that she should prefer this awful man to him! Sarah is the exact opposite of Ivory, and she represents the withdrawal of passion, a tactic that will wear her husband down and shrivel him in the end. Whitelaw is said to suffer from "a secret fatigue, a lack of any real optimism. His wife was surely aware of it, and why not? She was its principal cause." There are kinds of violence, emotional violence, in "Mojave," but most of all there is the loneliness felt by the two men, who are framed against the vast solitude of the desert.

Answered Prayers

"Unspoiled Monsters" is by far the largest segment of *Answered Prayers*, and is the first to appear in the book. It introduces the reader to P. B. Jones, Capote's unflattering portrait of himself as a sleazy opportunist with aspirations of becoming a recognized writer. But *Answered Prayers* is not so much about him as about the world of the rich and famous and its discontents. In a way it is about the American dream and the dry rot beneath its surface. Jones is a young drifter who takes a Greyhound bus to New York, where he begins to cultivate influential people like Turner Boatwright, the fiction editor of an exclusive women's magazine. Through Boatwright he meets the distinguished American fiction writer Alice Lee Langman, apparently inspired by Katherine Anne Porter. Jones attaches himself to her, ruthlessly using her to advance his career.

When Langman dies, Jones (or Jonesey, as he is sometimes called) takes up with Denham "Denny" Fouks, a real person and an early acquaintance of Capote's when he was living in Paris. Fouks, a Southerner, was famous in certain quarters as the most beautiful young man in the world, and was kept by a series of European millionaires. Fouks's story soon leads to the much publicized gigolos of the time, like Porfirio Rubirosa, and playboys like Prince Aly Khan. Jones speaks of the European scene in dour terms. "'When I think of Paris,'" he remarks, "'it seems to me as romantic as a flooded *pissoir*, as tempting as a strangled nude floating in the Seine.'"

Fouks becomes a drug-addicted wreck at a very early age. His "answered prayers" lead eventually to nightmares of emptiness and abandonment, evoked in the Father Flanagan passages:

> Once I spent a year meditating in a California monastery.... Looking for this ... Meaningful Thing.... And all that ever came of that putrid torture was ... Father Flanagan's Nigger Queen Kosher Café. There it is: right where they throw you off at the end of the line. Just beyond the garbage dump. Watch your step: don't step on the severed head. Now knock. Knock, knock. Father Flanagan's voice: "Who sent ya?" Christ, for Christs sake, ya dumb mick. Inside ... it's ... very ... relaxing. Because there's not a winner in the crowd. All derelicts.... The Nigger

Queen Kosher Café . . . restful as the grave, rock bottom. That's why I
drug: mere dry meditation isn't enough to get me there . . . hidden and
happy with Father Flanagan and his Outcast of Thousands. . . .

Denny, at age twenty, is bound for a rehab clinic at Vevey, but there
seems no hope for him.

Casualties and glamour are linked throughout the book, which
draws on Capote's own life. Speaking of his opportunistic nature, Jones
(Capote's stand-in) visits people, and cultivates connections, in Europe.
These passages read as if they belong to a memoir, and they do in fact
reuse material from Capote's earlier essays and travel sketches. Several
pages are devoted, for instance, to Jones's acquaintance with Natalie
Barney, "the premiere American expatriate" and salon hostess to the
Parisian art world that included Jean Cocteau, André Gide, Pablo
Picasso, Marcel Proust, and Gertrude Stein. The section on Colette
similarly draws on Capote's own meeting with her, and the parts about
Albert Camus are taken from life. These European passages seem too
much like advertisements for himself, but Capote's observation of people do seem acute: Alice B. Toklas "smoothing her fragile mustache";
Camus's "troubled, perpetually listening expression"; Jean-Paul Sartre
and Simon de Beauvoir propped in a corner "like an abandoned pair
of ventriloquists' dolls."

A curious thing about "Unspoiled Monsters" is that it assimilates
different styles—moving, for instance, from the elegant and cultured
to the low-life and bawdy. It also has more humor in it than one would
expect in a composition so given over to pessimism and gloom. A character named Victoria Self is encountered fairly early on, and she is like
the divided consciousness of the work itself. A graduate of a prestigious
women's college and a stickler for good manners, she operates a
prostitution ring that services both men and women. No questions are
asked as along as outward appearances are kept up.

After arriving in New York with hardly any money, Jones becomes
one of Victoria's employees. Reduced to living at a YMCA in the Times
Square area, he is contacted by Miss Self to walk the dog of a famous
American playwright named "Mr. Wallace" who is staying at the
Plaza Hotel. The dog hasn't been housebroken and the playwright, a
thinly disguised version of Tennessee Williams, lives among the filth
the dog has created. He is another in the procession of characters who
aspire to or even create beauty but whose personal lives are not at all

beautiful. Victoria is such a person, and her name, Self, seems to indicate that what is true of her is also true of Capote.

In this same section, Jones holds a conversation with a friend about Proust and the concept of the unknowable nature of truth. He wants to tell him that illusion, "the by-product of revealing artifice, can reach the summits nearer to the unobtainable peak of Perfect Truth. For example, female impersonators. The impersonator is in fact a man (truth), until he re-creates himself as a woman (illusion)—and of the two, the illusion is the truer." This conversation may seem like a digression, but it is relevant to the unfolding narrative and particularly to Capote's treatment of Kate McCloud, a chief character in "Unspoiled Monsters."

Jones first hears of Kate through a friend, Aces Nelson, whose prep school roommate was a youth named Harry McCloud. His parents owned much of the state of Virginia, and among other things maintained a stable of hunting horses. He seemed to have everything—wealth, good looks, success in athletics. Yet there was something a little odd about him, and when Aces pressed him to reveal why he had never spoken of a girlfriend, he finally confided that he was infatuated with a girl but could not marry her because she was only twelve years old.

Kate is a character who is larger than life. The tomboy daughter of the McCloud's Irish groom, she beguiled the McClouds who, in a sense, adopted her as a member of their family. She was tutored and nurtured in all the graces, which set off her exceptional beauty. When she was scarcely eighteen she and Harry were married. "'She was perfect,'" Aces tells Jones. "'Harry worshipped her; so did his parents. But they had overlooked one small factor—she was shrewd, she could outthink any of them, and she was planning far beyond the McClouds.'" He became insanely jealous of Kate, and began creating shocking scenes in his mind, accusing her of having affairs with other men, including even his father and younger brother; he demanded that she admit she was a whore, and in bed with her held a knife to her throat throughout the night. She divorced Harry and went to live in Europe, leaving him to live out the remainder of his life in a mental institution.

Kate goes on to marry Axel Jaeger, the richest man in Germany. When Jones meets her in the Swiss Alps, he feels that she is absolute perfection, a woman for whom he "would lie, steal, commit crimes that could have, and still could, put me in prison for life." It would be incorrect to say that "Unspoiled Monsters" is strewn with Gothic imagery, but some does appear, and at times shockingly, in connection with characters who might seem to have their prayers answered. The earlier conversation about Proust and the inaccessibility of truth can be noted in Kate, whose husband, Harry, is driven mad in his attempt to claim her. Other characters who appear to have attained enviable success not only lose it but are actually destroyed. Boatwright, the homosexual editor in New York who seems to be equipped with all the right advantages, is beaten to death by a heroin-crazed Puerto Rican hustler and is left with his eyeballs unhinged and dangling down his cheeks.

The next chapter, "Kate McCloud," is the shortest and least cohesive of the three sections that make up *Answered Prayers*. Jones (a surname so extremely common that it suggests he has little personal identity) tells the reader that he has never belonged anywhere or to anyone. He tells how he despised the nuns at his orphanage and ran away and was picked up on the highway by a gay masseur who taught him his trade; how he then came to New York and attempted to write a novel in a YMCA where incessant sex was going on; and went to work for Miss Self. Glimpses of his Forty-second Street surroundings have at times a William Burroughs-like dream quality. Doorways are lined with "nodding" heroin addicts and male hustlers; fourteen- and fifteen-year-old Puerto Rican boys call out to be taken home for ten dollars ("'Fuck me all night!'"). A young gay man lies unconscious in a gutter in front of an "S & M bar," surrounded by leather-jacketed young hoods howling with laughter as they urinate on him until his clothing is drenched.

In a following sequence the scene shifts to the smart East Side, where a party is being given for Montgomery Clift, but different as this setting is it has a similar implication of decay. Dorothy Parker, Tallulah Bankhead, and Estelle Winwood have been invited—a mistake since all of them are alcoholics. A sense of miasma is emphasized by the arrival of Clift. Dorothy Parker gasps at his appearance. "'He's so beautiful,'" she exclaims, "'Sensitive. So finely made. The most beautiful young man I've ever seen.'" But his emerging problems have already addicted him to alcohol—so much so that when he is handed a drink he has to struggle to hold it in his shaking hands.

Oddly, Kate McCloud hardly appears in this chapter that is named for her. The rich and famous, Kate included, are depicted aboard their yachts or pursuing other expensive diversions. But this class of people are treated only marginally. In the final chapter, "La Côte Basque," however, they are brought into full focus.

A principal character in "La Côte Basque" is Lady Ina Coolbirth, an American who has come by her title through marriage to a British chemicals tycoon. Jones runs into her in front of the fashionable La Côte Basque restaurant in the east Fifties, where she has been stood up by her friend Perla Apfeldorf. Jones agrees to fill in for her. When they enter the establishment they are catered to personally by the proprietor, M. Soulé, who seats them by the entranceway, a prime location that provides a view of the other customers as they arrive. "La Côte Basque" is a story that Capote seems destined to have written. He was, after all, well acquainted with the class of people who frequented New York's prestigious restaurants, and knew their habits and snobberies. He was himself a devotee of gossip, but in the story he looks upon the scene with a jaundiced eye. Over lunch, the diners tear each other to pieces.

Many of the choice items of gossip making the rounds in the room have to do with sex—how, for instance, one of the women in their circle (doctor Whitestone's wife) had an abortion as a result of her affair with the restaurant's handsome young wine steward. The abortion was performed by her husband, who had been brought to believe that he was responsible for her condition; the gossipers find all of this quite tacky. The narrative operates like a camera that circles the room picking up the conversations of the diners. Ina herself is not spared in regard to her marriage to the much older Lord Coolbirth. One of the women says she "'can't imagine Cool wanting to get into those rusty knickers.'" Another has been to a party with Princess Margaret. "Her mother's a darling," she remarks, "but the rest of that family!" The Bouviers and the Kennedys are widely discussed and dissected. Jacqueline is "'very photogenic, of course'" a woman comments, "but the effect is a little . . . unrefined, exaggerated.'" Jones remarks that Jacqueline does not strike him as being a bona fide woman, but as "an artful female impersonator impersonating Mrs. Kennedy."

"La Côte Basque" is more stylish than some other parts of the book, but like them it can also be grotesque, as in the case of a society wife who has been caught in a sexual act with a German shepherd dog. The section of "La Côte Basque" that raised an uproar and caused Capote to be repudiated by practically the whole of café society was not the most shocking episode in the book. It concerned Babe Paley and her husband's infidelities, and was meant chiefly as a rebuke to William Paley for his mistreatment of Babe, one of Capote's most cherished friends. While staying in a suite at the Plaza Hotel, Paley, fictionalized here as Sidney Dillon, is portrayed as a clumsy philanderer as he desperately attempts to remove menstrual stains from the bedsheets in the middle of the night while expecting the return of his wife at almost any time. The incident, as it happens, was true, and was told to Capote in confidence; moreover, Capote makes it clear who the people involved were.

Actually, Johnny Carson, the comedian-host of the *Tonight Show*, received much worse treatment. He, too, mistreated his wife Joanne, another intimate friend of Capote's. Carson appears in *Answered Prayers* as Bobby Baxter, a "midnight clown/hero" who is a sadist beneath his "huckleberry grin." He tortures his wife by stepping out on her, disappearing, and then calling her long distance and putting a young tart on the line to tell her what a good time they are having. Bobby Baxter's prayers may have been answered, but what they have divulged is his smallness and meanness.

But the worst instance of attained dreams is the case of Ann Woodward, who appears in the book, thinly disguised, as Ann Hopkins. Hopkins (like Woodward) achieved notoriety when she shot her husband David one night in the supposed belief that he was an intruder. The Hopkins family belonged to the upper echelons of Newport society. Hilda Hopkins, an austere, matriarchal figure in the family, could hardly have been more different from her daughter-in-law, whose louche and calculating past is sketched by Capote. On the eve of his divorcing her, David was shot to death in what Ann claimed was an accident. In fact, at the time of the shooting David was taking a shower; the glass door of the shower was shattered by bullets. The influential Hopkins family wanted no scandal at any cost, and the local police covered up for them.

Officially David Hopkins's death was judged to be an accident. Hilda Hopkins, like a character in a Balzac novel, pretended to grieve with the widow, protecting the grandchildren and the good Hopkins name. Ann Hopkins is the most Gothic of the characters whose stories are told in "La Côte Basque." Originating from a shady background, she schemed her way into a prominent family but remained what she has always been—a woman without a conscience. The story did have some unexpected reverberations. It has been speculated that Ann

Woodward may have managed to read the story in an advance copy of *Esquire* just before it came out on the newsstands, and as a result committed suicide by jumping out of an upper-story window.

Capote was never able to finish *Answered Prayers*, and what there was of it left people perplexed. It seemed vicious and bitter, and not entirely coherent. But even in the fragments that make up *Answered Prayers* there is a coherent theme of the misery of the successful and envied. Capote was supposedly rewriting the disillusionment that overcomes the narrator at the end of Marcel Proust's great novel *Remembrance of Things Past*; Proust's fashionable and exclusive turn-of-the-century Parisians become Capote's "beautiful people" in the American 1970s. But something obviously went wrong, and in a way the novel never progresses, being one case after another of broken and disillusioned lives. Capote's unfinished novel, one feels, is ultimately about himself.

Capote had been taking notes on New York café society for years, and envisioned a novel about it that would be his masterpiece. By the time he was ready to write it, however, he came up against a severe case of writer's block. He was treated by at least four psychiatrists, none of whom could tell him why the condition had befallen him; he had always been a nervous person, and had tried to calm his nerves with alcohol, which made things worse. By the 1970s his drinking was out of control, and to this was added the use of drugs. It was the smashup of his dream of being a "great American writer"—for that is what he did aspire to. Capote was a tormented man in later life—full of anger and guilt, which is what *Answered Prayers* is so much about: the golden boy brought to grief, or shrunk in stature to the size of P. B. Jones, a hanger-on or fake. But even in this strange, fragmentary work about failure one finds fascinating glimmerings of another of Capote's changes of style. He seems to be exploring American experience in a new way, even drawing a little closer to the Beat poets, to their sense of a wandering alienation and aloneness in the American night. It is also a work that focuses not merely on the individual but also on society itself, even if that society is in a stage of breakdown.

Although Capote's later years were difficult and troubled, he continued to have a high level of visibility. He had become associated in the public mind with Andy Warhol and the outré world of Studio 54. There was little difference in their age, but Capote had arrived earlier than Warhol, and from as far back as the publication of *Other Voices,*

Other Rooms he had been Warhol's idol. Warhol had been enraptured by the photograph of Capote on the jacket of *Other Voices*: young, attractive, flamboyantly homosexual, and famous, everything that Warhol longed to be. From his home in Pittsburgh, Warhol sent him fan letters without ever receiving a reply.

After that he came to New York and stalked Capote at closer range, not merely sending him letters every day but also finding his address and haunting the entrance to his building in hopes of seeing him come in or out. Capote was twenty-three at the time and Warhol was twenty; what divided them was not years but fame and worldly success. Unlike Capote, Warhol was an unknown, a nullity.

After a period of loitering in front of the building, Warhol began calling on the telephone. It was not answered by Truman Capote, however, but by his mother Nina, who told him to stop bothering her son. But Warhol persisted and somehow won Nina over. He joined her at a tavern where over drinks she told him of the disappointment her son had been to her. She invited him to join her at her apartment, and it was here that Warhol first met Truman Capote upon his return later in the afternoon. "He seemed," Capote would recall to Victor Bockris, "one of the most hopeless people that you just know *nothing's* ever going to happen to . . . a hopeless born loser, the loneliest, most friendless person I'd ever seen in my life."

Warhol's first gallery showing was dedicated to Capote, being a collection of his drawings based on his writings; and to crown the occasion Capote and his mother came to see it. When at a later time Capote began to hear that Warhol was being talked about favorably in art circles, he was quite surprised. "I never had the idea," Capote went on, "that he wanted to become an artist. I thought he was one of those people who are interested in the arts. As far as I knew he was a window decorator . . . let's say a window decorator type."

Later in his career Warhol became what he had so desperately admired in Capote—a cynosure, a figure who attracts attention and admiration. By 1977 Studio 54 became the new center of club life. Catering to the young jet setters and the suddenly famous, it became the playground of both Capote and Warhol who grew closer together. After publishing "La Côte Basque" and being repudiated by his café society friends, Capote found that he could retain his presence as a celebrity through his association with Warhol and Warhol's magazine, *Interview*. Bob Colacello, the magazine's editor, believed that both were "consummate geniuses at manipulating society. Brilliant at it, absolutely brilliant at it" (as quoted in Bockris's biography).

Capote's collaboration with *Interview* began with Warhol's following him around in the course of his day and letting him speak for himself. Warhol put him on the cover of the magazine. It attracted attention, and a whole series featuring Capote followed with the caption "Conversations with Capote." As Colacello tells it in George Plimpton's *Truman Capote*, these articles, it was agreed, had to be the first feature in every issue and the caption had to be designed in a certain way, with "Conversations" in black ink and "Capote" in red ink, and there could be no advertising opposite any of these pages. During this time Capote was in and out of clinics to cure his addictions, but nothing worked; then in 1979, summoning all his strength of will, he was able to free himself of them—for at least a year. During this time he was able to write again, and some of what he produced in this period was good. There were fourteen new pieces, and many of them appeared in *Interview*. But as Colacello points out, once they were brought out in his collection of new work, *Music for Chameleons*, Capote distanced himself from the magazine.

Different as they were, Capote and Warhol had one absolutely essential thing in common: they had the ability to fascinate the American public. Writers are not usually public personalities; there are exceptions like Mark Twain, but for every Twain there are a hundred Herman Melvilles. Capote had the unusual ability to project his innermost self onto the public mind: he was unique. There was always a flamboyance about him, like the long scarf he wore rakishly, and this flamboyance was also in his work. It can be seen in his characters Cousin Randolph, Miss Bobbit, and Holly Golightly. Much of his work is about private experience, but it is about private experience he shared with millions.

There was a flamboyance about Andy Warhol, too. One thinks of him with sparklers glittering in his white wig, surrounded by his "velvet underground" (the term originated with a band Warhol discovered and promoted before being used to designate—correctly or not—Warhol's immediate entourage). One thinks of him at the Factory, his offices in which celebrities mingled with Greenwich Village bohemians, and where "outrageous" movies were made or planned by Warhol and Paul Morrissey that made the sexually provocative Joe Dallesandro an underground star. Warhol was always discovering new and previously unknown people and giving them names like Viva and Ondine.

There was a lot of the child in him, just as there was in Capote, and both of them craved attention and wanted to be famous. Warhol is remembered for his commenting that "in the future everyone will be famous for fifteen minutes," but he wanted to be famous all the time. He and Capote were alike in their theatricalization of the self, which sets them off from social plodders and permits them to reject received social modes of conduct; in this way it is perhaps a reflection of gay sensibility.

Capote, in particular, can be seen in the context of his controversial late Victorian predecessor Oscar Wilde. In the December 2, 2007 issue of the *New York Times Book Review*, Charles McGrath has compared many of Capote's essays and sketches to Wilde. "In many ways," he writes, "the Capote of this book [*Portraits and Observations*] is not the heroic reporter of the two recent movie verions of his life but, rather, a Gothic, *fin-de-siecle* kind of writer who would have fitted right in with Beardsley, Wilde and Ernest Dowson. You don't read him here so much for character . . . or vivid description as for atmosphere and filigreed prose."

This "filigreed prose" is part of the aesthetic Capote inherited from Wilde. Wilde is supposed to have said, when being processed through American customs, "I have nothing to declare except my genius." Whether he actually said this is disputed, but if he didn't say it he should have, because the comment goes to his very essence. He was consummately flamboyant. It was typical of him that he should announce that he and his mother, Lady Wilde, had decided to found a society for the suppression of virtue. He was flamboyant when he came to America in the 1880s to lecture astonished coal miners on "beauty." He was flamboyant in letting his hair grow long and in lecturing while holding flowers in his hands. His plays were flamboyant in the sharpness and elegance of their wit. Wilde had considerable personal charm and, although mocked by some, could mesmerize an audience. Like Capote and Warhol, he craved attention and fame.

Capote had been aware of Wilde from an early age: when he and Phoebe Pierce dashed off to Manhattan in their teens they quoted lines from Wilde, who represented sophistication, art, and defiance—not to mention the green carnation. Later in life Capote became interested in Wilde's letters, and wished he had been present to be transfixed by his famously witty conversation. In other respects Wilde was not a fortunate role model. He became notorious, enduring imprisonment and a lonely and nearly anonymous exile in France, where he died at the age of forty-six. If Capote shared with Wilde a certain connoisseurship and sense of "acting" before the public, his career, too, led to a great fall.

* * * * * *

In his later years Capote kept up the pretense of his still being at work on *Answered Prayers* while he became increasingly addicted to alcohol and drugs and produced almost nothing. His breakdown became public knowledge. In one speaking engagement, he was so inebriated that he fell off the stage, and in a television interview his speech was so slurred that he should never have been allowed to continue. Nor did he have anything resembling a home life; he moved restlessly and pointlessly, it seemed, from one locality to another. He and Jack Dunphy were no longer having sexual relations, and Capote's new partners were ill chosen. The most important one, with a family man named John O'Shea, involved Capote in total chaos that included a savage beating by O'Shea.

Capote's drinking excesses might be compared to those of Dylan Thomas in the 1950s when, with his most inspired work of the preceding decade now in an irrevocable eclipse, he drank himself to death on the American lecture circuit and in Greenwich Village. Capote had been intent on being a great American writer, and when the writer's block happened the nerve-wracking intensity he put into his writing became the negative energy of self-destruction. How desperate the situation had become is illustrated by an observation of the English writer-editor Alan Pryce-Jones in Plimpton's *Truman Capote*: "He was truly in the autumn of his days the very last time I saw him; he suddenly walked right out in the middle of traffic without looking at all. He was absolutely out. Spaced out. . . . He was walking at random through traffic. He made no sense at all. He didn't know who one was." As Alan Schwartz notes in Plimpton's book, a CAT scan done at that time showed that Capote's brain had actually shrunk as a result of the abuse of drink and drugs.

His health was disintegrating rapidly. He developed epilepsy and collapsed in the lobby of the United Nations Plaza, in other public places, and on his way to his house at Sagaponack on Long Island, where he was found lying in the road. Severely depressed and subject to hallucinations, he required frequent treatment at the Southampton Hospital and numerous other hospitals and clinics both in and away from New York. In his invalid and despairing state he was looked after by a few friends and by Jack Dunphy; but Dunphy, who was never a sympathetic man, decided that he had had enough and flew off to Switzerland. On August 23, 1984, Capote was flown to Los Angeles to be nursed by Joanne Carson in a spare room of her apartment. In an extremely wasted condition, he longed for death, and the end was not long in coming. It is possible that he may even have committed suicide through an overdose of drugs. Whether or not this was actually the case, Leo Lerman noted in one of his diary entries, Capote's compulsive abuse of alcohol and drugs had been a form of suicide.

Chapter Nine
Capote in Retrospect

In the nearly twenty-five years since his death, Capote continues to cast his spell over the public; he has been impersonated in major productions on both stage and screen. In the autumn of 1989 Robert Morse performed on Broadway in a one-man show called *Tru* that was a mood piece combining humor with an underlying sadness. Morse had starred before on Broadway in such shows as *How to Succeed in Business without Really Trying*, in which his trademark was his ebullience; but *Tru* called for subtlety and inwardness as well as the ability to ingratiate himself with the audience. His performance earned him a Tony, in addition to the Outer Critics Circle, Drama Desk, and Drama League Awards. Most of Morse's monologue in *Tru* was taken from Capote's own words in interviews and elsewhere, by the veteran playwright Jay Presson Allen, who adapted, among other works, Muriel Spark's novel *The Prime of Miss Jean Brodie*.

Morse's Capote is seen at the opening seated on a Victorian couch in the dim light of his apartment in the United Nations Plaza: he's wearing a loosely fitting sweater, sneakers, a Panama hat, and sunglasses. *In Cold Blood* has made him rich and famous, but since then he has published "La Côte Basque" in *Esquire* and it has cost him his devoted friendship with Babe Paley, Slim Keith, and many others. The time is Christmas Eve and he is alone in his apartment reflecting on his life. His monologue is constantly entertaining in its repertoire of touching passages from one or another of his stories and moments of amusing gossip. As he talks he breaks at times into a little dance step to the tune of numbers like "The Girl from Ipanema," "A Kiss to Build a Dream On," and "At Long Last Love." He even tap dances as he reminisces about the time in his youth when he danced for Louis Armstrong as he played "On the Sunny Side of the Street."

He is plucky, but as the evening grows on his mood grows darker, and he holds up a painting of himself as the wunderkind of American letters, and in a coup de théâtre plunges his fist through it. By the time he snaps out the lights of the apartment and, twirling his signature scarf about his neck, prepares to go out into the street, he is as stymied as one of his own characters. *Tru* manages to capture some of Capote's peculiar charm, partly through the warmth and wit of Morse's extraordinary impersonation. But if *Tru* was bittersweet, we now know that it was not nearly as dark as Capote's real life at the end.

Tru established Capote on the stage as a striking character, but it was in 2005 that a resurgence of interest in his life and career brought Capote to center stage in the performing arts. It was then that the movie *Capote*, focusing upon his *In Cold Blood* period, came out. Actually, there were two movies about Capote scheduled to be released at about the same time. Since it wasn't feasible to have them appear at once, one of them, called *Infamous*, had to wait its turn for almost another year. *Capote* opened with much fanfare to extremely favorable reviews. Surprisingly, it was the first time out for both the film's director Bennett Miller and its screenwriter Dan Futterman. Everyone benefited from the picture but most of all Philip Seymour Hoffman, who had the title role and was awarded an Oscar for the year's best acting performance.

Audiences were astonished by Hoffman's physical resemblance to Capote (in real life the actor looks nothing like the author), together with his catchy mannerisms—the oddity of his baby voice, his lisp, and flickering tongue. But Hoffman's performance was less a cunning impersonation than a subtle exploration of Capote's psyche. He comes through as a charismatic figure at Manhattan cocktail parties, someone to whom others gravitate, but he is also given a quality of loneliness, especially at the end. The picture was based on the Gerald Clarke's biography *Capote*, and stays very close to it.

Capote is a quiet movie that is also suspenseful, and Adam Kimmel's cinematography is unusually dark, creating a pensive, rather solemn mood as it moves further into psychological depths and Capote's personal dilemma. That isn't to say that the film has no lighter side. Kimmel can fill the screen with surprising visual images of calm beauty—buildings of striking architecture, wheat fields waving in a breeze, trains moving in a long straight line through deserted Midwestern expanses. At times these visual compositions are accompanied by the sound of a piano key struck softly, thanks to the soundtrack of composer Mychael Danna.

The restraint of the film can also be noticed in Catherine Keener's performance as Harper Lee, whose calmness is a counterweight to the Capote character's nervousness. Chris Cooper's Alvin Dewey is also perfectly acted, and the more so in his not seeming to be acting at all. The only character who can be accused off being miscast is Clifton Collins as Perry Smith. He is attractive and even gentle looking, whereas photographs of the real Smith show a young man who has been hardened by life and can be dangerous. In Capote's indelible portrait of him in the novel, Smith is sympathetic but also grotesque—a crippled dwarf on the verge of psychic explosion.

The other biographical film about Capote, *Infamous* (it was first called *Have You Heard?* and then *Every Word Is True*), was presented in August 2006 at the Venice Film Festival, and released in October 2006 in the United States. Written and directed by Douglas McGrath, who had previously adapted *Emma* and *Nicholas Nickleby* for the screen, it stars the English actor Toby Jones who, like Philip Seymour Hoffman in *Capote*, bears an extraordinary resemblance to Capote. *Infamous* is a brighter, splashier picture than *Capote* and spends more time, at least at the beginning, at Manhattan cocktail parties and exclusive restaurants like El Morroco, where it begins.

Gwyneth Paltrow upstages everyone in the opening nightclub scene with her rendition of the Peggy Lee ballad "What Is This Thing Called Love?" and at least two of Capote's "swans"—Sigourney Weaver as Babe Paley and Hope Davis as Slim Keith—are shown socializing with Capote at nightclubs. Another friend, Juliet Stevenson as Diana Vreeland, is shown as a hostess for the fashionable set at her apartment, which is decorated almost entirely in brilliant red.

There is no great difference between Toby Jones's Capote and Philip Seymour Hoffman's, but Jones's version is more effeminate. To attract attention he appears at Alvin Dewey's press conference in what looks like a woman's ankle-length housecoat; and his bedroom is decorated in shades of pink, with tufted pink material in the backing of the bed—which seems more like caricature than characterization.

Infamous is fortunate to have Sandra Bullock playing Harper Lee, for she is Lee to perfection, just as Keener had been in *Capote*. But Jeff Daniels is no match for Chris Cooper's Alvin Dewey, who has more character and consequently more interest. But McGrath's really serious casting mistake is his choice of Daniel Craig as Perry Smith; six weeks after *Infamous* was finished Craig became the new James Bond, and to have James Bond as Perry Smith makes no sense whatsoever.

Smith was the sentient one in the partnership with Dick Hickock. With his soft lisping voice that could hardly be heard; his artwork; his recurrent dream of a giant yellow bird that would swoop down from the heavens to save him from those who would harm him; his stunted legs (which, depending on the chair he was in, could not always reach the floor) all work against McGrath's "iron man" casting of Craig and make it seem garish and absurd. In *Infamous*, Smith even attacks the Capote violently in his cell, and stuffs a sock in his mouth as he prepares to rape him. Nothing like this incident ever occurred in real life, but never mind.

McGrath's contention in the film is that Capote's life became so intertwined with Smith's during the five strenuous years of Perry's imprisonment on death row that they became, in a sense, lovers; and that when Perry was executed Capote lost his creativity and will to live. This notion seems simplistic. Capote was shaken by the spectacle of Perry's being hanged, but there is nothing in his papers to suggest that he spent the rest of his life mourning for him, as the end of the picture implies. Instead of capturing Capote on film, *Infamous* calls attention to what an elusive figure he was.

* * * * * *

Capote's elusiveness was apparent from his beginnings as Truman Persons. Although markedly more intelligent than his classmates in Monroeville, Alabama, he could still be emotionally immature. He lived to quite an extent in an inner world in which he wrote precociously and secretly, yet as he reached his teens was also a talented dancer, especially in tap dance, and according to Phoebe Pierce was "a marvelous ice skater." That he had different selves, mature and childish, and could go from one to the other in a flash was noted during his residency at Yaddo, the artists' colony in Saratoga Springs, New York. His writing gives the impression of his being detached from others, and yet he could be surprisingly gregarious. He was drawn to women and perhaps more appreciative of them than any of his contemporary American writers; but he was not attracted to them sexually. He had a very keen sense of humor, but his writing was often dark. "A Christmas

Memory" is remarkable for its tenderness, but "Greek Paragraphs" includes a tale of a beautiful sixteen-year-old boy who is eaten alive by monstrous rats on a deserted Grecian beach. The style of his writing suggests that he possessed a great degree of composure, but friends say that he was a nervous man from the beginning. Even his appearance could give the impression of his being elusive; he himself said that he had a changeling's face that made him look different from photograph to photograph.

Yet if he was a man divided, Capote was also someone who was very concentrated within himself. Practically everything he wrote had some inner self-reference. In this regard he had something in common with Ingmar Bergman, whose films often, or perhaps even always, had some personal subtext. In particular Bergman seems to have had a compulsion to delve over and over into the marriage of his parents and to have had an intense fixation with his mother. Capote's fixation with his mother (who withheld her love) and his birth father (who withheld even his presence) is played and replayed in his imagination like a drumbeat. In many ways this dwelling upon his mother and father limited him as a writer; there were many aspects of experience that he didn't begin to explore. He wasn't an author given to working with large social canvases or complex ideas.

He was less a novelist, for that matter, than he was a short story writer, sketch and vignette artist, and essayist. He was wonderfully observant and a great imagist. Capote's most admired novelists, apart from Willa Cather, whom he alludes to frequently, included Gustave Flaubert, E. M. Forster, and Henry James—which says a great deal about his tastes and ideals. He was a poet in the fictional moods he created; although he did not leave an unusually large body of work, what he did has a chiseled perfection. Shortly before Norman Mailer died, he remarked that Capote didn't have an idea in his head. Capote did, but it had less to do with the intellectual concepts of Mailer and more with the thinking of James, of whom it was said in a famous remark that he had an imagination "so pure that no idea could violate it." Whatever can be said of Capote, he was never heavy-handed, as the "ideas" of Mailer can be. Capote was an observer with a really brilliant eye. In his essay "Cecil Beaton," he called attention to Beaton's "visual intelligence," and this may also be said of him.

It might be out of place to speak of Capote in terms as dangerously ineffable as "charm," but he did possess it—it is at the heart of his writing. The Queen Mother touched on at least some of the attributes of this gifted, unusual, tormented, and complicated man when she told Beaton that she "found Mr. Capote quite wonderful, so talented, so wise, so funny," and Beaton, with equal graciousness, replied, "'Yes, he's a genius, M'am.'"

Bibliography

Books by Truman Capote

Other Voices, Other Rooms. New York: Random House, 1948.

A Tree of Night and Other Stories. New York, Random House, 1949.

Local Color. New York, Random House. 1949.

The Grass Harp. New York: Random House, 1951.

The Muses Are Heard. New York: Random House, 1956.

Breakfast at Tiffany's. New York: Random House, 1956.

Observations (with Richard Avedon). New York: Simon and Schuster, 1959.

Selected Writings of Truman Capote. New York: Random House, 1963.

A Christmas Memory. New York: Random House, 1966.

House of Flowers. New York: Random House, 1968.

The Dogs Bark: Public People and Private Places. New York: Random House, 1968.

Music for Chameleons. New York: Random House, 1980.

One Christmas. New York: Random House, 1983.

Three by Capote. New York: Random House, 1985.

Answered Prayers: The Unfinished Novel. New York: Random House, 1987.

A Capote Reader. New York: Random House, 1987.

The Complete Stories of Truman Capote. New York: Random House, 2004.

Too Brief a Treat: The Letters of Truman Capote. Edited by Gerald Clarke. New York: Random House, 2004.

Summer Crossing. New York: Random House, 2006.

Portraits and Observations: The Essays of Truman Capote. New York: Random House, 2007.

Works Consulted

Beaton, Cecil. *The Best of Cecil Beaton.* Introduced by Truman Capote. New York: Macmillan, 1968.

———. *Memoirs of the 40s.* New York: McGraw-Hill, 1972.

———. *The Strenuous Years, Diaries 1948-55.* London: Weidenfeld and Nicolson, 1973.

Bockris, Victor. *The Life and Death of Andy Warhol.* New York: Bantam Books, 1989.

Brinnin, John Malcolm. *Sextet: T. S. Eliot, Truman Capote and Others.* New York: Delacorte, 1981.

Clarke, Gerald. *Capote: A Biography.* New York: Simon and Schuster, 1988.

Davis, Deborah. *Party of the Century: The Fabulous Story of Truman Capote and His Black and White Ball.* Hoboken, NJ: John Wiley and Sons, 2006.

Dunphy, Jack. *Dear Genius: A Memoir of My Life with Truman Capote.* New York: McGraw-Hill, 1987.

Grobel, Lawrence. *Conversations with Capote.* New York: New American Library, 1985.

Garson, Helen S. *Truman Capote.* New York: Frederick Ungar, 1980.

———. *Truman Capote: A Study of the Short Fiction.* Boston: Twayne, 1981.

Inge, M. Thomas, ed. *Truman Capote Conversations.* Jackson: University Press of Mississippi, 1987.

Lerman, Leo. *The Grand Surprise: The Journals of Leo Lerman.* Edited by Stephen Pascal. New York: Alfred A. Knopf, 2007.

Malin, Irving. *New American Gothic.* Carbondale: Southern Illinois University Press, 1962.

———. *Truman Capote's* In Cold Blood: *A Critical Handbook.* New York: Wadsworth, 1968.

Moates, Marianne. *A Bridge of Childhood: Truman Capote's Southern Years.* New York: Henry Holt, 1987.

Nance, William. *The Worlds of Truman Capote.* New York: Stein and Day, 1970.

Plimpton, George. *Truman Capote: In Which Various Friends, Enemies, Acquaintances, and Detractors Recall His Turbulent Career.* New York: Nan A. Talese, 1997.

Reed, Kenneth. *Truman Capote.* Boston: Twayne, 1981.

Rudisill, Marie, with James C. Simmons. *Truman Capote*. New York: William Morrow, 1983.

Shields, Charles J. *Mockingbird: A Portrait of Harper Lee*. New York: Henry Holt, 2006.

Stanton, Robert J. *Truman Capote: A Primary and Secondary Bibliography*. Boston: G. K. Hall, 1980.

Souhami, Diana. *Greta and Cecil*. San Francisco: HarperCollins, 1994.

Warhol, Andy. *The Andy Warhol Diaries*. Edited by Pat Hackett. New York: Warner Books, 1989.

Windham, Donald. *Lost Friendships: A Memoir of Truman Capote, Tennessee Williams, and Others*. New York: Paragon House, 1987.

Index